The Who : A Who's Who

The Who: A Who's Who

RICHARD BOGOVICH
with Cheryl Posner

McFarland & Company, Inc., Publishers
Jefferson, North Carolina, and London

LIBRARY OF CONGRESS CATALOGUING-IN-PUBLICATION DATA

Bogovich, Richard
   The Who : A who's who / Richard Bogovich with Cheryl Posner.
     p.   cm.
   Includes bibliographical references and index.

   ISBN 0-7864-1569-X (softcover: 50# alkaline paper) ∞

    1. Who (Musical group)   2. Rock musicians—England—
Biography.   3. Rock music—England—History and criticism.
I. Posner, Cheryl.   II. Title.
ML421.W5B64   2003
782.42166'092'2—dc21   2003001406

British Library cataloguing data are available

©2003 Richard Bogovich and Cheryl Posner. All rights reserved

*No part of this book may be reproduced or transmitted in any form
or by any means, electronic or mechanical, including photocopying
or recording, or by any information storage and retrieval system,
without permission in writing from the publisher.*

On the front cover: ©2002 Image Bank

Manufactured in the United States of America

McFarland & Company, Inc., Publishers
  Box 611, Jefferson, North Carolina 28640
  www.mcfarlandpub.com

CONTENTS

Preface vii

The Who: A Who's Who 1

Bibliography 205

Index 207

PREFACE

From its inception in the mid–1980s, the Rock and Roll Hall of Fame and Museum has inducted "early influences," i.e., performers "whose music predated rock and roll but had an impact on the evolution of rock and roll and inspired rock's leading artists." One of the purposes of this biographical dictionary is to show, in aggregate, how diverse such influences can be, by focusing on a particular band that was among the first dozen inducted into the Rock and Roll Hall of Fame. A related purpose is to provide a sense of the many other performers the band in question has in turn influenced over the years.

This reference work also offers insight into the varied relationships, including nonmusical ones, that a very popular band may develop over its career. These connections are illuminated in part by information about many (though certainly not all) of the performers who have recorded or performed live with one or more members of the Who, and others who have paid tribute to the Who by recording their own version of a Who song. Also profiled are some behind-the-scenes personnel. All told, a close reading of the book should provide an appreciation of the interconnectedness within the recording industry.

At a more basic level, however, this book is intended to be a source of interesting tidbits for people who like pop culture trivia. It is also designed to provide a hint of the humor for which members of the Who have been known, both on stage and off (the latter category including movie and television appearances, as well as anecdotes and commentary appearing in biographies and magazine articles over the years).

Readers who aren't very familiar with the Who might want to begin with the band's own entry toward the end of the book, and proceed to the individual entries for the band's core members, Roger Daltrey, John Entwistle, Keith Moon, and Pete Townshend.

There are many people who deserve thanks for helping this book become a reality. Most notably, Townshend family and Who expert Bill Bedzyk carefully read the first full draft and provided lengthy input. A partial list of others who offered encouragement and information includes Pam Woodward, Kelly Giles, Luke Pacholski, Anne Dvorak, Claire Schmidt, Dave Van Staveren, Brian Cady, Todd Kuzma, Sarah Streed, Karin Kwiatkowski, Phil Arvia, Dave Bruggeman, Terry Perreault, and Nick Bogovich, plus many people at the National Environmental Trust and the Boardman Law Firm.

THE WHO: A WHO'S WHO

Boldface references within the entries indicate persons or groups that have separate entries. Exception: Although separate entries are of course provided for the Who and its core members Roger Daltrey, John Entwistle, Keith Moon, and Pete Townshend, these names are not in boldface when mentioned elsewhere in the text.

Aaronson, Blair   Los Angeles-based jazz artist whose biggest claim to fame might very well have been as the pianist on "Don't Worry Baby" and "Back Door Sally" on Keith Moon's only solo album, 1975's *Two Sides of the Moon*. In 1981 he played synthesizer on the album *Looking Back with Love* by **Beach Boys** singer Mike Love. In the late 1990s Blair was the keyboard player and musical director for the Carnival Dogs, the house band at an LA blues venue called the Mint. He also released an album, *Studies in Solitude*.

AC/DC   Australian heavy metal band that first achieved American chart success in the late 1970s. AC/DC, the **Stranglers**, and Nils Lofgren (who had played with **Neil Young** and would later back Bruce Springsteen) were the supporting acts at a Who concert in London's huge Wembley Stadium on August 18, 1979, which was billed as the band's official London relaunch with new drummer **Kenney Jones** though they had played at North London's Rainbow Theatre on May 2. 77,000 fans filled Wembley to its legal limit. On September 1, AC/DC joined Cheap Trick, the **Scorpions**, the **Steve Gibbons** Band and other performers to support the Who before 65,000 fans at Nuremberg, Germany's Olympic Stadium. According to *The Who Concert File*, AC/DC was delighted to be asked onto the two bills, and guitarist Angus Young said Pete Townshend was the only guitarist to ever influence him. Conversely, when Townshend had an opportunity to act as a guest disk jockey for the BBC around that time, he selected AC/DC's "Highway to Hell" to play as one of his favorite records.

Acock, Bimbo   Saxophone player on "The Heart Has Its Reasons" on Roger Daltrey's 1987 solo album, *Can't Wait to See the Movie*. Peter "Bimbo" Acock has worked with a number of progressive rock artists, sometimes with his brother John. For example, Bimbo recorded with Peter Brown in 1970, was briefly in the Strawbs around 1978, backed Mike Oldfield on a tour of Europe in 1980, and recorded with **Rick Wakeman** a couple of times in the mid–1980s. He has also worked with Eddie Hardin, including on 1982's *Circumstantial Evidence* and on the 1985 Hardin/**Zak Starkey** *Wind in the Willows* project, which featured John Entwistle on one track. Bimbo backed Tom Robinson on albums in 1984 and 1986 and co-wrote a pair of songs on the latter. His more notable work in the 1990s included playing clarinet on Steve Hackett's *Guitar Noir* album in 1993.

Adam and the Ants   British "New Romantic" band that achieved success in America in the early 1980s and, according to Who biographer and longtime friend **Richard Barnes**, kept the Who's *Face Dances* album from reaching number one by selling just nine more copies of their *Kings of the Wild Frontier* LP. Barnes also said, however, that in the United States *Face Dances* and its first single, "You Better You Bet," went to number one in *Billboard*'s rock charts. The correct *Billboard* numbers are #4 for the album and #18 for the single (though the album reached #3 in the rankings of New York radio station WABC and the single #15 according to *Cash Box*). "You Better You Bet" reached #9 in the UK.

Adams, Bryan   Canadian rock star who co-wrote two songs with **Jim Vallance**, "Rebel" and "Let Me Down Easy," on Roger Daltrey's 1985 album *Under a Raging Moon*. "Let Me Down Easy" was released as a single and had a video made for it. Adams plays guitar in the video though **Robbie McIntosh** is credited in the album's liner notes.

Alcock, John   Co-producer, with John Entwistle, of Entwistle's second, third, and fourth solo albums. On *Whistle Rymes* and *Rigor Mortis Sets In* the credit was "Produced by John Entwistle versus John Alcock" but on the fourth, *Mad Dog*, Alcock received top billing in this rivalry. Shortly after finishing *Mad Dog*, Entwistle and Alcock teamed with several other prominent rock stars on the 1975 album *Flash Fearless Versus the Zorg Women Parts 5 & 6*. This supposed stage musical was an erotic science fiction spoof that ultimately did get staged in Los Angeles under a different title — the main change renaming the hero Captain Crash — but that was six years after the record and its colorful comic book insert were released. Entwistle was the album's most involved performer, singing lead on one song, "(Let's Go) To the Chop," and playing on all but one of the other tracks. **Alice Cooper** sang two songs, on one of which Keith Moon can be heard imitating Long John Silver. Other vocalists included Jim Dandy, the lead singer of Black Oak Arkansas, Maddy Prior, who fronted Steeleye Span, Jim Dewar, bassist and vocalist with **Stone the Crows** and Robin Trower's band, and Frankie Miller, who released half a dozen albums in the 1970s on the Chrysalis label. Guitar was provided by Justin Hayward of the **Moody Blues**. **Nicky Hopkins** played piano. Drummers included Bill Bruford of Yes and King Crimson fame, Carmine Appice of Vanilla Fudge, and Entwistle's once and future bandmates, **Graham Deakin** and **Kenney Jones**. Other contributors included guitarist Mick Grabham of Procol Harum, bassist **Johnny Weider**, sax player **Howie Casey**, keyboardist Chick Churchill of Ten Years After, pianists **Mike Deacon** and Hayward collaborator Kirk Duncan, and Roxy Music's **Eddie Jobson** on strings. Backing vocals were provided by **Lesley Duncan**, the **Chanter Sisters**, and Thunderthighs, who memorably backed **Lou Reed** on "Walk on the Wild Side." Around this time Alcock achieved his biggest commercial success as producer for Thin Lizzy. He later produced an album for the Runaways. In 1995 he started his own label, called Public Records.

Allison, John   One of John Entwistle's early aliases. This one appeared in at least one story on the **High Numbers**, though his real surname turned up in print at least once prior to that, in a newspaper article on the **Detours** that appeared on November 21, 1963.

Allison, Mose   Mississippi-born jazz pianist and singer whose 1957 debut album *Back Country Suite* featured a ten-part series of melodies by that name, the "Blues" segment of which evolved into the Who's live staple, "Young Man Blues." Allison's original was less than 90 seconds long. "Young Man Blues" and a song Allison covered on *Back Country Suite*, "One Room Country Shack," were considered for inclusion in the Who's *Tommy*. Mercy Dee Walton wrote the latter but it was Allison's version that the Who were introduced to in late 1963. The same is true of **Sonny Boy Williamson**'s "Eyesight to the Blind," which Allison covered in 1959, eight years after its release. Pete Townshend wrote liner notes for Allison's *Greatest Hits* album and tried to recruit him to sing a part on Pete's *Iron Man* album. Allison continued to release albums throughout the

1990s. His first after turning 70, 1997's *Gimcracks and Gewgaws*, included a 90-second song entitled "Old Man Blues."

Altham, Keith   Writer for the British pop magazine *Fabulous* and later for *New Musical Express* who eventually served as publicist for the Who. In the book *Before I Get Old* Dave Marsh recounted how in 1965 Altham was assigned to interview Keith Moon. The two Keiths eventually met immediately after a performance and Moon promptly pulled an axe out of a gym bag. Altham was speechless for a moment but then asked what the axe was for, to which Moon snarled, "That's for Roger. You 'aven't seen 'im, 'ave you?" In 1971 Altham attended the Who's experimental performances at London's Young Vic Theatre for Pete Townshend's aborted *Lifehouse* project and ultimately thought "it preempted things like *Clockwork Orange* and *2001*" and that Pete's concepts "were as good as those ideas." He appeared in the 1999 DVD that focused on *Who's Next* as the primary outgrowth of the original *Lifehouse* project.

The Altones   According to Pete Goodman in the July 1965 issue of the UK magazine *Beat Instrumental*, this was the name of a band to which Keith Moon belonged before joining the **Beachcombers**. Goodman, in a column that was reprinted in the July 1997 issue of the UK magazine *Record Collector*, wrote that Moon had no drumming lessons but "just hammered away until he reached sufficient proficiency to join a group called the Altones. Then came the Beachcombers, then the Who." Some sources indicate that the Beachcombers were the only group Keith was in other than the Who, but Tony Fletcher's definitive Moon biography detailed his time with a band called the **Escorts** (and also dispelled the myth that Keith never had lessons). Fletcher didn't mention any other bands by name but did state that Moon had been in a few and "attached himself to any group of similarly aged kids in the neighborhood who'd offered a gig. With one of them he'd even had his photo taken in someone's back garden, the guitars laid out neatly on the grass, Keith sitting on a drum stool at the back, looking lean and mean, his hair slicked back, in white shirt, tight black trousers and Cuban heel boots." This color photo appears early in **Richard Barnes**'s book, and a caption refers to the band as Keith's "first group, the Beachcombers," but presumably in error.

The Amboy Dukes   *see* Nugent, Ted.

Amen Corner   *see* Fairweather-Low, Andy.

Andersen, Hans Christian   Danish fairy tales author of the 1800s. Among his popular stories are "The Ugly Duckling," "The Snow Queen," and "The Red Shoes." Roger Daltrey and **Twiggy** starred in a 1987 filmed musical production of his poignant tale "The Little Match Girl."

Angie Youngster who released a single in 1979 that featured Pete Townshend as producer, guitarist, and chorus vocalist. Pete also appeared on the front and back of the "Peppermint Lump" picture sleeve. The song, the first recorded composition of **James Asher**, failed to chart, but musician and prolific online music critic Gary "Pig" Gold lists it among his top 25 singles of all time, calling it "a charming piece of softcore British kiddie-pop." Angela Porter, who was 11 years old when the 45 was released, had appeared many times on youth-oriented television shows in her native England.

The Animals British Invasion band known for its 1964 #1 hit, a version of "House of the Rising Sun." They had changed their name from the Alan Price Combo shortly after vocalist Eric Burdon joined in 1962. In 1964 they and the **Swinging Blue Jeans** opened for **Chuck Berry** at a concert that was the first large gathering of mods which Pete Townshend attended. The Animals met with approval from the mods because they were considered a "rhythm and blues group" but the Swinging Blue Jeans were booed off the stage. In mid–June of 1967, Burdon introduced the Who at the legendary Monterey Pop Festival by saying, "I promise you this group will destroy you in more ways than one." In 1968 Burdon's new Animals lineup charted with the song "Monterey," which proclaimed that "The Who exploded into fire and light." By late 1966 Burdon remained the only original Animal, though bassist Chas Chandler had stopped performing in order to manage the band plus a performer he brought over from America, **Jimi Hendrix**. Chandler negotiated with Decca Records on behalf of Hendrix but ended up signing with Track Records, the new label founded by the Who's managers, **Kit Lambert** and **Chris Stamp**. In 1972 and 1975 New Animals bassist **Johnny Weider** helped out with a couple of John Entwistle's side projects. When Pete Townshend worked for the prestigious Faber & Faber publishing house in the 1980s as a commissioning editor, Burdon's autobiography was among the books he commissioned. Burdon was one of several well-known performers, including Roger Daltrey, who sang on the 1999 **British Rock Symphony** CD.

Ann-Margret One of Hollywood's sex symbols of the 1960s and 1970s but also one of the few women ever to sing with the Who thanks to her memorable role as Mrs. Nora Walker in the movie version of *Tommy*. While filming the vivid scene in which soap suds, beans and chocolate poured out of a shattered television screen, she sustained a cut on the broken glass that required 24 stitches. She also lost two valuable rings during that shoot but they were found after the crew sifted through four thousand pounds of beans. In an America Online chat in February of 2000, Roger Daltrey said, "I had this gorgeous woman, the beautiful Ann-Margret, as my mother. The only way I was going to get through doing anything with her as my mother without getting [aroused] was to be deaf, dumb and blind." The soundtrack song "Champagne" is credited to the Who plus her. Though known for her movie work, including an Academy Award nomination for *Carnal Knowledge*, she did have a Top 20 single in 1961, "I Just Don't Understand." However, in his book *Before I Get Old* Dave Marsh called her singing on the soundtrack "insipid, weak and emotionless" and said that Pete Townshend had wanted either Cleo Laine or Georgia Brown, both cabaret jazz singers, for the role. In the book *The Story of Tommy*, written by **Richard Barnes** and Townshend, Daltrey said Ann-Margret "really should make a rock and roll album. I think she's excellent and she has really suffered from the image which some of her early films have given her. She has this cabaret-show business image, and she's really not like that at all."

Anya *see* Butler, Anya.

Arbus, Dave   Violin player at the end of the Who's "Baba O'Riley." His other claim to a bit of fame was in the British band East of Eden, an early progressive rock group. Two years after helping out on *Who's Next* he played violin on "The Way of the World" on Roger Daltrey's self-titled solo album.

Argent   This band, formed in 1969 by **Rod Argent**, included two other musicians who would go on to work with Roger Daltrey, **Russ Ballard** and Bob Henrit. Argent had a number one hit with "Hold Your Head Up" in 1972. Henrit drummed on Roger Daltrey's self-titled debut solo album in 1973. About a decade later Henrit replaced Mick Avory in the **Kinks**. In the late 1990s Henrit appeared in the VH1 cable TV network's *Behind the Music* profile of Keith Moon. He said that Roger thought Keith was looking for something that wasn't there, though Bob thought Keith knew that.

Argent, Rod   Founding member of the **Zombies** and leader of **Argent** who worked with Roger Daltrey and the Who around 1977. The Zombies' 1964 hit "She's Not There," which went to #2 on the American charts, was only the second song Argent wrote. He played keyboards on Daltrey's third solo album, 1977's *One of the Boys* and fellow ex–Zombie **Colin Blunstone** wrote one of that album's songs. Argent was also a guest on 1978's *Who Are You*, playing synthesizer on "Had Enough" and piano on the title track.

The Aristocrats A Who precursor formed by John Entwistle and Pete Townshend during their Acton County Grammar School days, after John and then Pete had left the **Confederates** and after they had switched from banjo and brass to bass and guitar, respectively. The Aristocrats were followed by the **Scorpions**.

Armatrading, Joan West Indies-born singer and lyricist who has long been popular among critics for blending folk, soul, reggae and rock. **Kenney Jones** drummed on her self-titled 1976 album as well as on her 1977 *Show Some Emotion* album, on which **John "Rabbit" Bundrick** also played. Frequent Who producer **Glyn Johns** was committed to working with her around the time that the *Who Are You* album was being recorded, and this scheduling conflict may actually have worked to the Who's benefit. The band's recording sessions weren't going well, and Johns wasn't getting along well with either Keith Moon or Roger Daltrey. When Johns's obligations to work with Joan Armatrading loomed larger, it was left to his assistant, Pete Townshend's brother-in-law **Jon Astley**, to produce several songs and this helped complete the album.

Artists United Against Apartheid *see* Van Zandt, "Little Steven."

Asher, James Drummer on "Jools and Jim" and "Keep on Working" on Pete Townshend's *Empty Glass* who much later had success creating new age music. Asher, a Who fan from Sussex, got his big break when his song "Peppermint Lump" was released as a single by **Angie** in 1979. He also wrote the B-side, "Breakfast in Naples," which was credited to Angie's Orchestra. Though this single didn't chart, it had been a Pete Townshend side project and thus led to Asher's work on 1980's *Empty Glass*. Pete mentioned this single in a *Guitar* interview in August of 1996 when talking about David Gilmour of **Pink Floyd** and Pete's solo song "Give Blood": "I actually had a demo which had a triplet echo thing but done on keyboard; you know, that kind of *did did-dit did-dit* thing that Dave has now become famous for, the syncopated echo. Actually, I had first used it on a track I had produced for a friend of mine, James Asher, on an album [sic] called *Peppermint Lump*. I also used it for 'And I Moved' off of *Empty Glass*." Prior to working with Townshend, Asher was "altogether obscure," as Dave Marsh put it in his book *Before I Get Old*. From 1989 to 1999 Asher released seven albums, including *The Great Wheel*, which went to #13 in *Billboard*'s New Age chart, and *Feet in the Soil*, which sold more than 100,000 copies worldwide.

Ashton, Tony   Keyboard player on two of John Entwistle's solo albums, *Rigor Mortis Sets In* and *Mad Dog*. He and John composed the music for "Cell Number Seven" on the latter album but the lyrics were John's. He got his start in the 1960s as organist and vocalist in the band Remo Four, which released an album in 1966 and backed up George Harrison of **Beatles** fame on his first solo album, 1968's *Wonderwall Music*. In 1971 the group Ashton, Gardner & Dyke had a #3 British hit with "Resurrection Shuffle," an Ashton composition. In 1972 he also replaced John "Poli" Palmer in **Family** for that band's final year. Around the time that he worked with Entwistle he linked with two former Deep Purple members in another trio, Paice, Ashton, and Lord. In the early 1980s he led the house band on **Rick Wakeman**'s TV talk show, *Gas Tank*. By the mid–1980s he was in ill health and maintained a low profile before turning to painting. One of his works served as the cover for the 1998 CD of the Eddie Hardin and **Zak Starkey** *Wind in the Willows* project. A year earlier he was well enough to tour briefly with British bluesman Long John Baldry. On June 16, 2000, a concert to celebrate Ashton's return to good health was held in London, and Entwistle, Hardin and Starkey were among the many well-known musicians who took part.

Asner, Ed   Seven time Emmy Award-winning actor most known for his role as Lou Grant, first on the legendary comedy *The Mary Tyler Moore Show* and then on the character's long-running spin-off, which was a drama. The 1991 CINAR/Golden Book cartoon "The Real Story of Happy Birthday to You" featured "the vocal talents of rock superstar Roger Daltrey as the harmonica toting Barnaby and Ed Asner as the wise old horse, Charlie."

Aspery, Ron   Woodwind player and pianist who played flute on the *McVicar* soundtrack in 1980 and saxophone on **Simon Townshend**'s *Sweet Sound* album in 1984. He has played with a number of artists, ranging from the Hollies in 1969 to Elvis Costello in 1994. In the 1970s Aspery was a member of the jazz-rock trio Back Door, which released four albums from 1973 to 1976, the last produced by Carl Palmer of **Emerson, Lake and Palmer**.

The Assembled Multitude   Band consisting of studio musicians recruited in Philadelphia by a musician and producer named Tom Sellers (who would later work with the Righteous Brothers, Poco and Hall & Oates, among others) that reached #16 on the American charts in August of 1970 with its version of the Who's "Overture from Tommy." *Tommy* had reached #7 among LPs in July of 1969. Around the time the Assembled

Multitude's 45 peaked, the Who's album release after *Tommy*, *Live at Leeds*, reached the top 10. Perhaps in part due to the Assembled Multitude 45 plus the *Live at Leeds* LP's long jam that borrowed from *Tommy*, the *Tommy* album itself reentered the charts and reached a new peak at #4, giving the Who two top 10 albums simultaneously.

Astley, Edwin *see* Astley, Ted.

Astley, Jon   Pete Townshend's brother-in-law, who has released albums under his own name and produced others. He began as an assistant engineer for frequent Who producer **Glyn Johns**, serving in this role on the 1977 Pete Townshend/**Ronnie Lane** album, *Rough Mix*. Astley's father, Ted, (see entry below) provided some orchestration for one album track. The two also collaborated on orchestrations for large ensembles. Not long after *Rough Mix* Johns was committed to working with **Joan Armatrading** around the time that the *Who Are You* album was being recorded, so it was left to Astley to produce "New Song," "Guitar and Pen," and "Sister Disco." Dave Marsh characterized these songs as "perhaps the least orthodox compositions on the record" in his book *Before I Get Old*.

In 1980 Astley co-produced the *Another Planet* EP for On the Air, the trio consisting of **Simon Townshend**, **Tony Butler** and **Mark Brzezicki**. With Phil Chapman, Astley produced the two **Steve Swindells** songs, "Martyrs And Madmen" and "Treachery," on Roger Daltrey's *Best Bits* album in 1982. He also produced Roger's cover of the **Spencer Davis Group**'s "Gimme Some Lovin'," the 1984 non-album B-side of Roger's twelve-inch UK "Walking in My Sleep" single. Jon produced the 1983 album *Promise Nothing* for his sister Virginia (see entry below) as well as her 1986 album *Hope in a Darkened Heart*. Jon had two albums of his own, 1987's *Everyone Loves the Pilot (Except the Crew)* which produced a hit single, "Jane's Getting Serious," and 1988's *Compleat Angler*. His daughters Layla and Zelda (see entry below) played recorder on the first and provided backing vocals on the second. In 1991 he played keyboards for the duo the **Law**, half of which was **Kenney Jones**. For Pete Townshend's *Psychoderelict* album in 1993 Astley co-composed the music for "Fake It" with **Billy Nicholls** and **Jon Lind** and Pete wrote the lyrics. Astley also played fairlight drums on that album.

In 1994 Jon worked with his daughters, his father, his sister Virginia and her daughter Florence on the 1994 **London Symphony Orchestra** *Symphonic Music of the Rolling Stones* CD. Astley had a major hand in the mid–1990s project to reissue the Who's catalog, with each album remastered and remixed and most supplemented with bonus tracks. However, he was credited with remastering work that was performed by Tim Young though Astley did indeed remaster *Odds & Sods*. In 1996 he co-produced the "Deep Love" remix of "My Generation," which John Atkins described in *The Who on Record* as "basically a new dance rhythm track (not by the Who) overlaid with a sampled edit of Roger Daltrey's lead vocals" from the *Live at Leeds* album. In 1997 he helped rework the **Simon Townshend** Band's *Among Us* album, which had been released on the Stir label in 1996 but was being more widely distributed by Rising Records. On the 1998 London Philharmonic Orchestra album *Who's Serious* Astley served as producer and arranged four of the tracks with help from his father.

Astley mastered all six discs for Pete Townshend's major release in early 2000, *Lifehouse Chronicles*. Astley has worked for a number of other artists besides the Who and its members, including on at least two projects each for **Eric Clapton**, Corey Hart, Tori Amos, and **Led Zeppelin**.

Astley, Ted Composer who was Pete Townshend's father-in-law. Edwin "Ted" Astley provided the music for movie comedies and Kenneth Clark's very popular cultural series *Civilisation* and wrote the memorable theme songs for the TV shows *Danger Man* (starring Patrick McGoohan) and *The Saint* (starring Roger Moore before his stint as James Bond). A version of the latter theme song recorded by the rock band Orbital made it to the top five of the British charts in 1997. Astley had often been the opening act when the Squadronaires, a band that included **Cliff Townshend,** would play in his hometown of Manchester.

Astley's earliest success came in the 1940s when a song he co-wrote, "I Never Could Tell," was recorded by **Vera Lynn** and Richard Tauber. He later joined a team of arrangers working on songs for Lynn and other top names of the era, such as Anne Shelton. His entry into television work came when he was asked to write the incidental music for the television series *The Adventures of Robin Hood*, which debuted in 1955, ran for 143 episodes, and did well on American TV. His film credits include *The Mouse That Roared*, a 1959 comedy starring **Peter Sellers**, and, presciently, a 1961 film called *A Matter of Who*. Royalties from his various endeavors made him the highest earner in the Performing Rights Society in 1967.

Pete Townshend married Astley's daughter Karen in 1968 but several years passed before the two musicians collaborated to any significant degree. Astley provided the orchestral score for "Street in the City" on the 1977 Pete Townshend/**Ronnie Lane** album, *Rough Mix*. Tony Gilbert was the orchestra leader. A year later he did the string arrangements for "Had Enough" and "Love Is Coming Down" on the *Who Are You* album. In the 1980s, he and Pete co-wrote the songs "Football Fugue," "Praying the

Game" and "The Ferryman" that eventually appeared on the album *Another Scoop*. On the latter track Pete used a "simple, droning, open-tuned guitar" and said that Astley later composed an "absolutely stunning impressionistic orchestral setting" for it. He was also credited on that album with the orchestral arrangement on "Brooklyn Kids." He also arranged the strings on **Simon Townshend**'s *Sweet Sound* album in 1984, which Pete produced.

Astley set the stage for projects like the **British Rock Symphony** by orchestrating some of the earliest collections of pop music to be performed by large symphony orchestras. For example, in 1978 he was arranger and conductor on the **London Symphony Orchestra**'s version of "Pinball Wizard," for which Pete Townshend supplied a short vocal. He also worked with son Jon (see entry above) on orchestrations for large ensembles and arranged for his daughter Virginia on her albums *Hope in a Darkened Heart* in 1986 and *All Shall Be Well* in 1992. He worked with Jon, Virginia, and three granddaughters (see entries below) on the 1994 London Symphony Orchestra *Symphonic Music of the* **Rolling Stones** CD. He helped Jon with his four arrangements on the London Philharmonic Orchestra album *Who's Serious*, which was released in early 1998. He was born in 1922 and died in May of 1998, on Pete Townshend's birthday. He was survived by his wife since 1945, Hazel, as well as by two sons and three daughters.

Astley, Virginia   Pete Townshend's sister-in-law, a pianist and flautist, whose distinct music has been dubbed "pastoralia" by *Wire* magazine. Her late–'70s band, the Ravishing Beauties, also included Kate St. John, the future Dream Academy singer, and Nicky Holland, who would work with Tears for Fears. Virginia played piano on Pete's 1982 solo album, *All the Best Cowboys Have Chinese Eyes,* and during the next year she spent 17 weeks high in the UK indie charts with "Love's a Lonely Place to Be" from her album *Gardens Where We Feel Secure*. Her brother Jon (see entry above) produced a quick follow-up project, *Promise Nothing*, as well as her 1986 album *Hope in a Darkened Heart*. Her father, Ted (see entry above), arranged for Virginia on the latter and on *All Shall Be Well* in 1992.

The title of that 1992 album was the same as a track on Pete's 1989 *Iron Man* album, his 1989 musical adaptation of the **Ted Hughes** tale; in the album's credits Pete thanked Virginia "for advice and experimental work." A song she co-wrote with Dave Stewart of **Eurythmics** fame, "Second Chance," appeared on the *Lily Was Here* soundtrack album in 1991 though not in the movie; the title track became a hit instrumental for saxophonist

Candy Dulfer. Virginia has recorded with her daughter Florence a few times, starting with *All Shall Be Well*, and the two were among the six Astleys to work on the 1994 **London Symphony Orchestra** *Symphonic Music of the Rolling Stones* CD. In 1996 she released another album, *Had I the Heavens*.

Astley, Zelda Pete Townshend's niece and the subject of the song "Zelda" on Pete Townshend's first double album of demos, 1983's *Scoop*. "I have no idea what it's about… the day I wrote it she had waved at me from the back seat of her father's car." Zelda and her sister Layla helped their dad Jon (see entry above) on his two albums in the late 1980s, *Everyone Loves the Pilot (Except the Crew)* and *Compleat Angler*. They played recorder on the first and provided backing vocals on the second. In 1994 they joined their father, their grandfather Ted, their aunt Virginia and their cousin Florence (see separate entries above) on the **London Symphony Orchestra**'s *Symphonic Music of the* **Rolling Stones** CD.

Atfield, Donald *see* Christian, Roger.

Atlas, Charles American bodybuilder whose long-running ads depicted a "98-pound weakling" who, after learning "dynamic tension" from a Charles Atlas course, suffers bullies no longer. *The Who Sell Out* has a brief Charles Atlas jingle urging the listener to become more manly, and John Entwistle is dressed as an Atlas success story on the cover. The photo's caption: "John Entwistle was a nine and a half stone weakling until Charles Atlas made a man of him at nine and three-quarter stone. Now those huggy bear biceps bring those beach beauties running. Put muscles among the mussels. Tense yourself skinny." For some reason, on the Canadian cover "Charles Atlas" was changed to "Isometrics." The American cover probably should have included an explanatory note that in Britain a "stone" equals 14 pounds, meaning that Entwistle purportedly bulged from 133 all the way up to 136.5 pounds.

Baba, Meher Spiritual master in India to whom Pete Townshend became quite devoted and who had a huge influence on Pete's lyrics. Baba was born Merwan Sheriar Irani in Poona, India on February 24, 1894, and from 1925 until his death in 1969 he maintained a vow of silence but lectured using a handheld alphabet board and hand gestures. Early on he was renamed Meher Baba, meaning "compassionate father," by a group of disciples. As such he was considered the reincarnation of Jesus Christ, Buddha, Mohammed, and all other great spiritual leaders. The most well known saying attributed to Baba was "Don't worry, be happy," shortened from his advice to "Do your best, then leave the results to me and don't worry — be happy."

In late 1967 or early 1968 **Mike McInnerney**, who created the cover of the *Tommy* LP, introduced his friend Pete Townshend to Baba's teachings, which he asserted were similar to beliefs Pete embraced. Fittingly, Baba was credited as "Avatar" (a deity's earthly incarnation) on the *Tommy* album. Pete also had regular contact with a senior disciple of Baba's in the London area, Don Stevens. On March 1, 1970, London's *Sunday Telegraph* printed a column by Pete entitled "Sterility of Drug Taking" in which he praised the work of Dr. Allan Cohen for helping young people get off drugs and noted that Baba's influence on him led him to reject drug use. Despite Pete's later failure to stay off drugs, his statement was rare among rock stars at that time. For several years after Baba's death Pete joined with various performers, including **Ronnie Lane** and **Billy Nicholls**, to generate three nonprofit albums devoted to Baba, *Happy Birthday*, *I Am*, and *With Love*. One Townshend song on *Happy Birthday*, "Day of Silence," referred to July 10th, the day his followers typically spent without speaking. Songs from the first two were used on Pete's first commercial solo LP, *Who Came First*. That album's alternate title for "Let's See Action," "Nothing Is Everything," referred to a book of Baba teachings entitled *The Everything and the Nothing*.

Baba influenced not only "Baba O'Riley" on *Who's Next* but also the second song on that album, "Bargain." (The title of the former paid tribute not only to Baba but also to avant-garde composer **Terry Riley**.) In his *Another Scoop* liner notes Pete Townshend said that the song "The Ferryman," which he composed with **Ted Astley**, "was written for an amateur production of Siddhartha performed at the opening celebrations for the Meher Baba Oceanic Centre in June of 1976." Pete's top solo hit, "Let My Love Open the Door," was inspired by Baba, and the inner sleeve of the album featuring that song, *Empty Glass,* featured a Baba quote: "Desire for nothing except desirelessness, hope for nothing except to rise above all hopes, want nothing and you will have everything."

A year later the Who recorded yet another song influenced by Baba's teachings, "Don't Let Go the Coat." Baba's name also surfaced in the titles of instrumentals on Pete's studio album of the 1990s, *Psychoderelict*. Other instrumentals in this series turned up on Pete's six-disc *Lifehouse Chronicles* boxed set in early 2000. At the same time he released the *Avatar* boxed set, which presented the *Happy Birthday*, *I Am*, and *With Love* albums on CD for the first time. Also included was a CD-ROM containing an eight-minute movie about Baba titled *O'Parvardigar*.

Baby Buddha Female punk band from San Francisco whose early 1980s LP, *Music for Teenage Sex*, included a cover of the Who's "My

Generation." In 1988 vocalist Kathy Peck, who was also bass player in the SF female punk band the Contractions, was a founder and the executive director of Hearing Education and Awareness for Rockers (H.E.A.R.), which educates about the dangers posed by amplified music. The organization's website lists its more prominent supporters among musicians, and named first is Pete Townshend. A *Washington Post* story on January 30, 1999, noted that H.E.A.R. gained visibility early "when Pete Townshend of the Who wrote it a $10,000 check and publicly acknowledged his own hearing loss." He presented that check during a Who concert in Oakland on August 30, 1989. An announcement for the Fourth International Noise Awareness Day, which was April 21, 1999, listed Pete, Les Claypool of Primus, and Lars Ulrich of Metallica among H.E.A.R. spokespersons.

Bacon, Kevin   Actor who became well known as the star of the 1984 movie *Footloose* and who starred in the only 1980s movie featuring a Roger Daltrey theme song. In 1986 Daltrey sang the Giorgio Moroder and Dean Pitchford composition "Quicksilver Lightning" for the movie *Quicksilver*, in which Bacon portrayed a stockbroker-turned-bike messenger. Among Bacon's most prominent recent movie roles was co-starring in the 1995 box office success *Apollo 13*, which used the Who's "I Can See for Miles" on its soundtrack. Another musical connection to the Who came at the start of an appearance on the TV show *Late Night with Conan O'Brien*: Bacon was welcomed on stage to the tune of the Who's "Cousin Kevin" as performed by the house band, the Max Weinberg Seven. Around the time of *Apollo 13* Bacon found himself with a unique claim to fame due to a game developed by students at Pennsylvania's Albright College. They devised a movie trivia game based on the premise of John Guare's play *Six Degrees of Separation*, that any two people on Earth can be connected via a series of no more than six relationships. Six Degrees of Kevin Bacon challenges players to link any given actor or actress to Bacon, who was hostile to the game until he met its originators.

Bad Company   British rock band that had a #1 hit in 1974, "Can't Get Enough," off its self-titled debut album. A year later guitarist Mick Ralphs, who had been in Mott the Hoople, played on "1951/What About the Boy" on the *Tommy* movie soundtrack. In 1977 bass player Raymond "Boz" Burrell played on "Heart to Hang Onto" and "Till the Rivers All Run Dry" on the Pete Townshend/**Ronnie Lane** collaboration, *Rough Mix*. He was credited on the UK album but, like **Charlie Watts**, not on the U.S. release. Burrell, formerly of King Crimson, had been in the band Boz's People in 1965 when Roger Daltrey was briefly kicked out of the Who. Rumor had it that Burrell would be Daltrey's replacement, but **Richard**

Barnes noted that Boz dismissed the notion by saying that "The Who are children playing with electronic toys." **Geoff Whitehorn** joined Bad Company in mid–1990 for a U.S. tour and stayed until the return of Ralphs in April 1991. That year Bad Company singer Paul Rodgers, who had originally been in Free, formed a short-lived duo with **Kenney Jones** called the Law. Around the turn of the century Rodgers performed with the **British Rock Symphony**, as did Daltrey, and both sang on the 1999 album. Rodgers was supposed to headline two BRS performances in New York on April 12 and 13, 2000, but he backed out. They featured **Billy Preston**, **Darlene Love**, Nikki Lamborn and **Simon Townshend**.

Bailey, Richard   Drummer on the *Tommy* movie soundtrack, on "Go to the Mirror." Bailey had drummed on a couple of **Jeff Beck** albums around the same time and later recorded with Mick Taylor, Billy Ocean, and Brian Eno, among many others.

Baird, Roy   Producer of several Who-related movies. He was assistant director of several films in the 1960s, including the James Bond spoof *Casino Royale* in 1967. In the mid–1970s he produced two films for director Ken Russell: *Mahler*, starring Robert Powell, and *Lisztomania*, Roger Daltrey's second starring vehicle. He shared duties with David Puttnam on the latter. Around this time he also served as executive producer of *Stardust*, which starred **David Essex**, **Adam Faith**, **Larry Hagman**, and Keith Moon. Baird's association with the Who became even stronger by the end of the decade when he produced *Quadrophenia* with **Bill Curbishley** and *McVicar* with Curbishley and Daltrey. He was also credited as executive producer of *The Who Rocks America* concert video in 1982. Ten years after *McVicar* Baird teamed with Curbishley and Daltrey again to produce *Buddy's Song*, which starred Chesney Hawkes. In 1988 Baird produced the television movie *Lenin: The Train*, which starred Ben Kingsley and Leslie Caron.

Baker, Ginger   Drummer with some of the most notable bands in rock history. Peter "Ginger" Baker joined Alexis Korner's Blues Incorporated in mid–1962 but by February of the next year had switched to the **Graham Bond** Trio, which was rounded out by bassist Jack Bruce. By March of 1966 they grew to become the Graham Bond Organisation and provided the B-side "Waltz for a Pig" so that the Who's "Substitute" 45 could be rushed to retailers. The B-side was attributed to either the Who Orchestra or simply the Who, and was written by someone named Harry Butcher. However, according to Harry Shapiro in his 1992 book *Eric Clapton: Lost in the Blues*, the song was actually written by Baker. Shapiro also said that **Eric Clapton** performed on that track, but there is some dispute about that. In a 1991 interview for the Graham Bond fanzine *GRAMBO*, Graham Bond Organisation sax player Dick Heckstall-Smith said that Baker wrote "Waltz for a Pig" and that its use as the B-side for "Substitute" probably resulted from some kind of deal with **Robert Stigwood**. He added, "I think that was one way that Ginger got enough bread to leave and start setting up something or other." By the summer he, Bruce and Clapton had formed the acclaimed group Cream, though it lasted little more than two years. Baker and Clapton then formed Blind Faith with **Steve Winwood** and Rick Grech, but they only released one album, in 1969. He spent much of the 1970s making albums with Ginger Baker's Air Force and the Baker Gurvitz Army. After Keith Moon's death in 1978, Baker was reportedly among the drummers who offered to fill in on at least a temporary basis. Baker's recording career was a bit more active in the '90s than in the '80s.

Baker, Ray Robert   Writer of "There's a Heartache Following Me," which Pete Townshend covered on *Who Came First*. It was a hit for **Jim Reeves**. Ray Baker & the Happy Travellers recorded a few bluegrass 45s but Baker is mostly known for collaborating with Reeves and managing Reeves's music publishing firms.

Ball, Kenny   Longtime prominent British trumpet player whose songs John Entwistle often played in one of his first bands. While a member of the **Confederates** Entwistle also joined a bigger and more active trad group, though it never had a name. This band mainly played songs by the bigger "trad bands," those led by Kenny Ball and **Acker Bilk**. Ball's biggest hit came in 1961 when "Midnight in Moscow" became a hit in the U.S. as well as in the UK.

Ballard, Russ   Frequent aide to Roger Daltrey's solo career and former lead singer of **Argent**, which had its biggest chart success in 1972 with the song "Hold Your Head Up." Ballard also wrote the song "Liar," which was a hit for Three Dog Night. Ballard played guitar on Daltrey's self-titled solo debut and also provided the piano solo for "The Story So Far" on that 1973 album. Ballard produced, played on, and wrote "(Come and) Get Your Love," "Proud" and "Near to Surrender" on Daltrey's follow-up, *Ride a Rock Horse*. Ballard provided another trio of songs for 1980's *McVicar* soundtrack, including the hit "Free Me." On Daltrey's 1985 and 1987 releases, *Under a Raging Moon* and *Can't Wait to See the Movie*, Ballard provided guitar and backing vocals on the song he wrote for each album, "Breaking Down Paradise" and "Hearts of Fire," respectively. In between those albums, toward the end of 1985, Daltrey was backed on a mini-tour by Ballard, **Alan Shacklock, Stuart Elliott, John Siegler,** former **Humble Pie** guitarist Dave Clempson, and Mark Williamson. Some of these tracks were released as B-sides on Daltrey singles in Europe.

The Band *see* Helm, Levon.

The Bangles *see* Hoffs, Susanna.

Barcelona, Frank *see* Barsalona, Frank.

Barclay, John   Trumpet player who has recorded with a number of noted performers since the mid–1980s, including Pete Townshend. He played brass, along with **Peter Beachill**, on the Who song "Dig" on Townshend's *Iron Man* album, his 1989 musical adaptation of the **Ted Hughes** tale. In the 1990s he and Beachill played on albums by Björk, Peter Gabriel, **Colin Towns**, and Kenny Wheeler. Others Barclay has recorded with include the Cure, **Tom Jones**, ex–**Beatle** Paul McCartney, **Oasis**, the Pet Shop Boys, and ex–**Police** singer Sting.

Barclay, Nickey *see* Fanny.

The Bards   1960s band based in the state of Washington that released several 45s in the second half of the 1960s, including one in 1967 on the Piccadilly label that had a version of the Who's "My Generation" paired with a song called "The Jabberwocky." Their next single, an arrangement of Curtis Mayfield's "Never Too Much Love," received some national airplay and gave the band the chance to tour with known acts such as the Dave Clark Five, the Turtles, and Paul Revere and the Raiders. A re-release of the "My Generation" 45 on the Panorama label was planned shortly thereafter but not issued. The Bards then released a couple of 45s on the Capitol label and ended the decade by recording an album, but it wasn't released until 1980. Their version of "My Generation" can be found on the compilations *Battle of the Bands Vol. 2* and *History of Northwest Rock Vol. 3*.

Barham, John   Musician who handled the brass arrangement on Roger Daltrey's 1975 solo album, *Ride a Rock Horse* and who earlier performed with ex–**Beatles** John Lennon and George Harrison. He also worked with Ravi Shankar and Gary Wright over the years.

Barker, Robert *see* Parker, Robert.

Barlow, Gary   Member of Take That, the teenybopper quintet that dominated the British pop charts during the first half of the 1990s, selling more than any English act since the **Beatles**. In the winter of 1998, the Associated Press reported that Roger Daltrey came to the rescue of a group of anglers whom Barlow barred from fishing on his estate in Cuddington, Cheshire. Barlow erected fences and "keep out" signs and told the Delamere Manor Fly Fishers that they could no longer use a lake on his property which their club had fished for more than 40 years. Daltrey, a respected trout farmer, offered to open his Lakedown Trout Fishery in Sussex to the club after hearing about the turn of events.

Barnacle, Gary   Longtime saxophone player for Level 42 who also played on Roger Daltrey's 1987 solo album, *Can't Wait to See the Movie*. He formed a duo called Leisure Process with Ross Middleton and since 1980 he has recorded at least twice each with Björk, the **Clash**, Phil Collins of **Genesis**, Elvis Costello, Maxi Priest, and **Tina Turner**.

Barnacle, Steve   Bass player who performed on Pete Townshend's *White City* album in 1985 as well as **Simon Townshend**'s *Sweet Sound* album the year before. His other album credits include backing **Rick Wakeman** in 1981, Erasure in 1986, and Spear of Destiny in 1987 as well as on BBC's Radio 1 in 1994.

Barnes, Richard   Longtime friend of the Who, whom he named, and author of what many believe is the definitive biography of the band, the *Who: Maximum R&B*. "Barney" met Pete Townshend when the two were attending Ealing Art School and the two fast friends eventually became roommates. In the liner notes for *Another Scoop* Townshend noted that he recorded two demos, for "Call Me Lightning" and the unreleased "You Don't Have to Jerk," during the winter of 1964 at the flat he shared with Barnes above his parents' home. In February of 1964 the **Detours** needed a new name because another act using the name had appeared on television. During an America Online chat in February of 2000, Roger Daltrey recalled the process of coming up with the new name: "Just one stupid night of being drunk and disorderly in Pete's flat, shouting out stupid names, from the Hair... oh, lots of ridiculous names. Merwin. Ladies and gentlemen, No One! And then Pete's art school friend came up, who said the Who."

Barnes also recalled offering "the Group" and "the Name" while Pete pushed for "the Hair." Barnes recalled that it was Daltrey who settled it the next morning rather matter-of-factly. By the end of June, shortly before the Who temporarily were renamed the **High Numbers**, Barnes secured a Tuesday night spot for 12 weeks at the Railway Hotel in Harrow, which helped them develop a following. It was there that Townshend accidentally broke and then angrily smashed a guitar one night. Two weeks later the crowd insisted he repeat the performance, which he gladly did, and Keith Moon followed suit by smashing his drum kit. Around this time the High Numbers had their first commercial recording session. Barnes played maracas on several takes of their cover of **Bo Diddley**'s "Here 'Tis" and recalled having "severely blistered hands and fingers for weeks afterwards."

In the wake of his Railway success Barnes contemplated creating a company to promote dances, to be named either "Fabulous Entertainments" or "Fabulous Promotions." Townshend later recalled this when looking to name his music publishing company, and thus "Fabulous Music Ltd" was born. Barnes and Townshend wrote the book *The Story of Tommy* in 1977 and a couple of years later came Barnes's book *Mods*. Barnes and old friend Russ Schlagbaum, who had worked for the *Faces*, attended the tragic Who concert in Cincinnati on December 3, 1979. Though they decided to wander around the venue instead of standing to the side of the stage, their shifting vantage point still did not make it immediately apparent to them that deaths had occurred, in a stampede for seats.

Barnes's book *Maximum R&B* was published in 1982 and was updated in the late 1990s. A third edition was prepared for the new millennium, with a new introduction by Townshend. Barnes has provided liner notes for several albums, including *Who's Better Who's Best* in 1988 and the reissued *Tommy* CD in 1996. In 1997 he also provided liner notes for the CD debut of Keith Moon's 1975 solo album and the first-ever release of John Entwistle's March 1975 Ox concert that was broadcast by the *King Biscuit Flower Hour*.

Barnett, Andy   Slide guitarist in **John McEnroe** and Pat Cash's 1991 backup band, the Full Metal Rackets, which featured Roger Daltrey on vocals. In the last half of the 1970s Barnett and future **Iron Maiden** member Adrian Smith were in the band Urchin, which released two singles. In 1984 Barnett backed successful Canada-born singer Corey Hart on his debut album. Just before Smith left Iron Maiden he reunited with Barnett for the 1989 Adrian Smith And Project (A.S.A.P.) album *Silver And Gold*, which featured **Zak Starkey** on drums. Two years later came Barnett's job in the Full Metal Rackets, which included two of Smith's former Iron Maiden bandmates. In 1997 Barnett produced and played various instruments on Rhino's *Children's Favorites* album.

Barney   *see* Barnes, Richard.

Baron, Steve   Songwriter and guitarist for whom Pete Townshend twice wrote paragraphs on the backs of album covers, *The Mother of Us All* in 1969 and *A Wanderer Like You* about five years later. Pete also produced Baron's 45 "Tell Me"/"California Friends" on the Bell label. Baron took part in New York's Greenwich Village folk revival of the early 1960s.

The Steve Baron Quartet, which had jazz and rock overtones in addition to folk, appeared on a public television show called *Eavesdropping on the New Rock* in mid–1967 but they didn't release an album for about two years. A prime chance to promote it was playing with **Leslie West**'s band Mountain and the Steve Miller Blues Band at New York's Fillmore East on Halloween and the night after. *A Wanderer Like You*, which was recorded in Nashville, reportedly represented Baron's last attempt to hit it big, and its failure to sell well prompted Baron to fade from the music scene after playing organ on Buzz Rabin's *Cross Country Cowboy* album in 1974. Baron's and Rabin's albums were both produced by much-in-demand session musician Pete Drake and shared a few musicians.

The Barron Knights British group that started out in the early 1960s like most others but soon shifted to parody. In the process, they released a Pete Townshend song that never surfaced on a Who or Pete release in the 20th century. That song was "Lazy Fat People," a Decca 45 in the U.S. and a Columbia 45 in the UK in 1967. It is thought that Townshend never played his demo for the Who. The Barron Knights had roughly a dozen singles enter the UK charts during a 20-year span starting in 1964, but their only appearance on the U.S. charts was in 1979 with a parody of Supertramp's "The Logical Song."

Barry, Dave Humorous American journalist whose life was the basis for the network television series *Dave's World,* which aired for four seasons starting in 1993. In his 1990 book *Dave Barry Turns 40* he poked fun at **Beatles** fans and paraphrased Pete Townshend while discussing the "legendary" sixties: "We lit candles and sat around listening to John Lennon sing, with genuine passion in his voice, about how he was the egg man, and *they* were the egg men, and *he* was also the walrus, and by God we know *exactly what he meant*. That was the level of hipness that we attained, in My Generation. Oh sure, people tried to put us down, just because we got around."

Barsalona, Frank Agent for the **Beatles**' first American tour who later became the Who's American agent. By that time "Frank the Tank" was the co-owner of, and the moving force behind, Premier Talent in New York. He began with American clients such as Mitch Ryder, Del Shannon, and Jay and the Americans and moved to British clients such as **Herman's Hermits** and the **Animals**. **Chris Stamp** and others tried for a while to secure the services of Barsalona but he always declined because he thought the Who had a stronger association with the off-putting Allan Klein than was in fact the case. Stamp then persuaded Premier financial manager and co-owner Dick Freedman to sign the Who while Barsalona was in California, much to Barsalona's chagrin. However, Barsalona's hostility was overcome when famous New York disc jockey Murray the K insisted that Mitch Ryder perform on his 1967 Easter show. Ryder didn't want to do the show so Barsalona tried to dissuade Murray the K by claiming that Ryder was such a fan of the Who and would only perform if they would be paid handsomely to appear as well. Barsalona expected that the inclusion of the Who, then little-known in America, would kill the deal, but it didn't. Thus, on March 22, 1967, the Who collectively set foot in the United States for the first time.

When Barsalona actually had the chance to watch the Who perform, his attitude about the band quickly changed to one of tremendous enthusiasm. Barsalona's amusing account took up four pages of Robert Stephen Spitz's 1978 book the *Making of Superstars: Artists and Executives of the Rock Music Business*. The Who performed five shows a day at the RKO 58th Street Theater from March 25 through April 2. *The Who Concert File* stressed that the Who did not appear on Murray the K's TV show *Coliseum* around that time, contrary to other reports. Following the Who's performances for Murray the K, Barsalona arranged for the Who to tour the U.S. In support of **Herman's Hermits** that summer.

In 1969, after booking Joe Cocker, Ten Years After and other Premier Talent acts for the now-legendary Woodstock festival, Barsalona argued with Pete Townshend and **John "Wiggy" Wolff** that the Who should play there as well. Barsalona and the band had previously agreed to avoid pop festivals, but Barsalona correctly sensed that Woodstock would be too important to skip. Barsalona remained a force to be reckoned with into the 1980s, by which time Premier Talent was also doing booking work for Bruce Springsteen and the **Pretenders**. U2 manager Paul McGuinness worked with Barsalona to introduce the Irish band to the United States in 1980 and 1981.

Barton, Gordon   Drummer on most tracks on John Entwistle's second solo album, 1972's *Whistle Rymes*, who faded from the music scene afterwards. In 1966 he was in the band Wild Uncertainty with Eddie Hardin. They recorded a collectible 45, a version of the **Everly Brothers'** "Man with Money," on **Shel Talmy**'s Planet label. This song resurfaced on the 1993 compilation *English Freakbeat Vol. 5*, which also includes a version of the Who song "It's Not True" by the **Untamed**. Barton then released an album a year from 1969 through 1971 as part of a band called Andwella's Dream.

Batt, Mike   British singer/songwriter who has served as arranger or producer for a number of other performers. Roger Daltrey has taken part in two of Batt's projects, the first in 1984 when Batt transformed **Lewis Carroll**'s epic nonsense poem "The Hunting of the Snark" into a musical. Daltrey portrayed the Barrister and sang lead on "The Pig Must Die." In 1998 Daltrey was one of about a dozen guest vocalists on Batt's *Philharmania* album, which featured the Royal Philharmonic Orchestra on 14 familiar rock songs. Daltrey sang ex–**Eagle** Don Henley's "The Boys of Summer." Rock musicians who helped Batt on the album included **Chris Spedding** on guitar and Henry Spinetti on drums. Midway between those two projects he handled the string arrangements on two Chesney Hawkes songs on *The One and Only*, the album from the Daltrey movie *Buddy's Song*.

One of Batt's earliest credits was as arranger for **Family**'s 1968 album *Music in a Doll's House*. In 1974 he started making very successful music for the Wombles, a group of musicians in furry animal costumes linked to the popular British TV series of the same name. A year later he had a Top 10 UK solo hit with the song "Summertime City" and produced the Steeleye Span album *All Around My Hat*. Among Batt's other credits are as producer of albums for Art Garfunkel in 1981 and 1990, keyboard player on the 1983 Hollies album *What Goes Around*, and arranger and conductor on the 1994 Indigo Girls album *Swamp Ophelia*. Around the same time he helped Justin Hayward of **Moody Blues** fame and the London Philharmonic Orchestra get their album *Classic Blue* on the British charts. More recently he has been taking part in a Wombles revival.

Baum, L. Frank   American writer whose most famous work remains his 1900 tale the *Wonderful Wizard of Oz*, which was the basis of the famous movie in 1938. In the mid–1990s a stage production recorded for television, the *Wizard of Oz in Concert: Dreams Come True*, starred **Jewel** as Dorothy, Roger Daltrey as the Tin Man, **Nathan Lane** as the Cowardly Lion and **Jackson Browne** as the Scarecrow. The soundtrack for this Children's Defense Fund stage and TV benefit was released in 1996. Baum, who was also a journalist, lived from 1856 to 1919.

Baverstock, Jack   Producer of the first 45 by the band that would be rechristened "The Who" a few months later. Baverstock supervised the four-song recording session by the **High Numbers** and certainly engineered the recordings but the production credit "I'm the Face"/"Zoot Suit" 45 went to **Peter Meaden** and Chris Parmeinter. The High Numbers must have been on good behavior because in 1965 Baverstock stormed out of a Pretty Things recording session after 30 minutes. He did, however, have a hand in the success of several other artists, including Wayne Fontana and the Mindbenders, Kiki Dee, Slade, and the Merseybeats before they shortened their name to the **Merseys**.

Baxter, Jeff "Skunk" Former guitarist for the popular acts Steely Dan and the Doobie Brothers who has teamed up with John Entwistle from time to time. In the fall of 1990 and into 1991 he and John were part of a supergroup called the **Best**. He and Entwistle also performed live on a limited basis with Mickey Thomas of **Jefferson Starship**. In March of 1996 at the House of Blues in Los Angeles, Baxter played rhythm guitar with the John Entwistle Band on the encore songs "Long Live Rock" and "Shakin' All Over." About two years later he joined them at the same venue during the encore songs "Summertime Blues" and "Shakin' All Over." Baxter was in Steely Dan from 1972 to 1975, when he and yearlong member Michael McDonald departed for the Doobies. In fact, Baxter had been doing double duty for about a year. Baxter left the Doobies in 1978, shortly after the release of their Grammy Award winning *Minute by Minute* album. Baxter then turned toward country music and backed Hoyt Axton and Dolly Parton on a few albums each by 1980. From 1980 to 1991 he backed such performers as Steve Goodman, Deniece Williams, and MC Lyte. Baxter wrote the theme song for the long running prime time soap opera *Beverly Hills 90210*, which aired throughout the 1990s. In 1999 Baxter indicated that he was considering a bid for Congress in 2000 as a Republican against two-term California Representative Brad Sherman. The Associated Press reported that a past of illicit drug use and sexual conduct wouldn't deter Baxter, who said, "I'm going to admit that I did all that stuff. But the most important thing is to learn from your past." However, Baxter later declined to run, leaving Sherman to face a challenge from actor Jerry Doyle, best known as Security Chief Michael Garibaldi on the science fiction series *Babylon 5*.

Bayless, Lily Actress in the vaudeville era whose appearance on a postcard inspired Pete Townshend to write the early Who song "Pictures of Lily." Lilian Bayless was also theater manager of the Old Vic Company in London early in the 20th century. The single she inspired, one of the first "power pop" records as Townshend dubbed it, reached #4. In the liner notes for Rhino's 1997 compilation *Poptopia! Power Pop Classics of the '70s*, Doug Fieger of the Knack acknowledged that Townshend coined that term (and cited the Who as a major influence). "Pictures of Lily" was the Who's first single on Track Records, the British label founded by their managers, **Kit Lambert** and **Chris Stamp**. The label had just made its debut with the **Jimi Hendrix** Experience's second single, "Purple Haze." According to **Richard Barnes**, when Pete Townshend was working on his 1982 solo album *All the Best Cowboys Have Chinese Eyes*, Pete wanted to pair it with a film to be called *Bilder von Lily*, which is German for "Pictures of Lily." However, he abandoned the project halfway through after reportedly spending 70,000 pounds.

Beach, Reb   Guitarist on Roger Daltrey's remake of the **Elton John**/Bernie Taupin song "Don't Let the Sun Go Down on Me" for the soundtrack of *The Lost Boys* in 1985. Beach characterized the experience to this author as "pretty cool" and also recalls it fondly because it netted him his first gold record. The next year Beach formed the successful pop-metal group Winger with bassist/front man Kip Winger, and later joined another high-profile pop-metal band, Dokken.

The Beach Boys   California band that began cranking out surf hits in 1962 and which Keith Moon worshipped. Their 1964 hit "Don't Worry Baby" was reportedly among Keith's all-time favorite songs, if not number one outright. About 10 years later the song, written by Beach Boy Brian Wilson and **Roger Christian**, was a single from Keith's only solo album. In 1966 Moon persuaded his mates in the Who to cover "Barbara Ann" on their five-song EP *Ready Steady Who*. The song had become a #3 UK hit for the Beach Boys in March of 1966 though it was written by Charles Fassert and first released by the Regents in 1961. In late 1977 an aborted studio version by the Who was filmed for the movie *The Kids Are Alright*.

In November of 1997, Beach Boy bassist/vocalist Bruce Johnston released from his personal archive an unpublished photo with Keith Moon in London in May of 1966. The two were outside of the Rediffusion television studios for a *Ready Steady Go* walk-on. If it is indeed true that the **Beatles** were inspired to create their *Sgt. Pepper's* album after hearing the 1966 Beach Boys album *Pet Sounds*, then this may have been precipitated by Moon that day. Johnston had flown to England to promote foreign distribution of his band's newly released album and was phoned by Moon, who wanted to hear it. Johnston told Moon to meet him at the Waldorf Hotel, and Keith brought John Lennon and Paul McCartney. Johnston said they spent hours playing cards and repeatedly listening to the album, and that John and Paul "were absolutely amazed." Moon, however, later said he felt *Pet Sounds* was too far removed from the style he loved. However, Pete Townshend had a completely different reaction. In the latter half of the 1960s and even years later he would speak quite highly of it. During a radio show in May of 1995 he called *Pet Sounds* the definitive and first concept album, adding that it's an even better example of the genre than *Sgt. Pepper's*.

It wasn't the only Beach Boys album he admired, however. On his first double album of demos, 1983's *Scoop*, his liner notes indicated that when recording the song "Goin' Fishin'" he was probably aiming for "the kind of atmosphere the Beach Boys had achieved on *Smiley Smile*" in 1967. According to Tony Fletcher in *Dear Boy*, Keith finally met all of the Beach Boys in late 1970 when he attended a concert of theirs in London. Just as Keith had found *Pet Sounds* to be a disappointment, he didn't care for the fact that the Beach Boys were "still into the Indian spiritual vibe," as Fletcher put it. Still, if the British music press had made an accurate prediction in 1971, Keith Moon would have realized one of his fondest dreams. An injury sustained by Beach Boys drummer Dennis Wilson led to rumors that Keith had been asked to serve as a temporary replacement.

The Beachcombers   Band which Keith Moon left in order to join the Who. Contrary to many sources and the band's name notwithstanding, they apparently were not a surf band and thus did not figure prominently in Moon's love of that pop subgenre. They also weren't Keith's only pre-Who band, as some sources state, because he had been in others, including the **Escorts** and, according to one source, a band called the **Altones**. Sometimes billed as Clyde Burns and the Beachcombers, a photo caption in Tony Fletcher's definitive Moon biography *Dear Boy* identified Moon's bandmates as Tony Brind, Ron Chenery (aka Clyde Burns), John Schollar, and Norman Mitchener. In late 1962 the band advertised in a local paper for a drummer to replace the one they'd recently ousted, named Alan Roberts. Because Keith was only 16 at the time, Alfred Moon accompanied his son to the audition, which the older Beachcombers thought should've embarrassed Keith. Several older drummers auditioned first, and though the Beachcombers were reluctant to take on someone whose age would make it difficult to get into pubs, Keith's persistence and explosive playing got him the job.

Moon amply demonstrated his sense of humor during his 18 months in the band, as indicated by one of John Schollar's memories that appeared in **Richard Barnes**'s book. "When we used to do Little Egypt, we used to carry Keith on in a basket and he'd do the talking intro bit dressed in a fez." **Chris Charlesworth** indicated in his 1982 biography of the Who that in 1963 Keith was the drummer when the Beachcombers released a song called "Mad Goose" on a 45 issued by EMI's Columbia label. This and other Beachcombers releases do exist, but they were apparently performed by one or more other bands using that name, including "Pat Wayne and the Beachcombers." In Fletcher's 1998 biography, for which Charlesworth served as editor, it is noted that Keith never got to release a record with the Beachcombers and that the band "only went into a studio once, and that in a dingy basement beneath a keyboard shop in North Harrow to make a tape of a few cover versions ('Poison Ivy' and 'I'm a Hog for You Baby' among them) that has long since disappeared." Ironically, original Who drummer **Doug Sandom** briefly served as drummer for the Beachcombers after Moon left to replace Sandom in the Who.

Beachill, Peter   Trombone player who has recorded with a number of noted performers since the mid–1980s, including Pete Townshend. He played brass, along with **John Barclay**, on the Who song "Dig" on Townshend's *Iron Man* album, his 1989 musical adaptation of the **Ted Hughes** tale. In the 1990s he and Barclay played on albums by Björk, Peter Gabriel, **Colin Towns**, and Kenny Wheeler. Others Beachill has recorded with include Grace Jones, **Tom Jones**, the **Moody Blues**, Sade, The The, and Was (Not Was).

Beard, Tony   Drummer on Roger Daltrey's 1987 solo album, *Can't Wait to See the Movie*. A year or two before that he backed such artists as the Dream Academy, Chris De Burgh, and Matthew Sweet, and in the 1990s his credits include albums for Foreigner, Judy Collins, **Laura Branigan**, **Bette Midler**, and former **Van Halen** frontman David Lee Roth.

The Beat   *see* The English Beat.

The Beatles   The most commercially successful band of the 1960s, starting with the top 20 UK hit "Love Me Do" in the autumn of 1962. "The Fab Four," as they were widely known, consisted of John Lennon, George Harrison, Paul McCartney, and Ringo Starr. After impressive chart success in the UK, the Beatles arrived in the U.S. in February of 1964 and thus touched off the "British Invasion," which saw numerous other groups from the UK become popular in the United States. In Steve Clarke's 1979 book *The Who in Their Own Words*, Roger Daltrey recalled that in 1963 the Who's immediate precursor, the **Detours**, "played Beatles songs for about six months and then we completely forgot that and went on a really heavy blues trip." In early 1964 the Detours became the Who but in the summer they were temporarily known as the **High Numbers** and had their only gig in support of the Beatles on August 16. In *The Who: Maximum R&B* **Richard Barnes** described how the High Numbers plus their aides **Kit Lambert**, **Mike Shaw**, and Barnes himself had to encounter a mob of Beatles fans after the Fab Four escaped via a tunnel. Barnes said Daltrey "bravely fought his way through the mob" while having his collar and a sleeve torn off, and then backed the band's van through the mob. He couldn't quite reach the stage door and the police present were powerless, so Roger's six comrades were pawed while climbing into the van.

After the High Numbers were rechristened the Who and released two popular 45s, Paul McCartney said that "The Who are the most exciting thing around." The next significant encounter of the two bands was after *New Musical Express* conducted its annual readership poll in 1965. This led to the winners performing on May 1 of the following year, at what Barnes called "the pop event of 1966," a concert that aired on television split over the following two Sundays. *NME*'s own review said the Who were more remarkable than the Beatles and the **Rolling Stones**. That same month Keith Moon took Lennon and McCartney to meet Bruce Johnston of the **Beach Boys**, who was in London to promote his group's new *Pet Sounds* album. The four listened to the album repeatedly. If it is true that the Beatles' *Sgt. Pepper's* album was inspired by *Pet Sounds*, then it was presumably this meeting that set the stage.

Toward the end of 1966 the Who's second album, *A Quick One*, included Moon's composition "I Need You," which sounded like it might have been influenced by the Beatles, though the supposed sarcasm of the song's lyrics was interpreted by some as a jab at the Fab Four. However, Keith denied that in the January 1967 issue of *Beat Instrumental* (in an article that was reprinted in the July 1997 issue of *Record Collector*). There must not have been any hard feelings because by mid–June Paul McCartney used his position on the "Board of Governors" for the Monterey Pop Festival to urge that the Who be added to the bill of this historic event. He also helped them get a prime spot on the concert's final day, June 18. Several days later Moon was part of the chorus on the Beatles hit "All You Need Is Love." In fact, it has been suggested that he can be glimpsed playing drums with a set of brushes during the live TV broadcast of the song that month. Later in 1967 McCartney read a rave review of the new Who single "I Can See for Miles" that praised the song's hard edge, and in an attempt to outrock the Who he wrote "Helter Skelter" for the Fab Four's self-titled album in 1968.

The Who figured twice in the Beatles' January 1969 rehearsals that led to the *Let It Be* album. There was talk of doing something akin to the Rolling Stones' *Rock & Roll Circus*, but Harrison noted the risk of getting shown up by a band like the Who (as happened to the Stones the previous month). The sessions brought tensions within the Beatles to a head, and, after a fight with Lennon, Harrison announced that he was quitting the group and left. Moments later the remaining band members started improvising some music and Lennon began to play and sing the "soon be home" refrain from the Who's "A Quick One While He's Away," presumably as a prediction about Harrison's eventual return. At one point Lennon even called out, "Take it, George" at a point where a guitar solo would have fit in. In mid–March of 1970 the Who were planning to appear at a charitable concert organized by Lennon for the National Council for Civil Liberties and Release, but the intended venue, the Royal Albert Hall, refused. Later that month the Beatles were mentioned in the Who's newly released single, "The Seeker," three weeks before the Fab Four broke up.

In the summer of 1971 George Harrison made a name for himself apart from the Beatles by organizing two all-star concerts in New York to benefit the nation of Bangladesh, and on September 18 the Who was the final act at the South London concert for Bangladesh. Also in 1971 Keith Moon and Ringo Starr appeared in **Frank Zappa**'s movie *200 Motels*. In 1972 Moon drummed as "Kief Spoon" on Lennon's *Sometime in New York City* album, and Ringo Starr sang the part of Uncle Ernie for **Lou Reizner**'s orchestral version of the Who's *Tommy*. In 1974, Moon, Starr and Lennon helped **Harry Nilsson** with his LP *Pussycats*. Ringo, Keith and Jim Keltner all drummed simultaneously on two tracks with Lennon producing. Lennon wrote the song "Move Over Ms. L" which appeared on Keith's only solo album in 1975, and Moon also covered the Lennon-McCartney song "In My Life."

When MCA Records rejected Keith Moon's plan to call his album *Like a Rat Stuffed Up a Pipe*, Moon opted for Ringo's idea, *Two Sides of the Moon*. Ringo had several roles, including drumming again with Keltner on the three unreleased **Steve Cropper** tracks that finally surfaced when the album was released on compact disc in the 1990s. Later in 1975 Ringo portrayed the Pope opposite Roger Daltrey as **Franz Liszt** in Roger's second movie, *Lisztomania*. The next year Keith Moon sang the Beatles' "When I'm Sixty Four" for the soundtrack of *All This and World War II*. In 1977, McCartney's song "Giddy" was recorded for Roger Daltrey's third solo album, *One of the Boys*, and later that same year the Who were filmed covering the Beatles' "I Saw Her Standing There" for possible use in their movie *The Kids Are Alright*. That footage remains unreleased, but scenes featuring Keith Moon and Ringo Starr did get used.

In September of 1978 McCartney was the host of the reception for the debut of the movie the *Buddy Holly Story*, which Keith Moon attended the night before his death. McCartney had spent most of the 1970s fronting the band Wings, and in 1979 Pete Townshend played on two tracks on their *Back to the Egg* album. That album's Rockestra appeared live at the Concerts for the People of Kampuchea late in the year, which McCartney spearheaded. The Who, with **Kenney Jones** on drums, played on December 28 and four songs ended up on a double album taken from the charitable performances. In July of 1985 McCartney and Townshend were in the chorus that sang the Beatles' "Let It Be" as part of the finale to the Live Aid benefit concerts, and both hoisted organizer **Bob Geldof** into the air.

The next year Townshend played guitar on McCartney's *Press to Play* album, along with Phil Collins of **Genesis** on drums, on the track "Angry." In the late 1990s John Entwistle was part of Ringo's third All Starr Band, and the Entwistle classic "Boris the Spider" appeared on a compact disc released by the Blockbuster Video chain. In 1999 the **British Rock Symphony** CD included a duet by Roger Daltrey and **Thelma Houston** on "Let It Be." On the BRS video that year Daltrey's duet partner for "Let It Be" was **Darlene Love**. Ringo's son, **Zak Starkey**, has lately been the drummer for the Who.

Beck, Jeff Influential British guitarist who was employing feedback about the same time that Pete Townshend was starting. According to Dave Marsh in his Who book *Before I Get Old*, Dave Davies of the **Kinks** also has some basis for claiming to be a feedback pioneer. Roger Daltrey, who hasn't always been a Pete Townshend loyalist when interviewed, told Gary Herman that "Townshend was the starter of it all, I don't care what anyone says. Well … I think Beck as well, about the same time, it's a bit dodgy between the two. But Pete went much further than Beck ever did. Pete wasn't interested in the technique of the guitar, he'd use a guitar in a completely different way from Beck. Beck would use electronics with technique and work it into one, whereas Townshend just banged the guitar and used the electronics, and I mean, no technique at all." He reemphasized in that statement for Herman's 1972 book *The Who* that "Pete was the original feedback merchant."

Early in his career Beck had backed Lord Sutch but really began to build his reputation after replacing **Eric Clapton** in the Yardbirds in 1965. Not long after **Led Zeppelin** founder Jimmy Page joined the Yardbirds Beck left to branch out on his own. On May 16 and 17, 1966, he arranged a session involving Page, Keith Moon, **Nicky Hopkins** and future Led Zeppelin member John Paul Jones. Most sources indicated that this session was in June or July of 1967 but the new chronology *Jeff's Book* set the record straight. The primary result of this session was the song "Beck's Bolero," which surfaced on the album *Truth* in 1968. Timpani drumming was credited to "You Know Who." In the meantime the Jeff Beck Group had solidified the first of several lineups by enlisting **Rod Stewart** and **Ron Wood**.

Beckett, Peter Liverpool native whose band Player had a #1 hit in the U.S. with "Baby Come Back" in late 1977. A decade later he was one of the backing vocalists on Roger Daltrey's 1987 solo album, *Can't Wait to See the Movie*. Beckett began recording in America in 1974 and co-founded Player a few years later. The band faded away after 1981. Beckett's compositions can be found on major motion picture soundtracks such as the *Karate Kid*, *Major League*, and *Cocktail*, and have been recorded by the Commodores, **Heart**, Janet Jackson, **Olivia Newton-John**, and Kenny Rogers, among others. In the early 1990s he joined the Australian group the Little River Band and then reformed Player in 1995.

The Bee Gees   Australian band started by the Brothers Gibb which had hits from 1967 to 1971, most after hooking up with **Robert Stigwood**, and which also took full advantage of the 1970s disco craze with him. Roger Daltrey was a member of a chorus backing Barry Gibb on his 1984 album *Now Voyager*, on the song "Fine Line." **Olivia-Newton John** was also part of that chorus.

Bell, Graham   Singer in several short-lived bands who sang the part of Mrs. Walker's lover in **Lou Reizner**'s all-star stage version of the Who's *Tommy* in 1972. In 1965 Bell joined the Chosen Few for the second of their two 45s. Bell also released a 45 in 1966. Founding member Alan Hull, later of Lindisfarne fame, left the Chosen Few around this time, and the remaining members, including **Mickey Gallagher**, changed the band's name to Skip Bifferty. A couple years later they recorded one album and in 1968 they recorded a 45 as Heavy Jelly before learning that another group was already using that name. Most of Skip Bifferty then went on to form Arc but Bell's major project of 1970 was singing on the *Every Which Way* album for a band formed by ex–Nice drummer Brian "Blinky" Davison. In 1971 Bell reunited with his former bandmates for the *Bell and Arc* album and his solo album came out the same year he sang for Reizner. He sang and played harmonica on Carol Grimes's 1974 album *Warm Blood* and released another solo single the next year. He maintained a low profile until engineering the 1995 Celtic/folk album *Tenterhooks* by Jez Lowe and the Bad Pennies.

Bell, Maggie   *see*   Stone the Crows.

Benson, A.C.   *see*   Elgar, Edward.

Benson, Jonathan   Assistant director of numerous movies who helped Roger Daltrey add lyrics to three **Franz Liszt** compositions for the soundtrack of Daltrey's second movie, Ken Russell's *Lisztomania*. Jonathan, who has sometimes been credited as John D. Benson, served as assistant director to Russell on *Women in Love* in 1969 and *Tommy* in 1975 just before his work on *Lisztomania*. Among his subsequent assistant director credits are **Monty Python**'s *Life of Brian* in 1979, *A Fish Called Wanda* in 1988, and *Jane Eyre* in 1996.

Berry, Chuck   One of rock and roll's trailblazers in the 1950s who was a big influence on Pete Townshend, along with Hank Marvin of the **Shadows**. Berry had a series of Top 10 hits in the late 1950s, including "Rock & Roll Music," "Sweet Little Sixteen," and "Johnny B. Goode." In 1964 a concert of his was the first large gathering of mods that Pete attended. One opening band, the **Animals**, met with approval from the mods because they were considered a "rhythm and blues group," but the rocker-like **Swinging Blue Jeans** were booed off the stage. On July 5, 1969, the Who received top billing above Berry for two performances at London's Royal Albert Hall. Berry protested mildly and was allowed to close the earlier of the shows. When the Who came on for the final set, trouble was caused by rockers who had been hanging around after the **Rolling Stones** gave a free concert in the area that afternoon. The arrival of a flock of police kept history from repeating itself, or worse. In the Who's 1979 movie *The Kids Are Alright* Pete can be seen imitating Berry's distinctive "duck walk" in a 1975 performance of the **Bo Diddley** song "Road Runner." With Keith Moon on vocals the Who covered "Johnny B. Goode" during their encore in Oakland on October 10, 1976. In 1986 Berry was among the first performers inducted into the Rock and Roll Hall of Fame.

The Best   Short-lived supergroup formed in 1990 that included John Entwistle, **Joe Walsh** and **Jeff "Skunk" Baxter** on guitars, Keith Emerson of **Emerson, Lake and Palmer** on keyboards, **Simon Phillips** on drums, and Rick Livingstone of the Canadian band Agent on vocals. In September the band performed at least twice in Japan, including once on television, and played in Hawaii.

Best, George   Legendary Manchester United soccer star whose biographical movie *Best* included Roger Daltrey in a supporting role as fellow footballer **Rodney Marsh**. Best led Manchester United to a win in the European Cup Final in 1968. He also played for the Los Angeles Aztecs of the North American Soccer League in the 1970s. The movie also starred Ian Bannen and **John Lynch** in the title role. Best himself was unable to attend the movie's premier in the spring of 2000 because he was recovering from liver failure.

Bethnal   London rock band that issued its only two albums in 1978, both of which were linked to Pete Townshend. On *Dangerous Times* they covered the Who's "Baba O'Riley" though with the misspellings "O'Reilly" and "Townsend" and with the line "don't bruise your eye" instead of "don't raise your eye." On the back cover of *Crash Landing* they thanked Pete Townshend. Bethnal was formed in 1972 and broke up in 1980. Only bass player Everton Williams resurfaced in any noteworthy fashion, as bass player on a couple of albums in the mid–1990s for Bernie Torme, guitarist for former Deep Purple vocalist Ian Gillan.

Big Country Band consisting of two Scottsmen, vocalist/songwriter/guitarist Stuart Adamson and guitarist Bruce Watson, and two Londoners, bassist **Tony Butler**, and drummer **Mark Brzezicki**. Around 1980 Butler and Brzezicki were in the trio On the Air with **Simon Townshend**. Meanwhile, in the early 1980s Adamson and Watson recorded some demos with the **Jam**'s Rick Buckler on drums, but by April of 1982 they had recruited Butler and Brzezicki as their permanent rhythm section. In the summer of 1983, Big Country released its debut album *The Crossing*. On the strength of the UK and U.S. hit single "In a Big Country," the band was named Best New Group in *Rolling Stone*'s year-end poll and was nominated for two Grammy awards. In 1985 Adamson was the only member not to back Roger Daltrey on "After the Fire" from his solo album *Under a Raging Moon*. In December Big Country opened for Roger at the New York City concert on his mini-tour. In mid–1989 Brzezicki left the group and **Simon Phillips** was among his replacements. Mark returned by 1993. The band remained very big in the UK in the last half of the '80s and still has a very large following there. Nevertheless, Stuart Anderson committed suicide in December of 2001. He was 43.

Bilk, Acker British clarinet player whose early 1960s hit "Stranger on the Shore" was the first song ever to reach number one simultaneously in England and the United States. John Entwistle often played his songs in one of his first bands. While a member of the **Confederates** Entwistle also joined a bigger and more active trad jazz group though it never had a name. This band mainly played songs by "Mr. Acker Bilk" and by **Kenny Ball**. "Acker" is a slang word meaning "mate;" he was born Bernard Stanley Bilk. He was among several guest performers in the **Spencer Davis** Group's 1966 movie *The Ghost Goes Gear*.

Biondolillo, Jimmy Arranged and conducted strings and horns on Roger Daltrey's 1984 solo LP, *Parting Should Be Painless*. The album was produced by Mike Thorne, with whom Jimmy is associated at present as well. Since 1984 he has produced for Hue & Cry, Honeychild, Ray Simpson (younger brother of Valerie, of Ashford & Simpson fame), and Valerie Ghent, who toured with Deborah Harry of **Blondie**. In addition, in 1998 he helped with a horn arrangement on a Tatsuro Yamashita album.

Birch, Dyan *see* Kokomo.

Bird, Ronnie French singer in the 1960s who successfully evoked

British Invasion artists while singing in his native tongue. He was among the first performers to cover a Who song, when "A Legal Matter" was translated by H. Wayaffe and became "Ne t'en fais pas pour Ronnie" on a 7" record of Ronnie's. Guitarist Mick Jones, who wound up in the successful band Foreigner, served in Bird's backing band for a while.

The Birdman   A nickname for Pete Townshend, which John Entwistle used in his 1975 solo song "Cell Number Seven," his account of the Who's night in a Montreal jail in late 1973.

Birkett, David   Bass player on "One Night Stand" on Keith Moon's only solo album, 1975's *Two Sides of the Moon. In* 1969 Birkett had played bass on Warren S. Richardson's self-titled album. (The Borderline/Delerium Records online "Fuzz, Acid & Flowers" archive, based on the Vernon Joynson book of the same name, theorized that Richardson was really future **Tubes** guitarist Bill "Sputnik" Spooner.) Birkett also played bass on the first Goose Creek Symphony album in 1970 but didn't play on later albums as that band turned increasingly toward country music. His biggest success came as producer of several albums for Iceland's most successful band, the Sugarcubes, whose singer Björk went on to even greater success on her own starting in 1992. Among the Sugarcubes albums Birkett produced was *Life's Too Good,* which was very well received and was quite popular on collegiate radio stations in 1988.

Black, Gene   *see* Bloch, Gene.

Blades, Jack   Bass player for Night Ranger and Damn Yankees who co-wrote the Roger Daltrey solo song "The Price of Love" with **David Foster**. Night Ranger thrived throughout the 1980s and Damn Yankees, which also included Tommy Shaw of **Styx** and **Ted Nugent**, released albums in 1990 and 1992. He played with Shaw again on albums in 1995 and 1998, and in 1999 Blades provided background vocals for the **British Rock Symphony**.

Blake, Peter   Artist who conceived of and designed the cover for the Who's *Face Dances* album. Blake's most famous album cover was for the **Beatles**' *Sgt. Pepper's Lonely Hearts Club Band.* It was Blake's idea to commission paintings of the members of the Who by top UK artists. Francis Bacon was perhaps the most notable artist to decline. Blake was among the four who painted new drummer **Kenney Jones**. Sculptor Clive Barker sketched a profile of John Entwistle; given Entwistle's grim sense of humor, it would have been appropriate if Barker were the same person as the Clive Barker of horror movie fame. Blake created the poster for the 1985 Live Aid benefit, at which the Who appeared. In 1995 he was approached about providing the cover for the *Beatles Anthology* collection but he chose not to.

Bloch, Gene Guitarist, along with Devin Powers, on John Entwistle's long-delayed solo album, *The Rock*, which was released in 1996. Bloch didn't tour with the band in 1988 after the album was finished, but Powers did. In 1985 Bloch teamed with Holly Night and the Wilson sisters to write the hit "Never" for **Heart**. In 1986 Bloch was a member of the group Device, which released one self-titled album. Bloch, who has also gone by "Gene Black," backed Berlin and **Rod Stewart** that same year. More recently he has backed such performers as Cher and **Tina Turner**.

Blondie Band fronted by former Playboy bunny Deborah Harry, which had a few number one hits from 1979 to 1981. Shortly after Keith Moon's death in September of 1978, Blondie drummer Clem Burke kicked his drums over at the end of the band's set as a tribute. In 1985 Burke played on Pete Townshend's solo album *White City*.

The Blossoms *see* Love, Darlene.

Blues Project *see* Kooper, Al.

Blunstone, Colin Singer for the British Invasion band the **Zombies** whose song "Single Man's Dilemma" appeared on Roger Daltrey's third solo album, 1977's *One of the Boys*. Fellow Zombie **Rod Argent** performed on that album. After the Zombies broke up at the end of 1967 he recorded under the name Neil MacArthur and made several solo albums in the 1970s under his own name. In 1998 he began a comeback, which included covering the Yes song "Owner of a Lonely Heart" on **Mike Batt**'s *Philharmania* album.

Boddicker, Michael Keyboard and synthesizer player for an astounding list of performers who programmed the synthesizer for the song "The Price of Love" on Roger Daltrey's 1987 solo album, *Can't Wait to See the Movie*. The song was also used on the soundtrack of the movie *Secret of My Success*, which starred Michael J. Fox. Since 1969 Boddicker is credited on at least three albums for each of the following artists: **Barbra Streisand**, Michael Jackson, Quincy Jones, Lionel Richie, Neil Diamond, Julio Iglesias, Rickie Lee Jones, **Laura Branigan**, the Pointer Sisters, **Leo Sayer**, Manhattan Transfer, and Randy Newman.

Boland, Neil Chauffeur for Keith Moon who was killed at the beginning of 1970. Cornelius Boland hadn't been serving as Keith's driver for long when he took Keith, his wife Kim, "Legs" Larry Smith of the **Bonzo Dog Doo-Dah Band** and his girlfriend Jean Battye to a disco outside London. Keith was the guest of honor at its grand opening. Also in attendance but driving separately were brothers Jack and Jimmy McCulloch (Jimmy was in **Thunderclap Newman**). Many skinheads were present and afterwards about 30 of them surrounded Keith's limo. During the resulting turmoil Boland exited the car to try to clear a path and was apparently knocked down though nobody inside the vehicle realized. Moon, meanwhile, attempted to get the car clear of the crowd despite not knowing how to drive. Boland was crushed in the process. Though the death was ultimately ruled accidental, it was very traumatic for Moon. Tony Fletcher's definitive Moon biography *Dear Boy* gives a gripping account of this event and noted that 18-year-old and 15-year-old skinheads were charged in the incident.

Bolton, Steve "Boltz" Guitarist for an incarnation of Atomic Rooster who played with the Who throughout their 1989 tour, though **Joe Walsh** had expressed interest in the job. The original Atomic Rooster lineup in 1969 included Crazy World of **Arthur Brown** drummer Carl Palmer just before **Emerson, Lake and Palmer** was formed, but by the time Bolton joined in 1972 the band had already gained and lost various members. Bolton recorded one album with them that year, *Made in England*, but that lineup parted company within two years. He then played on Headstone albums in the 1970s and Paul Young albums in the 1980s. Other artists he has backed include Matthew Sweet in 1986, Richard Wright in 1996, and Mary McLaughlin in 1997.

Bond, Graham British R&B pioneer who facilitated the release of the Who's "Substitute" 45 by providing a B-side for the record. Depending on the pressing, the Graham Bond Organisation's recording of "Waltz for a Pig" was credited to "The Who Orchestra" or the Who itself. Though attributed to someone named Harry Butcher, the song was reportedly written by **Ginger Baker**. During the Who's dispute with producer **Shel Talmy** the band released its new song "Substitute" on **Robert Stigwood**'s young Reaction label with a version of "Circles" retitled "Instant Party" on the B-side. According to **Richard Barnes**, this was intended by the Who to provoke legal action by Talmy, who did indeed obtain an injunction against the 45. The Who reached an agreement with Talmy not to record for a while, but got around the injunction by being in Bond's band. Bond had been a member of Alexis Korner's Blues Incorporated in 1962 but by February of 1963 had formed the Graham Bond Trio with Jack Bruce and Ginger Baker (both of whom would later team with **Eric Clapton** in the trio Cream; Bond and Stigwood helped Cream in the studio). By year's end they were a quartet and an Organisation. The band didn't outlast the 1960s, and by 1970 its namesake was a member of Ginger Baker's Air Force. Bond, who was hospitalized for a month in 1973 after a nervous breakdown, was reportedly eager to revive his career when he was found dead beneath a motionless train in May of 1974. He was 36.

The Bonzo Dog Doo-Dah Band   Satirical septet that had several members with connections to the Who. The band was formed in 1965 and two years later appeared in the **Beatles** movie *Magical Mystery Tour*. Their only hit song, "I'm the Urban Spaceman," came out in 1968. At some point they shortened their name to the Bonzo Dog Band and on June 13, 1970 they opened for the Who in Los Angeles. However, before the year was out they split up. Bonzo vocalist Viv Stanshall, who died in a fire in 1995 at the age of 51, had been a very good friend of Keith Moon's. In fact, at the time of his death he was reportedly writing a screenplay about Moon. They became very close after causing backstage mischief throughout the second annual Isle of Wight festival in 1969. Keith then produced Viv's 45 "Suspicion"/"Blind Date," a fact noted in a *New Musical Express* article on the "fearful duo" in its issue of December 19, 1970. Similarly, *Melody Maker* dubbed them a "dangerous duo" after such subsequent stunts as goofing around in Nazi uniforms.

According to the *Rolling Stone Encyclopedia of Rock & Roll*, John Entwistle and **Eric Clapton** backed Stanshall in the studio "on occasional singles." The mid–1970s double album the *History of the Bonzos* includes the aforementioned pair of songs plus a photo of Moon in Nazi garb. A recording of Viv performing Keith's contribution to the movie *Tommy*, "Fiddle About," appeared on a vinyl bootleg years ago. Viv and Bonzo pianist Neil Innes joined Moon as the "Latin American percussion section" on the song "No. 29" on Entwistle's first solo album, 1971's *Smash Your Head Against the Wall*. Innes later wrote songs for **Monty Python's Flying Circus** and was a member of the Rutles, a group formed with Monty Python's Eric Idle as a Beatles spoof.

Bonzo drummer "Legs" Larry Smith was also a close friend of Keith Moon's and was present when Moon's chauffeur, **Neil Boland**, was killed. Bonzo co-founder Roger Ruskin Spear, who attended Ealing Art School at the same time as Pete Townshend, mentioned him in the liner notes of his solo album *Electric Shocks* and recruited him to play guitar on his *Unusual* album on a version of "Pinball Wizard." In late 1974 John Entwistle told *Rolling Stone*: "There's quite a lack of humor in the business and I'd like to correct that. Thank God for **Sha Na Na** and the late Bonzo Dog Doo-Dah Band."

The Boomtown Rats *see* Geldof, Bob.

Boruff, David Highly regarded saxophone player who played that instrument as well as synthesizer on "The Price of Love" on Roger Daltrey's 1987 solo album, *Can't Wait to See the Movie*. The song was also used on the soundtrack of the movie *Secret of My Success*, which starred Michael J. Fox. Since 1995 Boruff has overseen an internet service for studio musicians called the Musicians Network Group, or MuseNet for short. "The Reverend" picked up a number of studio credits in the 1980s and 1990s, including on at least two albums each for **Barbra Streisand**, Neil Diamond, Celine Dion, **David Foster**, Juice Newton, and John Wetton. He also played on the **British Rock Symphony** album in 1999.

Bowie, David Androgynous pop star whose long and successful recording career dates back to his native England in the mid–1960s and whose path has crossed the Who's several times. Bowie was born David Robert Jones but scrapped his surname when Davy Jones of the Monkees became a major celebrity. Bowie covered two early Who songs on his 1973 album *Pinups*, "I Can't Explain" and "Anyway Anyhow Anywhere." In the issue of *Melody Maker* dated November 17, 1973, it was reported that Bowie had turned down a role in the movie version of the Who's *Tommy*. He had been offered both the Acid Queen and the Pinball Wizard. Bowie guested on three Keith Moon solo recordings that turned up as bonus tracks when *Two Sides of the Moon* was released on compact disc in 1997. On Bowie's 1980 album *Scary Monsters* Pete Townshend played guitar on the song "Because You're Young." According to **Richard Barnes**, when Townshend first presented his record company with the raw materials that eventually became his 1982 album *All the Best Cowboys Have Chinese Eyes*, the label's reaction was quite negative but Bowie was with him and urged him to persevere. Nevertheless, Townshend rewrote half of the experimental material, which consisted of "rhythm tracks and poetry over the top." In 2001 the CD entitled *Substitute: The Songs of the Who* included a new version of "Pictures of Lily" by Bowie.

Bown, Alan Leader of the popular Alan Bown Set and trumpet player on Roger Daltrey's 1975 solo album, *Ride a Rock Horse*. Bown's group, sometimes simply called "The Alan Bown!" started releasing singles in 1965 and had recorded a dozen by 1971 despite major chart success. Vocalists for Bown's band included **Jess Roden** and Robert Palmer; Palmer had success as a solo artist many years later. After the group broke up in the mid–1970s, Bown shifted to the management side of the recording industry.

Boz's People *see* Bad Company.

Bradbury, Ray Famous American science fiction writer known for such novels as the *Martian Chronicles* (1950) and *Fahrenheit 451* (1953). In a long interview in the April 19, 1980 issue of *New Musical Express,* Pete Townshend discussed the possibility of Bradbury writing a film script for *Lifehouse.* Almost two full decades would pass before this ambitious project saw the light of day in some form, namely a radio play, book, and six-CD boxed set.

Branigan, Laura American pop singer with a powerful voice and four octave range who had a few big chart hits in the first half of the 1980s, beginning with "Gloria." on her second album, released in 1983, she covered the Who's "Squeeze Box."

Brecht, Bertolt German dramatist and poet, born in 1898. **Kurt Weill** supplied the music for the *Threepenny Opera*, which debuted in 1928. It was based on **John Gay**'s the *Beggar's Opera*, from 200 years earlier. During the Nazi era he lived in Denmark and the U.S. and from 1948 until his death in 1956 he directed East Germany's Berliner Ensemble. Roger Daltrey played the Street Singer in the 1989 movie *Mack the Knife*, an adaptation of the *Threepenny Opera*. Roger launched into the title song just before the appearance of stars **Raul Julia** and **Richard Harris**. *Rolling Stone* reviewer Peter Travis liked Daltrey's rendition of the song but thought his character was overused to take advantage of Daltrey's celebrity. In 1983 Roger had played Macheath in a BBC production of the *Beggar's Opera*.

Brecker, Michael Philadelphia-born tenor sax player whose countless number of studio session credits includes Roger Daltrey's 1984 solo LP, *Parting Should Be Painless*. He has performed multiple times with a variety of musicians including George Benson, James Taylor, **Paul Simon**, and **David Sanborn**. Born in 1949, his album credits began while he was in his teens. For 25 years, starting in 1972, he was credited on about a dozen albums each year, and in some years as many as 30 or 40.

The Breeders Female-dominated group that covered the Who's "So Sad About Us" on their four-song *Safari* CD in 1992. This was two years after their critically acclaimed debut album, *Pod*, which was merely expected to be a one-shot side project for Kim Deal of the Pixies and Tanya Donelly of Throwing Muses, with both on guitar. Donelly left to form the group Belly shortly after *Safari*, but the Pixies broke up around this time as well so Deal has continued off and on in the Breeders with her twin sister, Kelley.

The British Rock Symphony Fluid lineup of known and

unknown singers belting out classic rock songs backed by an orchestra and choir. Roger Daltrey often headlined BRS concerts, and **Simon Townshend** was occasionally featured as well. The driving forces behind the creation of the BRS were concert producer David Fishof and conductor/musical director Keith Levenson. The BRS made its American debut at a sold-out New York show on April 22, 1998. In addition to Daltrey, helping to unveil the BRS were **Peter Frampton, Paul Shaffer, Phoebe Snow, Leslie West** and **Zak Starkey**. In 1999 a BRS CD was released, and it included Daltrey duets with Ann Wilson of **Heart** on the **Led Zeppelin** song "Kashmir" and with **Thelma Houston** on the **Beatles** song "Let It Be." The CD also included **Alice Cooper** covering the Who's "5.15" and Tommy Shaw of **Styx** fame covering the Who's "See Me, Feel Me/Listening to You." Rock musicians in the backing band included Starkey, Simon Townshend and **"Rabbit" Bundrick**, among others. A video from some UK performances with a few different noted vocalists was later released. It included Daltrey and Cooper teaming up to sing "5.15" and the **Rolling Stones**' "Start Me Up." This time Daltrey's "Let It Be" duet was with **Darlene Love**.

Simon Townshend actually appeared on camera more often than Daltrey, in part by virtue of taking lead vocals on two Beatles songs, "Blackbird" and "Norwegian Wood." On the latter he was backed on vocals by Alvin Fields, who also backed Daltrey on "See Me, Feel Me." Zak Starkey again handled drumming chores. Perhaps not wanting to remind Australia of its origins as a British penal colony, the tour of that nation in 2000 was billed as the "Ultimate Rock Symphony."

Broudie, Ian *see* The Lightning Seeds.

Brown, Arthur   Perhaps the oddest performer signed to the Who's Track Records label, though his band, the Crazy World of Arthur Brown, was stable enough to have a #2 hit in the U.S. In 1968 with the song "Fire." **Kit Lambert** was producer and Pete Townshend associate producer of the song and the band's eponymous album. According to **Richard Barnes**, Pete's first attempt at a rock opera, to be called *Rael*, was conceived with Arthur Brown in mind as the hero. An approximation of the plot survived in the song of that name on *The Who Sell Out*. Pete had become a fan of Brown's after he gained a reputation for rock frontman theatrics, including culminating 1967 shows by seeming to set his hair ablaze. By late 1969 keyboardist Vincent Crane and drummer Carl Palmer left the Crazy World band to form Atomic Rooster, a band which later included **Steve Bolton**. Within a year Palmer made his shrewdest career move by becoming part of **Emerson, Lake and Palmer**. From 1970 to 1973 Brown fronted the electronic rock band Kingdom Come, which released three albums. In 1975 Brown had a role in the Who movie *Tommy* during "Eyesight to the Blind" but his name tended to be omitted from the acting and singing credits. One of the few new studio recordings by the Who after 1982 was a version of "Fire" on Townshend's *Iron Man* album in 1989.

Brown, Charles   Influential African-American blues balladeer who co-wrote the 1946 hit "Driftin' Blues," which Pete Townshend covered on his 1987 album *Another Scoop*. Brown, a skilled classical pianist, was born in Texas in 1922. His first session as part of Johnny Moore's Three Blazers produced "Driftin' Blues," though the version Townshend originally heard was performed by **John Lee Hooker**. In 1947 the trio debuted a perennial favorite, Brown's "Merry Christmas, Baby," but a year later saw Brown leave to form his own trio. Brown then had two #1 rhythm-and-blues records, "Trouble Blues" in 1949 and "Black Night" in 1951. However, his releases over the next decade or so were generally less successful and Brown eventually retired. Knowledge of his career jumped in the early 1980s and he recorded several creditable albums prior to a tour with Bonnie Raitt in 1990. In 1992 he and Raitt recorded together, and two of their efforts turned up on Brown's *Someone to Love* CD. He also opened for her in 1995. Not long after his death in early 1999 Brown was inducted into the Rock and Roll Hall of Fame.

Brown, James   America's "Godfather of Soul," who had much success as a singer from the late 1950s into the 1970s. During an America Online chat in February of 2000, Roger Daltrey talked about the songs the Who used to cover in its early days, and foremost in his thoughts were James Brown songs. Daltrey said he "used to do all those song selections in those days." However, Pete Townshend was also very familiar with Brown's work thanks to the impressive collection of his friend **Tom Wright**. The Who ended up recording no fewer than four of Brown's compositions in 1965, including "Please Please Please" and "I Don't Mind" on the *My Generation* album and "Shout and Shimmy" for the B-side of the UK "My Generation" 45. The fourth was "Just You and Me, Darling," which the Who recorded for a BBC program. Brown's version of "Night Train" was used on the *Quadrophenia* soundtrack in 1979. After a leg injury cut short a potential career as a baseball pitcher, Brown and friend Bobby Byrd joined a Georgia gospel group called the Swanees and soon persuaded them to change their name to the Famous Flames. After two years of touring they released their first single in 1956, the aforementioned "Please Please Please," which over time sold a million copies. They had a #1 hit on the U.S. R&B chart in 1958 with "Try Me" and throughout the

1960s Brown was regularly hitting #1 on the R&B singles chart and often landing in the top 10 or 20 of the pop chart as well. In 1986 Brown was among the first performers inducted into the Rock and Roll Hall of Fame.

Brown, Vicki   One of the two nurses singing during "It's a Boy" in the *Tommy* movie. The other was **Margo Newman**, her fellow background vocalist on a couple of **Olivia Newton-John** albums around that time. Brown's other big break a few years before the *Tommy* movie was as background vocalist for Carly Simon, and she has recorded with a number of other famous artists over the years, including twice each with **Bryan Ferry** and the **Small Faces**. Other examples of her session work worth noting are Murray Head's *Say It Ain't So* and **Pink Floyd** guitarist David Gilmour's solo album *About Face*.

Browne, Jackson   Singer who has had periodic success since his #8 hit in the U.S. in 1972, "Doctor My Eyes." Perhaps most notably, his album *Hold Out* went straight to #1 in 1980. Early in his career Browne wrote or co-wrote songs for the Byrds, Bonnie Raitt, Linda Ronstadt, and the **Eagles**. In the mid–1990s he appeared as the Scarecrow alongside Roger Daltrey's Tin Man on stage in the *Wizard of Oz in Concert: Dreams Come True*. The soundtrack for this Children's Defense Fund benefit was released in 1996.

Browne, John   One of John Entwistle's early aliases, perhaps the last one he used. *New Musical Express* used this name at least twice after the Who released "Anyway Anyhow Anywhere" though the publication also noted his real name one of those times.

Brzezicki, Mark   Drummer for **Big Country** who has also had a long association with Pete as well as **Simon Townshend**. Around 1977 he, Simon, and **Tony Butler** formed On the Air, which released a couple of records before Mark and Tony joined Big Country in 1982. In the meantime, Mark drummed on "A Little Is Enough" on Pete's 1980 solo album *Empty Glass*. He was also credited with drumming as Mark "Brrrescekkiagghh" on Pete's 1982 solo album, *All the Best Cowboys Have Chinese Eyes*. A year later he was credited as the "inimitable" drummer on "Body Language" on Pete's first double album of demos, *Scoop*. In 1984 he drummed on Simon Townshend's *Sweet Sound* album, and in 1985 he drummed on Pete's album *White City* and on Roger Daltrey's album *Under a Raging Moon*. In mid–1989 Mark left Big Country for a while and toured with a reformed Procol Harum. Among his replacements in Big Country was **Simon Phillips**. Mark rejoined the band by 1993 in time for its first American performances in seven years. Mark co-wrote the song "Flame" with

Simon Townshend, Gavin Lewis, Josh Phillips-Gorse, and Jaz Lochrie. It appeared on Pete's *Psychoderelict* album in 1993. Not surprisingly, he also drummed on the album.

Bundrick, John "Rabbit"   Keyboard player from Texas who has had a long association with the Who. His nickname came from some early bandmates who thought his teeth resembled a hare's. Rabbit's big break was taking part in a 1969 session for fellow Texan Johnny Nash, who had charted since the late 1950s but wouldn't hit #1 until recording "I Can See Clearly Now" in 1972. Rabbit followed Nash to Sweden and there became close friends with Bob Marley. In the early 1970s Traffic percussionist Rebop Kwaku Baah took Rabbit to see the band Free, and Rabbit was so impressed that he made working with them a priority. As a result, Rabbit recorded an album with three members of Free as a side project in 1971–72 and became a member of Free himself in time to land two of his compositions on their 1973 album *Heartbreaker*.

Rabbit was quite busy around this time, releasing solo albums in 1973 and 1974 and recording once or twice with such performers as Traffic drummer Jim Capaldi, Donovan, **Andy Fairweather-Low**, and **Sandy Denny**. After *Heartbreaker* two members of Free left to form **Bad Company**, while Free guitarist Paul Kossoff and Rabbit eventually formed Back Street Crawler. However, Kossoff soon died of a heart ailment, and the band shortened its name to Crawler. **Geoff Whitehorn** was among the members of this short-lived but well-regarded band. A factor in their 1979 breakup was Pete Townshend's increasing interest in collaborating with Rabbit. They first worked together on the 1977 Townshend/**Ronnie Lane** collaboration *Rough Mix*, on which Rabbit played organ on "Nowhere to Run," "Rough Mix" and "Keep Me Turning" and Fender Rhodes on "Heart to Hang Onto."

Rabbit was soon recruited to play on *Who Are You*, which was released in 1978, but he broke his arm soon after the recording sessions began. In 1979 Rabbit took part in the first of several Who tours and came close to being an official member of the band around the time that **Kenney Jones** was named the Who's new drummer. On July 13, 1979, Rabbit was part of the first band Pete Townshend formed outside of the Who, for the "Rock Against Racism" benefit. The other musicians were Kenney, **Tony Butler** and **Peter Hope-Evans**. In 1980 Rabbit played keyboards on the *McVicar* soundtrack and on Pete's *Empty Glass* album. Though Rabbit didn't receive credit for playing on *Face Dances*, the first Who album recorded with Kenney, Pete did thank him "for help and inspiration" on the album's underrated closing track, "Another Tricky Day."

The next year Rabbit played on Townshend's contribution to the *Music & Rhythm* compilation, the track "Ascension Two." In 1985 Rabbit played on Pete's album *White City* and was part of Pete's **Deep End** band shortly thereafter. In 1989 he played piano on "A Friend Is a Friend" on Pete's *Iron Man* album, his 1989 musical adaptation of the **Ted Hughes** tale. A noteworthy claim to fame for Rabbit outside of the Who in the early 1990s was supplying the piano music for John Goodman's memorable Jerry Lee Lewis imitation in the 1991 movie *King Ralph*. In 1993 Rabbit played keyboards on Pete's *Psychoderelict* album and on Pete's subsequent *Live* video. In 1994 he played on Roger Daltrey's CD *A Celebration — The Music of Pete Townshend and the Who*. As the decade wound down he played piano and organ on the London Philharmonic Orchestra's 1998 album *Who's Serious* and was one of the rock musicians among the **British Rock Symphony**. The year 2000 found him and **Zak Starkey** touring with the three surviving members of the Who. Rabbit and Zak also toured with the Who in 2002, shortly after John Entwistle's death.

Burchill, Julie Critic for *New Musical Express* who, along with critic Tony Parsons, were the targets of Pete Townshend's pointed solo song "Jools and Jim" in 1980. Townshend spoke at length about the song in a *Trouser Press* interview and noted that he was responding to printed statements by the pair, including Parsons's comment that rock 'n' roll was better off with Keith Moon dead. However, Townshend also had some kind words for the duo, and said he "changed the title from 'Jools and Tone' to 'Jules and Jim' because it's not directly about them; it's about taking a stance and believing what you read. It's just another 'don't believe what you read' song." Nevertheless, many years later Townshend's somewhat unflattering *Psychoderelict* character of Rosalyn Nathan was presumed to be based on Burchill.

Burdon, Eric *see* The Animals.

Burke, Clem *see* Blondie.

Burnett, Chester *see* Howlin' Wolf.

Burnett, T-bone Respected singer and songwriter who became an increasingly popular producer as well. He began working with Bob Dylan in 1975 and released his first solo album in 1980. In 1982 he was an opening act for the Who. Pete Townshend, Ry Cooder, and Richard Thompson were guests on his 1983 album *Proof Through the Night*. He started touring with Elvis Costello in 1984 under the name the Coward Brothers and worked on Costello's *King of America* album in 1986. Since then Burnett has cut back on his solo career and focused on producing such artists as the BoDeans, Bruce Cockburn, Counting Crows, Marshall Crenshaw, Los Lobos, Sam Phillips, and the Wallflowers.

Burrell, Boz *see* Bad Company.

Burridge, Emily   Cellist who played on Roger Daltrey's 1992 solo CD, *Rocks in the Head*, on "Unforgettable Opera." She has also performed with George Michael, Robert Palmer, the **Pretenders** and the Psychedelic Furs.

Buscemi, Steve   Actor known most for quirky roles in offbeat movies such as in Quentin Tarantino's *Reservoir Dogs* in 1992 and *Fargo* in 1996. The long-running HBO horror anthology series *Tales from the Crypt* aired a 1993 episode entitled "Forever Ambergris" in which Buscemi appeared and which featured Roger Daltrey as a well known photographer named Dalton.

Butcher, Harry *see* Baker, Ginger.

Butler, Anya   When **Kit Lambert** and **Chris Stamp** created their New Action company, the only other people involved were **Mike Shaw** and Kit's friend Anya. Her best friend happened to be married to **Shel Talmy**, and she and Shaw first approached him about working with the Who.

Butler, Peter "Dougal"   Keith Moon's chauffeur and personal assistant during much of the 1970s. During the autumn of 1967 Butler, a former mod, became one of the Who's roadies. By late 1969 he'd been dubbed "Dougal" by Pete Townshend and was John Entwistle's chauffeur; **Neil Boland** had taken on those duties for Keith Moon. Two more years later Dougal took over from Peter "Chalky" White as Moon's driver. Dougal was mentioned in John Entwistle's solo song "Cell Number Seven" on his 1975 *Mad Dog* album. The song was about the Who and a number of associates being jailed briefly for some post-concert hotel destruction in Montreal on December 2, 1973. On a happier note, Dougal appeared on the cover of Keith's only solo album, *Two Sides of the Moon*. In the early 1980s Dougal published his recollections of his times with Keith in a book entitled *Moon the Loon* in the UK and *Full Moon* in the U.S. Around this time he also managed the band Mono Pacific, one of the first joined by **Zak Starkey**. It was reported in the 1990s that Robert DeNiro, among others, was interested in basing a movie on Dougal's book. Most recently, Dougal appeared in the VH1 *Behind the Music* episode that profiled Keith.

Butler, Tony   Bass player for **Big Country** who has played on several of Pete Townshend's solo albums. Butler was among the musicians who backed **Simon Townshend** at a concert in 1977. Shortly thereafter he, Simon, and **Mark Brzezicki** formed On the Air and released a couple of records before Tony and Mark joined Big Country in 1982. On July 13, 1979, Butler was part of the first band that Pete Townshend formed outside of the Who, for the "Rock Against Racism" benefit. Also in this band were **Kenney Jones, John "Rabbit" Bundrick** and **Peter Hope-Evans**. On Pete's 1980 album *Empty Glass* Tony played bass on all but two tracks, "And I Moved" and "Keep on Working." He also played bass on Pete's 1982 album, *All the Best Cowboys Have Chinese Eyes*, and shortly thereafter on the **Pretenders**' hit single "Back on the Chain Gang." In 1985 he also played bass on Townshend's album *White City* and on the Townshend composition "After the Fire" on Roger Daltrey's solo album *Under a Raging Moon*.

Butler, Yancy   Actress whose TV series that debuted in 2001, *Witchblade*, featured Roger Daltrey as a guest star. Yancy's father Joe, a drummer, was in the Lovin' Spoonful with **John Sebastian**. In an early acting role she portrayed an android police officer in a 1992 NBC show called *Mann And Machine*, which was set in the future. In one episode her partner talked about seeing the Who on another reunion tour. In the next two years she appeared in the movies *Hard Target* with Jean-Claude Van Damme and *Drop Zone* with Wesley Snipes. Another notable credit was being a regular on the TV series *Brooklyn South*, a police drama, in 1997.

Byrd, Charlie   Jazz guitarist noted for mixing in aspects of classical techniques and for helping to introduce Brazilian bossa nova music to English-speaking listeners. From the late '50s until his death in 1999 he released a large number of albums. On his 1971 album *For All We Know* he covered the Who's "See Me, Feel Me." In the 1950s and '60s Byrd was an associate of such noted performers as Andrés Segovia, Woody Herman, and Stan Getz. In 1973 he wrote a popular guitar instruction manual and also formed the group Great Guitars with **Barney Kessel** and Herb Ellis.

Byrd, Ricky   Lead guitarist with **Joan Jett** and the Blackhearts who later worked with Ian Hunter, formerly of Mott the Hoople. In between he helped out on Roger Daltrey's 1992 solo album *Rocks in the Head*. In addition to playing guitar and providing backing vocals, Byrd co-wrote the song "Love Is" and co-wrote and produced the song "Who's Gonna Walk on Water." In the early 1980s, around age 20, Byrd had already made tentative plans to work with Steve Marriott of the **Small Faces** and had begun to write songs with John Waite of the Babys when he met and began a long association with Jett. According to an interview on Byrd's own website, rickybyrd.com, Daltrey contacted Byrd just after he left the Blackhearts. "Being a kid who grew up in the Bronx and waited in line five hours to see the Who, I was like, wow." Byrd thus celebrated a birthday by recording with Daltrey at Abbey Road Studios in England where he said Roger gave him one of Pete Townshend's famous Les Pauls as a gift. Daltrey took Byrd on a radio and TV promotional tour and they did acoustic versions of Who classics as well as the new material. At a Carnegie Hall benefit, Byrd recalled turning to Daltrey during a sound check and joking, "hey, ain't cha gonna swing the mic?" Roger laughed while holding a cordless microphone, but during that night's show Byrd said, "I feel this big whoosh buzzing right by my ear, I look to my right and Roger's got this big grin on his face and the mic is swinging by my head."

Capehart, Jerry *see* Cochran, Eddie.

Carin, Jon Keyboard player who performed on six **Pink Floyd** albums from 1987 to 1995 and who has worked with members of the Who. In 1985 Carin played on one of **Bryan Ferry**'s solo albums and backed him at that year's huge Live Aid benefit. Around the time that he started recording with Pink Floyd he also worked with the Psychedelic Furs. Carin played guitar as well as keyboards on Roger Daltrey's 1994 CD *A Celebration — The Music of Pete Townshend and the Who*. A few years later he began performing as a duo with Pete Townshend, providing keyboards, drum tracks and backing vocals. This culminated in Pete's 1999 *Live* CD. Two songs which he helped Pete perform at Shepherds Bush Empire in 1998, "Won't Get Fooled Again" and "Who Are You," turned up on Pete's six-disc *Lifehouse Chronicles* boxed set in 2000. Carin produced those tracks.

Carlsen, Dave The name under which Keith Moon's friend Dave Clarke (no relation to the frontman of the Dave Clark Five) recorded the album *Pale Horse* in the early 1970s. Clarke was recording an album for CBS Records and coaxed Moon to drum for him. Moon did, but according to Tony Fletcher he was criticized by CBS's Dave Margereson for being a day late for his first recording session. A second argument between Margereson and Moon prompted CBS to drop Clarke. The album was released on the Spark label in 1973 and featured several guests besides Moon, including **Spencer Davis** and the **Jimi Hendrix** Experience's bass player, Noel Redding. Proceeds from the song "Death on a Pale Horse" were earmarked for a mentally handicapped children's charity "courtesy of Noel Redding, Keith Moon, Dave Carlsen and CBS Records." Clarke went on to play keyboards in the Noel Redding Band, which released two mid–1970s albums, *Clonakilty Cowboys* and *Blowin'*. In 1995 thirteen of the band's recordings that were caught up in legal red tape were released on the CD *Missing Album* with liner notes by Redding and Clarke.

Carroll, Lewis   Pseudonym of Victorian author and mathematician Charles Lutwidge Dodgson, who authored the fantasy novels *Alice's Adventures in Wonderland* (1865) and *Through the Looking-Glass* (1872). Carroll's epic nonsense poem "The Hunting of the Snark" was transformed into a musical by **Mike Batt** in which Roger Daltrey portrayed the Barrister and sang lead on "The Pig Must Die."

Casey, Howie   Saxophonist on John Entwistle's third solo album *Rigor Mortis Sets In*, on the songs "Gimme That Rock 'n' Roll," "Do the Dangle" and "Hound Dog." He also played tenor sax on John's next album, *Mad Dog*. He also played sax on the **John Alcock**/John Entwistle *Flash Fearless* album. Casey worked with the **Beatles** in their early days and Paul McCartney recruited him for Wings tours in 1975 and 1979. He also played on a number of Wings recordings. In 1995 he recorded an album with **Roy Young** and Tony Sheridan, another early Beatles associate.

Cash, Pat   *see*   McEnroe, John.

Cassidy, Shaun   Teen idol of the late 1970s thanks in large part to a roll on the *Hardy Boys* TV series. Like his half-brother and fellow teen idol David Cassidy, Shaun also had success as a singer. On his 1980 album *Wasp* he was backed by **Todd Rundgren** and his band Utopia on a well-done version of the Who's "So Sad About Us."

Cavaleri, Nathan   Young Australian guitar prodigy who was backed by John Entwistle at a Los Angeles Guitar Institute concert before he'd even reached his teens. He had made his American debut in 1992 at a San Francisco concert celebrating the 25th anniversary of *Guitar Player* magazine. **Skunk Baxter**, with whom Nathan performed, said he had "never seen anyone play with that much heart." By the end of 1994 he had played with Mark Knopfler of Dire Straits, blues great Albert Collins, and Booker T. and the MGs. A couple of years later, at the age of 13, he toured with guitar legend B.B. King.

Cerveris, Michael   American actor and musician most known for starring in the Tony Award winning show *The Who's Tommy* in the 1990s. During the summer of 1993 he joined Pete Townshend on stage a few times, including for a *Tommy* medley in San Diego. One of Cerveris' early breaks was playing an English guitar student on the TV series *Fame* in the late 1980s. He soon appeared in other series such as the *Tracey Ullman Show*, *Quantum Leap*, and *Dream On*. Following *The Who's Tommy* he originated the role of Thomas Andrews in the Broadway musical *Titanic*. Michael's official website is amazing-journey.com, a clear nod to *Tommy*.

Chambers, Martin *see* The Pretenders.

Chandler, Chas *see* The Animals.

The Chanter Sisters   Lead vocalists, along with **Juanita Franklin**, on John Entwistle's song "Mad Dog" in 1975. The three singers also provided backing vocals on the rest of the *Mad Dog* album, John's fourth solo release. Despite the obviously feminine vocals on "Mad Dog," Entwistle was asked by a French television show to mime the song for a broadcast. He declined. Doreen and Irene Chanter also sang on the **John Alcock**/John Entwistle *Flash Fearless* album. The Chanter Sisters released four of their own albums from 1970 through 1978 and played keyboards in addition to singing on them. Their numerous credits include backing **Manfred Mann** a few times from 1973 to 1978, Whitesnake in 1978, Justin Hayward of the **Moody Blues** in 1980, and John Cale of Velvet Underground fame in the 1970s and 1990s.

Chapman, Graham *see* Monty Python's Flying Circus.

Charlesworth, Chris   Rock journalist, biographer, and, since 1984, editor of UK rock book publisher Omnibus Press. He has written extensively on the Who and had a hand in the reissuing of the Who's back catalogue during the 1990s. Charlesworth was with *Melody Maker* from 1970 to 1977, then spent two years as tour manager for a New York-based company whose clientele included the Who and the **Rolling Stones**. He also spent some time as head of press with Stiff Records and then RCA before turning his attention to writing rock biographies.

Chen, Phil *see* Streetwalkers.

Chicago   Band that spanned the last three decades of the 20th century while sliding from rock to orchestrated ballads. It achieved success on its earlier albums by adding brass and woodwinds to its rock songs, such as "25 or 6 to 4," but over time the group moved toward a softer sound, such as on its 1982 #1 hit "Hard to Say I'm Sorry." Keyboard player and unofficial leader Robert Lamm was the pianist on the song "Unforgettable Opera" on Roger Daltrey's 1992 solo album, *Rocks in the Head*.

The Chieftains   Award-winning group that has popularized traditional Irish music around the world. The Chieftains were formed in 1963 but started to gain their widest notice in the 1980s by working with prominent musicians and singers from other musical genres. They also exposed audiences to dancers Michael Flatley and Jean Butler before both gained notice in Riverdance. The Chieftains won a Grammy for 1991's *An Irish Evening*, which featured Roger Daltrey and Nanci Griffith as guests. The

Chieftains can be heard on "Baba O'Riley" and "After the Fire" on Daltrey's 1994 CD *A Celebration — The Music of Pete Townshend and the Who*. They were joined for those songs by Sinead O'Connor.

Christian, Roger   Songwriter who collaborated on songs for the **Beach Boys** and Jan and Dean that were also recorded by Keith Moon and the Who. Christian co-wrote the 1964 Beach Boys hit "Don't Worry Baby" with band member Brian Wilson. The song was reportedly among Keith's all-time favorite songs, if not number one outright, and about a decade later it was a single from Keith's only solo album. Christian, Donald Atfield, and Dean Torrence wrote the song "Bucket T" for a 1964 Jan and Dean album. The Who recorded a version that was released on the five-song EP *Ready Steady Who* in November of 1966. As the A-side of a 45, "Bucket T" was a #1 hit for the Who in Sweden. Without Torrence, who was half of Jan and Dean, Atfield and Christian wrote the hit "The Little Old Lady (From Pasadena)" for that surf duo.

Chyna   London singer who has worked with Peter Gabriel, **Eric Clapton**, and Pete Townshend, among others. At the age of 17 she debuted with the reggae band Silk Tones and later sang with African jazz bands. In 1986, as Coral Gordon, she backed Gabriel on his hits "Sledgehammer" and "Big Time" and was one of five backing vocalists in Townshend's **Deep End** band. In 1989 she shared lead vocals on "All Shall Be Well" and "New Life/Reprise" on Pete Townshend's *Iron Man* album, his 1989 musical adaptation of the **Ted Hughes** tale. Her character was the Crow. Some of Townshend's income from "All Shall Be Well" was paid to the Lincoln Trust, a nonaggressive antiapartheid group including white South Africans; some from "New Life" was paid to black African educational charities. Chyna provided vocals for the Who on its 1989 reunion tour, most notably on the song "Acid Queen." She then formed a band to tour England and developed a large following. The singer Seal became one of her biggest fans during this time and asked her to support him on tour in 1995. A few years prior to that she co-wrote the song "Don't Be a Stranger," which was a #3 hit in the UK for Dina Carroll in 1993. In 1998 she sang on Clapton's *Pilgrim* album and took part in the subsequent tour. Chyna had some lead vocal duties during Pete Townshend's *Lifehouse* concert at London's Sadler's Wells in early 2000.

Clapton, Eric   British rock and blues guitarist who has long been successful as a solo artist as well as in such 1960s groups as the Yardbirds, Cream, and Blind Faith. When Cream was just starting out it played support for the Who on September 15, 1966. Keith Moon and Clapton were among numerous performers to back John Lennon of the **Beatles** at a concert at London's Lyceum to close out 1969. In the early 1970s, however, heroin addiction prompted Clapton to withdraw to his Surrey home for the better part of two years. Pete Townshend introduced him to Dr. **Meg Patterson**, who helped him overcome his problem. Thanks to encouragement from Townshend, a nervous Clapton reemerged in January of 1973 at a couple of concerts at London's Rainbow Theatre. Backing him were Townshend, **Ron Wood**, drummer Jim Karstein (of the Crickets and Delaney and Bonnie) and four members of Traffic, including **Steve Winwood**. The resulting album was engineered by **Glyn Johns**, who produced Clapton's *Slowhand* and *Backless* albums a few years later. Clapton toured the U.S. in 1974, and Townshend and Keith Moon were guest performers at three shows in August. In 1975 Clapton appeared in the movie *Tommy*, singing and playing guitar on "Eyesight to the Blind." He also played guitar on the soundtrack's version of "Sally Simpson."

Keith Moon joined Clapton during a Los Angeles concert in August of 1975, along with Carlos Santana and Joe Cocker. They played "Why Does Love Got to Be So Sad," "Teach Me to Be Your Woman," and "Badge." During the first half of 1976 Townshend played on Clapton's recording of the unreleased song "The Path" and was credited on Clapton's *No Reason to Cry* album. In 1977 Clapton was the lead guitarist on the title track of the Pete Townshend/**Ronnie Lane** collaboration, *Rough Mix*. He also played on "Till the Rivers All Run Dry," "April Fool" and "Annie," and co-wrote the latter with Lane and Kate Lambert. In April Townshend was again a guest of Clapton's at a Rainbow concert. That year Clapton also received special thanks for an unspecified reason in the credits of Roger Daltrey's third solo album, *One of the Boys*. In October of 1989, Townshend and Clapton appeared together on the UK television talk show *Saturday Matters* and performed an acoustic version of the **Muddy Waters** song "Standin' Around Cryin'."

On July 24, 2000 Clapton answered questions for an America Online chat, including one about his scene in *Tommy*. Clapton said he could only recall bits and pieces due to "the brandy and other substances that were being introduced into my system, along with the rest of the guys." He said he didn't enjoy being in front of a camera. "But I remember the director or his assistant called me up afterwards and said we need to shoot one more scene, so I deliberately shaved my beard off. He said that's no problem, just come down and we'll stick another one on. They did, hair by hair. And it took like three hours." Clapton said his other strong memory was "hanging out with Moon who was a complete and utter lunatic. And we had a lot of fun together. I was very close to Keith. And I'm very close to Pete. It was Pete's baby, making that movie, so he took it a little bit more seriously than I wanted to or Keith wanted to. And we were desperately trying to sabotage the whole thing all of the time. And he wasn't that pleased. But a lot of the time he would get into it. But I mean, I love those guys and I felt very honored that Pete wanted me to be involved." Earlier in 2000 Clapton was inducted into the Rock and Roll Hall of Fame based on his solo career. He had already been inducted with the Yardbirds in 1992 and with Cream in 1993 and thus became the first performer honored on three different occasions.

Clarke, Dave *see* Carlsen, Dave.

The Clash British punk band that rose to prominence in the late 1970s, and caught the eye of Pete Townshend in part because of their overtly political nature. The Clash played for the Rock Against Racism benefit in July of 1979, as did Townshend, and six months later he joined them onstage during one of their concerts, during the encore. In 1982 **Glyn Johns** mixed their *Combat Rock* album and the Clash were an opening act for the Who. By the middle of the decade they had disbanded. In mid-2001 Clash guitarist Joe Strummer released an album called *Global a Go Go*, with Roger Daltrey providing vocals for the title track. Strummer died of cardiac arrest in late 2002 at the age of 50.

Clayton, Merry African-American singer who portrayed the Acid Queen in **Lou Reizner**'s all-star stage version of *Tommy* in 1972. In the late 1960s Clayton sang for Joe Cocker, the **Rolling Stones**, and **Neil Young**. In the 1970s she sang for B.B. King, **Barbra Streisand**, Carole King, and Lynyrd Skynyrd and had a handful of solo albums. A noteworthy credit in the 1980s was providing vocals on **Big Country**'s 1988 album *Peace in Our Time*. During the 1990s she focused on gospel music and sang with Chrissie Hynde of the **Pretenders** on a tribute album cover of the **Doors** song "Touch Me." Hynde and Clayton were joined by Clayton's husband, Curtis Amy, who had played the saxophone solo on the original version of the song.

Clempson, Dave "Clem" *see* Humble Pie.

Cochran, Eddie Youthful musician whose brief career included the hit singles "Summertime Blues" and "C'mon Everybody," both of which were covered by the Who. Cochran met and began working with songwriter Jerry Capehart around 1950 and more than five years passed before their partnership started paying off with successful singles. They wrote "Summertime Blues" in March of 1958 and it was an international hit. Later in 1958 "C'mon Everybody" reached the top 40 in the U.S. and was quite popular in the UK as well. Cochran played and sang all the parts on both hits and thus proved to be one of the first musicians to demonstrate studio overdubbing mastery. In 1960, at the age of 21, Cochran died in a car accident on his way to the airport in London. The Who's version of "Summertime Blues" from their 1970 *Live at Leeds* album proved to be quite popular. They had also recorded a studio version for a BBC show in 1967. In 1967 the Who also recorded a studio version of another Cochran/Capehart song, "My Way," which finally surfaced as a bonus track on the *Odds and Sods* CD in 1998. The Who performed "C'mon Everybody" on tour in 1968. Cochran was inducted into the Rock and Roll Hall of Fame in 1987.

Cole, B.J.   One of popular music's most accomplished steel guitar players. Brian "B.J." Cole backed his fellow countryman Roger Daltrey on the song "Thinking" on Roger's 1973 solo debut, *Daltrey*. Over the years Cole worked with such performers as **Elton John**, Tammy Wynette, Emmylou Harris, **Leo Sayer**, Jerry Lee Lewis, Gerry Rafferty of **Stealers Wheel**, Dave Edmunds, and k.d. lang.

Cole, Gary   Actor who portrayed the lead role of Jack Killian in the American TV series *Midnight Caller* and who later demonstrated amazing voice mimicry as the dad in the two big screen *Brady Bunch* movies. In the 1991 *Midnight Caller* episode entitled "Can't Say N-N-No" Roger Daltrey guest starred as Danny Bingham, who was a former lover of actress Lisa Eilbacher's character, the manager of the San Francisco radio station where Killian hosted a late night talk show host.

Cole, Richard   Driver for the Who starting in October of 1965 and later tour manager for **Led Zeppelin**. When John Entwistle and Keith Moon talked with Cole about leaving the Who to form a group called "Lead Zeppelin" it was Cole who later suggested this name to Jimmy Page. According to Tony Fletcher, in early 1966 Cole lost his job with the Who due to one traffic ticket too many, and he went to work for the Yardbirds. When Jimmy Page was left in charge of that disintegrating band in mid-1968, it was Cole who suggested the name for the band's successor. John Entwistle said that he had mentioned the name "Lead Zeppelin" to Cole in 1966, but Fletcher said Cole heard it in the summer of 1968 when he happened to meet Entwistle and Moon in New York City.

Collins, Frank *see* Kokomo.

Collins, Mel *see* Kokomo.

Collins, Phil *see* Genesis.

The Confederates   The first band in which John Entwistle and Pete

Townshend played together, in 1959 when both were barely in their teens and not long after they met at Acton County Grammar School. Entwistle played brass and Townshend banjo. Their only live appearances were at the Congo Club, an Acton church teen center. Pete said they played songs like "Marching Through Georgia" and "Farewell Blues." The other core members of this traditional jazz band were Alf Maynard on banjo, Chris Sherwin on drums and Phil Rhodes on clarinet. Entwistle started playing with a bigger and more active trad group, albeit one lacking a name, and eventually he left the Confederates for good. This other band mainly played **Kenny Ball** and **Acker Bilk** songs, and due to hard work more so than talent managed to make some decent money for a while: Townshend played with them one New Year's Eve and received eight pounds, a half-share of the band's earnings, and he considered that a surprisingly good amount. Townshend told **Richard Barnes** that this unnamed group was already dominated by Alf Maynard, so Pete wasn't able to play with them regularly. The Confederates ultimately broke up after a fight between Sherwin and Townshend during which the young drummer sustained a concussion. Townshend was then shunned by schoolmates and took up the guitar in his free time, influenced in part by Hank Marvin of the **Shadows** and **Chuck Berry**. Meanwhile, the instrumental hits of Duane Eddy prompted John Entwistle to take up the bass. Entwistle and Townshend soon reunited to form the **Aristocrats** and then the **Scorpions**, with pals Pete Wilson and Mick Brown.

Conway, Deborah Australian singer and actress who shared lead vocals on "I Won't Run Anymore" and "All Shall Be Well" on Pete Townshend's *Iron Man* album, his 1989 musical adaptation of the **Ted Hughes** tale. Prior to that she was in a band called Do Re Mi. Since 1991 Conway has released a solo album every two or three years. On one of them, 1995's *Ultrasound*, she worked with Paul Hester of Crowded House.

Cook, Paul *see* The Sex Pistols.

Coombes, Rod *see* Ro Ro.

Cooper, Alice Well-known American male rock singer, born Vincent Furnier, whose stage name reportedly came from a Ouija board. Before he was well known Cooper opened for the Who at a concert in Michigan on October 11, 1969. His shock-rock theatrical band had several Top 40 hits from 1971 to 1973, peaking at #7 with "School's Out" in 1972. He also reached the Top 20 with a different backing band a few times later in the decade and has consistently maintained a following. In 1975 Cooper worked with John Entwistle and other musicians on **John Alcock**'s *Flash*

Fearless project. Cooper sang on two tracks, including one on which Keith Moon can be heard imitating Long John Silver. In late 1976 Cooper and Moon were among the celebrities who appeared in Mae West's final film, *Sextette*. In 1978 the album cover for Cooper's *From the Inside* had small tabs that could be opened, and a picture of Moon was behind one of them. When Roger Daltrey celebrated his 50th birthday in 1994 with two shows at New York's Carnegie Hall, Alice was among the guest performers. Aptly, the man with the woman's name and known for wearing makeup sang "I'm a Boy." A few years later Daltrey sang the Cooper hit "No More Mr. Nice Guy" on the tribute album *Humanary Stew*. On the **British Rock Symphony**'s 1999 CD Cooper covered the Who's "5.15" and in the 1999 BRS video he and Daltrey teamed up on that song and the **Rolling Stones**' "Start Me Up." In January of 2000 Cooper was a guest on the VH1 cable TV series *The List* for an episode that purported to determine the three greatest pop/rock songs of all time. Cooper nominated the Who's "My Generation," which ended up finishing behind only "Stairway to Heaven" and "American Pie." The episode ended with a "My Generation" jam by the band Train.

Copeland, Stewart *see* The Police.

The Count Five Psychedelic garage band that emerged from California to become one-hit wonders when their song "Psychotic Reaction" reached #5 in 1966. They recorded covers of two Who songs, "My Generation" and "Out in the Street." A live version of "My Generation" was also released, on their album *Psychotic Reaction Live*.

Courtney, David Writing partner of **Leo Sayer** for 10 years who thus had a hand in some of Roger Daltrey's solo work. Courtney had been a drummer for **Adam Faith** but by 1972 was attempting to set up a talent agency. Sayer responded to an ad Courtney placed, and the two established a writing partnership. This led to Courtney's roles as producer, pianist, and songwriter for Daltrey's self-titled debut solo album in 1973. Courtney and Sayer co-wrote all but two of the songs; Courtney and Faith wrote the other two. The single "Giving It All Away" became a top five hit for Daltrey in the UK. Courtney and Sayer also wrote "There Is Love," a non-album B-side that surfaced on CD in the 1990s as a bonus track. The album that Sayer had recorded at Daltrey's studios was entitled *Silverbird*, and it was released shortly after *Daltrey*. *Silverbird* gave Sayer a top five hit of his own in the UK, "The Show Must Go On." Sayer recorded at least part of his second album, *Just a Boy*, at Daltrey's facility as well and it gave the songwriting duo its first big hit in the U.S., "Long Tall Glasses."

For a few years Courtney and Sayer parted company, so Courtney alone wrote the song "Dear John," another non-album B-side that was among the bonus tracks on Daltrey's *Ride a Rock Horse* CD. Courtney and early **Shadows** drummer Tony Meehan produced Daltrey's third solo album, 1977's *One of the Boys*. Courtney, Meehan and Daltrey wrote "Satin and Lace" and "Doing It All Again." Courtney also co-wrote "The Prisoner," which was inspired by a meeting between Roger and **John McVicar**. Besides Faith, Sayer and Daltrey, Courtney has worked with the likes of **Pink Floyd**'s Dave Gilmour, ex–**Beatle** Paul McCartney, Toto and **Steve Cropper**. In 1993 Courtney produced the Faith/Daltrey duet "Stuck in the Middle." Courtney spent much of the 1990s in his hometown of Brighton focusing on experimental music and television projects.

Covey, Julian Leader of a progressive rock/blues band called the Machine who drummed for the Who in mid–1967 after Keith Moon had strained his stomach muscles while goofing around during the Who's previous performance on May 27 and/or during a recording session on May 28. Covey filled in on May 29 and June 3. **Chris Townson** of **John's Children** was recruited to help out on June 4 and 5. *The Who Concert File* notes that about a year earlier, from May 21 through 27, 1966, "an unknown deputy drummer filled in" for Keith because he was recovering from being accidentally hit in the face with Pete Townshend's guitar on May 20. Covey's band was known to have played at the Marquee in 1965. According to the *Tapestry of Delights*, Covey's real name was Phil Kinorra and he gained early experience playing with noted keyboard player Brian Auger. Julian Covey and Machine released one 45, "A Little Bit Hurt" backed with "Sweet Bacon," and the A-side turns up on compilations from time to time. Machine member John Moreshead had played with **Johnny Kidd** and the Pirates and went on to play with Aynsley Dunbar. Machine later included Jim Cregan, who later joined **Family**, and Dave Mason, who would later be in Traffic.

Covington, Joey *see* Jefferson Airplane/Starship.

The Crazy World of Arthur Brown *see* Brown, Arthur.

Creedence Clearwater Revival Dominant American singles band in 1969 and 1970. In that span CCR's top five hits included "Proud Mary," "Bad Moon Rising," "Green River," "Down on the Corner," "Travelin' Band," "Up Around the Bend," and "Lookin' Out My Back Door." The Who covered CCR's "Born on the Bayou" during its 1989 tour; at a concert in Wisconsin, Roger Daltrey said the song was the only thing he could remember from Woodstock. CCR disbanded in the autumn of 1972, and frontman John Fogerty took many years off before having some solo success on the charts in the 1980s and 1990s. In 1993 CCR was inducted into the Rock and Roll Hall of Fame.

Cropper, Steve   Prolific songwriter, producer, and guitarist who briefly worked with Keith Moon. At the age of 20 Cropper's band the Mar-Keys garnered a gold record for the 1961 instrumental "Last Night," but his most notable guitar work was as a member of Booker T. and the MGs into the mid–'70s. Their version of "Green Onions" was used on the *Quadrophenia* soundtrack in 1979. His songwriting credits include hits for various singers, such as "Soul Man," "Knock on Wood," "In the Midnight Hour," and "(Sittin' on) The Dock of the Bay." He opened his own studio in Memphis in 1969 and produced such artists as **Jeff Beck**, the Temptations, José Feliciano, Joe Cocker, Poco, and John Prine. He has also done session work for the likes of **Rod Stewart** and **Sammy Hagar**. After Keith Moon's only solo album, 1975's *Two Sides of the Moon*, turned out to be a producer's nightmare, Cropper was recruited to direct and produce a second album for Moon in September of that year. Three tracks from this aborted album were first released in 1997 as bonus tracks when *Two Sides of the Moon* was released on compact disc. Two of them, "Do Me Good" and "Real Emotion," were written by Cropper. "Naked Man" was written by Randy Newman. Guest performers on the three tracks included **David Bowie** and **Ron Wood**. On top of all these other claims to fame, from 1978 to 1981 Cropper was part of the *Saturday Night Live* spin-off the Blues Brothers. Booker T. and the MGs were inducted into the Rock and Roll Hall of Fame in 1992.

Crow, Sheryl   Popular rock performer beginning with her debut album, *Tuesday Night Music Club*, in 1993. She has strapped on an accordion to perform the Who's "Squeeze Box" live, and in 2001 the CD entitled *Substitute: the Songs of the Who* included a version of "Behind Blue Eyes" by Sheryl. There has been talk for many months of a CD release of a 1973 Who concert in Philadelphia that was recorded by the *King Biscuit Flower Hour*, and at one point it was reported that Sheryl interviewed Roger Daltrey to provide bonus material.

The Crowd   The name given in 1985 to a very large number of singers and musicians, including John Entwistle, who recorded a version of "You'll Never Walk Alone," the Rodgers and Hammerstein number from the 1945 musical *Carousel*. All proceeds from the sale of the twelve inch single went to the Bradford City Disaster Fund, which was established after a fatal fire at the city's soccer stadium. The project was spearheaded by Gerry Marsden of the 1960s British group Gerry and the Pacemakers.

The Crystals *see* Love, Darlene.

Curbishley, Bill   Longtime employee and ultimately manager of the Who. Curbishley had befriended **Mike Shaw** and **Chris Stamp** during their school days, and he joined Stamp and **Kit Lambert**'s New Action company in 1970. About a year later Shaw and Curbishley designed the cover of *Meaty, Beaty, Big and Bouncy* though the photography was handled by **Graham Hughes**. Due to growing animosity between Roger Daltrey on the one hand and Lambert and Stamp on the other, Daltrey anointed Curbishley as his personal manager for his 1973 debut solo album, *Daltrey*. Roger soon insisted that Lambert and Stamp turn over managing responsibilities of the Who to Curbishley, and then many months were spent disentangling the Who contractually from New Action and Track Records. *Quadrophenia* was the last new Who album on which Lambert and Stamp were credited, as executive producers. One of Curbishley's next projects was serving as executive producer, along with **Rick Wakeman**'s manager Brian Lane, of Roger Daltrey's second movie, 1975's *Lisztomania*.

Around 1977 Bill and wife Jackie read about **John McVicar** in a Sunday newspaper and spent three years raising the funds for Roger Daltrey to portray John in the movie *McVicar*. Bill produced the *McVicar* movie with **Roy Baird** and Roger. Shortly before **Peter Meaden**'s suicide in August of 1978 Meaden and Curbishley were managing the **Steve Gibbons** Band. **Judas Priest** became one Curbishley's clients in 1983. In 1986 Bill was co-producer of a video for Pete Townshend and his **Deep End** band, and Jackie was one of the executive producers. Pete listed Bill under "management" on his 1993 live video. In 1991 Curbishley, Baird, and Daltrey produced the Roger Daltrey/Chesney Hawkes movie *Buddy's Song*. In issue #51 of the British periodical *Punch*, dated March 28–April 10, 1998, John McVicar wrote about a conversation with one Lord Taverne, who asked McVicar about an "ex-con with whom he knew I was friendly, Bill Curbishley. This conversation was in 1981, and Curbishley was then manager of the Who, but he'd served a long prison sentence in the Sixties for a crime he didn't commit. In his capacity as a Home Office minister at the time, Taverne had responsibility for Curbishley's case. He asked me if Curbishley was innocent. I said yes; he had absolutely nothing to do with the robbery for which he was sentenced to 15 years. Taverne nodded sadly and replied: 'I thought so, but there was little I could do. It didn't help that the trial judge was alive…'." In 2000 Curbishley arranged for ex–**Led Zeppelin** guitarist Jimmy Page and the Black Crowes to minimize tour expenses by often playing in venues the night before or after the Who did so.

Dale, Dick Legendary surf guitarist whose pioneering style influenced and was borrowed by performers who had much more chart success than did his Del-Tones. His most notable followers were Keith Moon's beloved **Beach Boys**, who covered two of Dale's songs on early albums of theirs. Dale provided the surf guitar and solo on the song "Teenage Idol" on Moon's only solo album, 1975's *Two Sides of the Moon*. Dick Dale and his Del-Tones were mentioned by Moon during one of his "Life with the Moons" comedy bits while serving as a guest disc jockey on the BBC.

Daltrey, Roger Energetic lead singer for the Who. In his teens Daltrey founded and led the **Detours**, the band that eventually became the Who. Roger Harry Daltrey was born to Irene and Harry Daltrey in London on March 1, 1944. They had wed in 1936. Harry Daltrey worked for a bathroom fixtures manufacturer but served in the military in World War II. By the end of 1947 Roger had two sisters, Gillian/Jill and Carol. During an America Online chat in February of 2000 he commented on growing up in postwar England: "We had nothing. We really had nothing. We had our asses hanging out of our trousers. We just got roofs put back on our houses, and windows. Really, it was that bad. So you can't just measure the age in years." In 1955 the Daltrey family moved from the Shepherd's Bush area to a nicer neighborhood nearby, Bedford Park in Acton. During his last year at Victorial Primary School in Shepherd's Bush, his "eleven-plus" exam scores put him at the top of his class. Due to his family's new home he switched to Acton County Grammar School.

In *Before I Get Old* Dave Marsh quoted both of Roger's parents regarding Roger's sudden loss of interest in his schooling. This apparently resulted from the clash between Roger's humble origins and the more upper-class lifestyles of the pupils in his new neighborhood. Roger eventually fell in with a gang of similarly disaffected youths but rock music soon presented him with a way out. Around that time Roger was exposed to the music of Elvis Presley and **Lonnie Donegan** and decided to build his own guitar. He eventually formed the Detours with some friends. He built his next guitar, another acoustic one, with help from an uncle who was a carpenter. Roger was the lead guitarist of the Detours, who practiced at the home of Reg Bowen, the rhythm guitarist. According to Marsh, Roger's father bought him an Epiphone guitar in 1959 because Roger was so serious about his music. But Roger became even less serious about his schooling, and was expelled from Acton County Grammar by the end of the year.

Roger soon landed a job as a sheet metal worker and took the opportunity to build an electric guitar, which he recalls sufficing for about three years. During the America Online chat he talked about that project: "I was working in the sheet metal work factory, and it was really difficult to hide all the wood shavings, because I used to make guitars behind the carpenter's back. And wood shavings and metal shavings don't quite look alike. He put up with a lot." Roger managed to hold that job for about five years. In 1961 or 1962 Roger coaxed John Entwistle into the Detours, and in short order Entwistle managed to bring Pete Townshend in as the new rhythm guitarist. Both had been one grade below Roger's at Acton County Grammar. Marsh quoted Townshend as saying that he was well aware of Roger while they were both at Acton County Grammar and that "Roger was the best guitarist, a very basic guitar player but very confident and very fluid in a way." According to *The Who Concert File*, in July of 1962 **Doug Sandom** became the Detours' drummer.

In February of 1964 Daltrey, Entwistle, Townshend and Sandom changed their band's name from the Detours to the Who. However, more changes were just around the corner; in May Keith Moon became the drummer and in July the band changed its name to the **High Numbers**. In November they reverted to the Who. Their first two 45s as the Who, "I Can't Explain" and "Anyway Anyhow Anywhere," were both successful. Shortly after the Who released its third single, the mythic "My Generation," Daltrey was kicked out of the band temporarily. Rumor had it that Boz Burrell, then in the band Boz's People and later a member of **Bad Company**, would be Roger's replacement. Pete Townshend and **Kit Lambert** also considered merging the three remaining members of the Who with **Paddy, Klaus and Gibson**. The huge success of "My Generation" provided the impetus to readmit Roger. It was a sensible move not only because it was Roger's distinctive voice on the band's biggest hit but also because early on Daltrey had demonstrated "a natural instinct for structuring live performances," as Dave Marsh noted in *Before I Get Old*.

In addition to being credited with helping Townshend write "Anyway, Anyhow, Anywhere" in 1965, in 1966 Daltrey wrote "See My Way" for their second album, *A Quick One* (released as *Happy Jack* in the United States). A few years later he wrote "Here for More," the B-side of the 1970 Who 45 "The Seeker." Daltrey also co-wrote "Early Morning Cold Taxi" with Cy Langston in 1967. The song was intended for the Who's third album, *The Who Sell Out*, but it wasn't officially released until that album had bonus tracks added to it in 1994. Throughout the 1960s as the Who were developing a reputation for wild partying while touring, Daltrey decided that he could only be at his best by maintaining a relatively healthy lifestyle.

In September of 1972 Roger hit #13 with "I'm Free" from **Lou Reizner**'s all-star cast version of *Tommy* performed at London's Rainbow Theatre. That same year Daltrey started living on a farm in East Burwash and opened a recording facility that **Adam Faith** started using that year to record **Leo Sayer**'s first album. This ultimately led to Roger's first solo album, *Daltrey*. Its first single, "Giving It All Away," reached the top five in the UK in 1973. The album reached #45 in the U.S. but there "Giving It All Away" only reached #83. In 1975 *Ride a Rock Horse* reached #14 in the UK and #28 in the U.S. The single "Written on the Wind" reached #46 in the UK charts but wasn't released in the U.S. In 1977 Roger's *One of the Boys* LP hit #45 in the UK and #46 in the U.S. The single "Avenging Annie" only reached #88 in the U.S. In 1980 the **McVicar** soundtrack reached #22 in the U.S. and #39 in the UK. It yielded two singles: "Without Your Love" reached #55 in the UK but peaked at #20 in the U.S. and "Free Me" hit #53 in the U.S. but climbed into the top 40 in the UK.

Of his albums in the 1980s—*Parting Should Be Painless*, *Under a Raging Moon*, and *Can't Wait to See the Movie*—the second was definitely the most successful. His underrated 1992 album *Rocks in the Head* was only released in the U.S. Roger toured on a limited basis in 1985 and more broadly in 1994. Since starring in *Tommy* in 1975 he has had a number of movie roles, including in *Lisztomania*, *McVicar*, *The Little Matchgirl*, *Mack the Knife*, *Buddy's Song*, and *Cold Justice*. On television he has had recurring characters on *Highlander* and *Rude Awakening*.

On March 21, 2001, Ben and **Simon Townshend** performed live with Roger in Vail, Colorado, to benefit the U.S. Disabled Ski Team. Roger recently provided vocals for the title track of former **Clash** guitarist Joe Strummer's album *Global a Go-Go* and appeared in the VH1 cable TV series *Strange Frequency*. Roger and Jackie Daltrey were married secretly in the 1960s while she was expecting their child, Simon, and they divorced in 1968. Roger married American Heather Taylor in the fall of 1970. They have two daughters and a son: Rosie, Willow and Jamie.

Daniels, Phil   Actor probably known most for portraying the main character Jimmy in the movie version of *Quadrophenia*. Daniels, who was born in 1958, had been acting for at least three years when he made his movie debut in 1978 as a misfit in the *Class of Miss MacMichael*. He had a few movie roles in the 1980s and 1990s but may have received more attention by recording with the band Blur in 1994. In 2000 he provided the voice of the rat Fletcher in the acclaimed "claymation" movie *Chicken Run*.

Davis, Bette   Well known American movie star in the middle of the

20th century. She was a guest on the **Smothers Brothers** show in September of 1967 and fainted offstage into **Mickey Rooney**'s arms when Keith Moon's drums exploded at the end of the Who's performance of "My Generation." This famous television moment starts the movie *The Kids Are Alright* and was ranked by the cable channel VH1 as the 10th greatest rock 'n' roll moment in history.

Davis, Cam *see* Fanny.

Davis, George British prisoner who was the subject of the "George Davis is Innocent" campaign, which counted Roger Daltrey among its numbers. Davis had been jailed for a number of armed robberies in the 1950s, but suspicions that he was framed resulted in widespread graffiti and vandalism in the 1970s. During 1975 Who concerts Daltrey wore a "George Davis is Innocent" shirt. Davis was released in 1976.

Davis, Miles Influential jazz trumpeter whose instrumental "Walking" was performed by Pete Townshend's **Deep End** band during its Brixton, England concert, which was released on video. In the mid–1940s Davis met saxophonist Charlie Parker in St. Louis and a year later Davis sought him out in New York when Davis's father sent him to that city's renowned Julliard School of Music. Davis became Parker's protégé as well as his roommate and bandmate for a while. By 1955 Davis formed the first of several influential groups that he would lead. His quintet from 1963 to 1968 included pianist **Herbie Hancock**. Davis's 1970 double album *Bitches Brew* sold over 400,000 copies and led to a few years of touring the U.S., Europe and Japan before big audiences. Davis later married actress Cicely Tyson. Pete Townshend was first exposed to Davis's music thanks to the impressive collection of Pete's friend **Tom Wright**. In a speech on September 14, 1997, at the London ceremony unveiling a Blue Plaque in honor of **Jimi Hendrix**, Pete Townshend said that Jimi "was up there with Miles Davis and Charlie Parker as a virtuoso, an innovator…"

Davis, Spencer Leader of the Spencer Davis Group, which launched the career of **Steve Winwood** and had a big hit in the mid–1960s with "Gimme Some Lovin'." Roger Daltrey covered that song as a B-side for the 1984 12-inch single of "Walking in My Sleep." The Spencer Davis Group joined with the Who and many other artists to perform at what **Richard Barnes** called "the pop event of 1966," a concert that included many of the UK artists who ranked high in a *New Musical Express* poll from 1965. The band's popularity also led to a movie in 1966, *The Ghost Goes Gear*. The band was formed in Birmingham, England, in 1963, but within four years Winwood left to form Traffic and was replaced by Eddie

Hardin, who would work closely with **Zak Starkey** in the 1980s. Davis led another Spencer Davis Group during the first half of the 1970s but their records didn't sell. Davis and Keith Moon played on **Dave Carlsen**'s *Pale Horse* album, which was released in 1973. In 1975 Davis played acoustic guitar on "Crazy Like a Fox" on Keith Moon's only solo album, *Two Sides of the Moon.*

Deacon, Mike   Keyboard player during John Entwistle's March 1975 solo concert that was broadcast by the *King Biscuit Flower Hour.* However, when this concert was finally released on disc, in 1997, his name was spelled "Decan." Around that same time Deacon played piano on the **John Alcock**/John Entwistle *Flash Fearless* album. He also played with Suzi Quatro and Kiki Dee.

The Dead   *see*   The Grateful Dead.

Dead Sea Fruit   Band that released a 45 in the U.S. and UK in 1967 that featured a song called "Kensington High Street," which for years was thought by dedicated Who fans to be a Pete Townshend composition — e.g., it is listed as such in Ed Hanel's handy reference work *The Who: The Illustrated Discography.* This was plausible, given that the song was credited to someone named "Townsend" (a common misspelling of Pete's surname in those days). However, it was later discovered that one of the band members was named John Errington-Townsend.

Deakin, Graham   Drummer on John Entwistle's first and fourth solo albums, *Rigor Mortis Sets in* in 1971 and *Mad Dog* in 1975. He and John co-wrote the instrumental "Jungle Bunny" on *Mad Dog.* Deakin was the only musician to back John both on the album and when John's band Ox toured in support of it. A March 1975 date that had been broadcast long ago on the *King Biscuit Flower Hour* was finally commercially released in 1997. In 1975 Deakin also drummed on the **John Alcock**/John Entwistle *Flash Fearless* album and the *Tommy* movie soundtrack, on "Sally Simpson" and "Do You Think It's Alright?" His only other noteworthy session work was on the 1975 **Moody Blues** spin-off by Justin Hayward and John Lodge, *Blue Jays.*

Decan, Mike   *see*   Deacon, Mike.

Deep End   Pete Townshend's live band from November of 1985 into early 1996. It played in London for charitable purposes and on January 29th performed once at Cannes in France. Later in 1986 came the release of the album *Pete Townshend's Deep End Live!* Long and short videos were also released. The Deep End lineup for these videos consisted mainly of musicians and backup singers with whom Pete has collaborated on several other occasions: David Gilmour of **Pink Floyd**, **Simon Phillips**, **John "Rabbit" Bundrick**, **Chucho Merchan**, **Jody Linscott**, **Peter Hope-Evans**, the **Kick Horns**, **Billy Nicholls**, **Gina Foster**, Coral Gordon (see **Chyna**), Ian Ellis and Chris Staines.

Denny, Sandy   Leading British folk-rock singer who sang the part of the nurse in **Lou Reizner**'s 1972 production of *Tommy*. Denny had two stints in the revered band Fairport Convention and backed **Led Zeppelin** on a couple of their albums. She died in 1978 from injuries she sustained while falling down a stairway.

Des Barres, Pamela   A budding actress in the 1970s who can stake a claim to being rock music's most famous groupie. As Miss Pamela Miller in early 1971 she shot scenes for the **Frank Zappa** movie *200 Motels*, as did Keith Moon. In December of that year she and Moon developed a romantic relationship that lasted from 12 to 18 months. In January of 1974 Keith was supposed to shoot a cameo for the movie *Arizonaslim*, which starred Pamela, but he never showed. His replacement was Michael des Barres, who became her husband in real life. Her 1987 book *I'm with the Band* included several stories of time she spent with Keith Moon, and the two appeared in several of the book's photos.

The Detours   Band that eventually became the Who. Many sources indicate that the Detours were formed by Roger Daltrey in 1962, shortly after he was expelled from the Acton County Grammar School. However, accounts in other sources, such as Dave Marsh's book *Before I Get Old*, imply that the Detours were formed by Roger in 1959 and that John Entwistle succeeded in drawing Pete Townshend into the band in 1961. In fact, during an America Online chat in February of 2000, Daltrey said: "I started the band when I was 14 with John Entwistle. Pete joined a year later. I think Keith joined when I was 17, and then within two years it had taken off." Daltrey turned 14 in 1958, four years before 1962. In any case, vocalist Colin Dawson helped lead guitarist/trombone player Daltrey assemble the original lineup, which included Harry Wilson on drums and Reg Bowen on rhythm guitar. Daltrey, who was a year ahead of Entwistle and Townshend at Acton County Grammar School, persuaded Entwistle to jump from the **Scorpions** to become the fifth member of the Detours, and Entwistle in turn soon succeeded in bringing Townshend in to replace Bowen. *The Who Concert File* shed light on a brief period not touched upon in most if not all of the Who's biographies, when a female joined the band: "Colin Dawson introduced his girlfriend, **Angela Dives**, to the band and persuaded Roger to augment the Detours with Angela on vocals, maracas and tambourine on selected numbers. For a short time the band called themselves Dale Angelo & the Detours. No one is certain where the Dale came from but Angelo was a variation of the band's newest member." After reverting to a five-man traditional jazz and Top 10 band, the next lineup change was replacing drummer Harry Wilson with **Doug Sandom** in July or August of 1962. Sandom, a very experienced drummer, gave his bandmates a surge of confidence and they soon were signed to the area's leading booking agency, Commercial Entertainments, which was managed by Bob Druce and Barry Foran. Their first documented engagement for Druce was in Broadstairs, Kent on November 23, 1962. In Steve Clarke's book *The Who in Their Own Words* Daltrey said that the band "went through about four lead singers and various people coming in with strange instruments...." According to *The Who Concert File*, around the end of January 1963, Colin Dawson was replaced by Gabby Connolly. He had been the bass player for a group called the Bel-Airs. Gabby sang instead of playing bass and was only with the Detours for a few months because the Detours decided to model themselves after **Johnny Kidd** and the Pirates, who were a quartet. Roger thus took over on vocals and Pete became the lead guitarist. However, for awhile the Detours reverted to a quintet by adding a second guitarist named Peter Vernon Kell.

At some point **Cliff Townshend** arranged with acquaintance Barry Gray for the Detours to have their first recording session (and their only one before becoming the Who). This might have occurred as early as mid–1963 though *The Who Concert File* suggested it took place in the first half of 1964. The location was Gray's home recording studio. The band recorded Pete Townshend's first published song, "It Was You." The tape from this session was probably destroyed long ago, or has been misplaced all these years. **Richard Barnes** recalled that it was "very powerful for a first recording but sounded too much like a **Beatles** song." However, "It Was You" was recorded by the **Naturals** and reportedly by the Fourmost. A year would pass before Pete would present another composition to the band. The Detours ended the year on a positive note by opening for the **Rolling Stones** in the London area on December 22, 1963, and again on January 3, 1964.

It was on the first of these dates that Townshend saw Stones guitarist Keith Richards rotate his arm like the hand of a clock while warming up. Townshend has acknowledged he developed his trademark "windmill" motion during concerts from seeing Richards do this, but down the road Richards didn't recall doing this nor did he mind that Pete mimicked him. On January 30, 1964, a band called Johnny Devlin & the Detours appeared on the TV show *Thank Your Lucky Stars* and Daltrey's Detours knew they had to change names quickly. In February they were renamed the Who between two of their weekly appearances at West London's Oldfield Hotel. On March 7, less than a month after changing their name to the Who, the band played at the wedding reception of ex–Detour Harry Wilson's sister Joan.

Dickinson, Peter   Award-winning author whose 1979 book *Hepzibah* came with a flexi disc that was produced by Pete Townshend's Eel Pie label, and for which Pete provided lyrics over a **Billy Nicholls** melody. Dickinson was born in 1927 and was an assistant editor and reviewer for *Punch* magazine from 1952 to 1969. He has won 16 awards for his young adult fiction work.

Diddley, Bo   Well known American R&B guitarist whose signature rhythm turned up in the Who's "Magic Bus," as well as other rock classics. He was born Ellas Bates in Mississippi in 1928 but became Ellas McDaniel after being adopted. He took his stage name from the term for a single-stringed African guitar. He played in Chicago for quite awhile before backing **Chuck Berry** on a few recordings starting in 1955, including "Memphis." His first single, "Bo Diddley," quickly established him as a successful R&B performer, and "I'm a Man" was also a successful 45 for him in 1955. His biggest success on the pop charts was in 1959 when "Say Man" landed in the top 20. Pete Townshend was exposed to Diddley's songs in the impressive collection of his friend **Tom Wright**. The Who often performed Diddley songs back when they were still called the **Detours**, and when they were known as the **High Numbers** recorded Diddley's 1960 song "Here 'Tis." This track surfaced on the Who's boxed set *30 Years of Maximum R&B* in 1994. The Who's studio cover of "I'm a Man" appeared on their UK *My Generation* album in 1965, and in 1975 the Who performed a live version of "Road Runner" that appeared a few years later in *The Kids Are Alright*. "Road Runner" was another Diddley number from 1960. Keith Moon was among the artists who played on the 1976 tribute to Diddley entitled *The 20th Anniversary of Rock and Roll*. According to *The Who Concert File*, it was "Road Runner" which Moon blazed his way through in 1964 to instantly earn his place in the Who. On their 1987 U.S. album *Two's Missing* the Who's version of "I'm a Man" was incorrectly attributed to **Kit Lambert** and **Chris Stamp**, the Who's managers when it was recorded in 1965. More importantly, 1987 was also the year that Bo Diddley was inducted into the Rock and Roll Hall of Fame.

Dives, Angela   The only woman to belong to a band that was a precursor to the Who. *The Who Concert File* shed light on this brief period, which is not touched upon in most if not all of the band's biographies:

"Colin Dawson introduced his girlfriend, Angela Dives, to the band and persuaded Roger to augment the **Detours** with Angela on vocals, maracas and tambourine on selected numbers. For a short time the band called themselves Dale Angelo & the Detours. No one is certain where the Dale came from but Angelo was a variation of the band's newest member." An article on the Detours in the *Gazette and Post* newspaper from November 21, 1963, quoted her as the blonde president of the Detours fan club, which at the time was reported to have 30 members and three new applicants daily: "They have a good sense of humour. They laugh and crack jokes on stage. And they can play very good harmonies." The article went on to note that when not dealing with fan mail, Angela operated an accounting machine. Colin Dawson was no longer in the Detours at that point in time.

Dixon, Willie *see* Howlin' Wolf; Waters, Muddy.

Dokken *see* Beach, Reb.

Donegan, Lonnie Top hitmaker during the British "skiffle" craze around 1956 and 1957 and thus a strong influence on young Roger Daltrey. Skiffle music had been around for at least three decades and was characterized by jazz songs that featured kazoos and washboards plus other makeshift "instruments." Anthony Donegan chose to go by "Lonnie" as a nod to bluesman Lonnie Johnson and played with Alexis Korner in Ken Colyer's "pure" jazz band in 1955. Donegan outlasted the skiffle fad by turning to a music-hall style.

The Doobie Brothers *see* Baxter, Jeff "Skunk."

The Doors Popular Los Angeles band of the late 1960s and early '70s that retained a following long after the death of frontman Jim Morrison in the summer of 1971. The Doors had a #1 single, "Light My Fire," from their self-titled debut album in 1967. On August 2, 1968 the Who played on the same bill as the Doors in Flushing, New York, and as the Doors were ending their performance some scuffling in the audience left a girl injured. According to *The Who Concert File*, this was what prompted Pete Townshend to write the song "Sally Simpson" for *Tommy*.

Dozier, Lamont *see* Holland/Dozier/Holland.

Drains, Bijou Pete Townshend's alter ego, apparently, on at least two occasions. Townshend played bass for **Thunderclap Newman**'s *Hollywood Dream* album but Drains received the credit. By coincidence, in a November 1970 issue of *Rolling Stone* Pete had to deny that he and **Thunderclap Newman**'s Speedy Keene were the same person. Bijou Drains was also credited with providing the "gulp" on the 1977 Townshend/**Ronnie Lane** collaboration, *Rough Mix*. On a possibly related note, in 1971 **Mike Heron** was backed on a song by "Tommy and the Bijoux," one of whom is widely assumed to have been Townshend.

Duncan, Lesley   British singer/songwriter who had Pete Townshend in the chorus on her 1969 single, "Sing Children Sing." Duncan began releasing 45s in 1963 but didn't get a big career boost until **Elton John** recorded her composition "Love Song" on his *Tumbleweed Connection* album in 1971. She was thus able to release some albums in the 1970s, beginning with *Sing Children Sing*, but none sold particularly well. Among her credits on other performers' albums in the 1970s are serving as a backing vocalist on the **John Alcock**/John Entwistle *Flash Fearless* album and singing lead on one song on the **Alan Parsons** Project album *Eve*. After that 1979 album Duncan faded from the music scene although she did release albums in 1982 and '86.

The Eagles   Very successful American rock band from the early 1970s onward. The Eagles recorded their first two albums with **Glyn Johns**. Their self-titled debut in 1972 went gold on the strength of the single "Take It Easy." For their third album, 1974's *On the Border*, they switched to **Bill Szymczyk**, who would later produce the Who's *Face Dances* album. **Joe Walsh** joined in 1976, in time for the Eagles' third consecutive #1 album, *Hotel California*. Starting in 1982 the band's two remaining founders, Glenn Frey and Don Henley, began to pursue solo careers that produced a number of top 10 hits. Frey had hits in 1984 and '85 with "Smuggler's Blues," "The Heat Is On," and "You Belong to the City." Henley experienced even more success with "Dirty Laundry" in 1982, "Boys of Summer" and "All She Wants to Do Is Dance," in 1984, and "The End of the Innocence" and "Heart of the Matter," among others, in 1989. The Eagles' much-publicized "Hell Freezes Over" reunion tour spawned a #1 album in 1994. They were inducted into the Rock and Roll Hall of Fame in January of 1988. That year Roger Daltrey covered "Boys of Summer" as one of about a dozen guest vocalists on **Mike Batt**'s *Philharmania* album, which featured the Royal Philharmonic Orchestra on 14 familiar rock songs.

Egan, Joe *see* Stealers Wheel.

Elgar, Edward   Composer whose "Pomp & Circumstance" is traditionally played at graduation ceremonies in the U.S. With words by Arthur C. Benson, this is the song that the Who irreverently attached to a version of "My Generation" that surfaced as a bonus track on *A Quick One* in 1995. Sir Edward Elgar was an Englishman who lived from 1857 to 1934, and his composition has served as a second national anthem for his country since Benson added lyrics around 1902, shortly after Elgar unveiled the music.

Elliman, Yvonne   Singer who made a big splash in the movie *Jesus Christ Superstar*. In 1969, while in her late teens, Elliman moved from Hawaii to London and was soon discovered by **Andrew Lloyd Webber** and **Tim Rice**. She immediately hit it big in the movie version of their *Jesus Christ Superstar* and won a Golden Globe award. The soundtrack also provided her with the hit "I Don't Know How to Love Him." In 1973 Yvonne recorded a version of the Who's "I Can't Explain" on which she received help from Pete Townshend. Her new husband, RSO Records president Bill Oakes, introduced Elliman to **Eric Clapton**, whom she backed on the hit "I Shot the Sheriff." She was a member of Clapton's band for the next five years. The soundtrack of the 1977 movie *Saturday Night Fever* included a song by Elliman that would reach #1, "If I Can't Have You." She wasn't able to replicate this success and soon returned to being a backing vocalist. In 1997 **Fatboy Slim** transformed her cover of "I Can't Explain" into the popular instrumental single "Going Out of My Head."

Elliott, Stuart   Drummer who got his start as a member of Cockney Rebel from 1974 to 1978 and who performed on numerous albums by the **Alan Parsons** Project and by Kate Bush from the late 1970s into the 1990s. In 1980 he drummed on the *McVicar* soundtrack. Toward the end of 1985 he backed Roger Daltrey on a mini-tour in America, along with **Russ Ballard**, **Alan Shacklock**, and others.

Eltworth, John   Author of the 1971 *Who's Next* track "My Wife" according to some dubious albums released around 1980. John Entwistle often saw his surname spelled "Entwhistle" in the 1960s but crediting one of his songs to someone named "Eltworth" took the cake. The records and tapes in question consisted of all but two of the songs from *Who's Next*, and, depending on the country, were titled *Going Mobile*, the *Who Anthology*, *Who Rocks Harder*, and even *Who's Next*.

Emerson, Lake and Palmer   Successful progressive rock band that mixed in as many classical elements as any of their peers. Keith Emerson was still in his late teens when he got his professional start in Gary Farr and the T-Bones, at the same time that longtime John Entwistle friend Cy Langston was in that band. Emerson formed the Nice in 1967 but broke up that band to work with Greg Lake and Carl Palmer. Lake had played with King Crimson, and Palmer had drummed in the Crazy World of

Arthur Brown. One of ELP's first public appearances was at 1970's Isle of Wight Festival, on a different night than the Who. Each of their first five albums sold enough to earn the band gold records, and they thrived until the late 1970s. After Keith Moon's death, Palmer was reportedly among the drummers who offered to fill in on a temporary basis. ELP split at the end of 1979. Palmer soon joined the supergroup Asia, and in 1985 he was one of the drum soloists who honored Keith Moon on the title track of Roger Daltrey's 1985 album *Under a Raging Moon*. In 1990 Keith Emerson was in the supergroup the **Best** with John Entwistle.

The English Beat   Ska group simply called the Beat when formed in 1978 but which added "English" to avoid confusion with an American group by that name. Their 1982 hit "Save It for Later," written by guitarist Dave Wakeling, was covered by Pete Townshend on his 1985 album *Deep End Live!* Within a year the band broke up, with two members later forming Fine Young Cannibals and another pair General Public.

Entwistle, John   The Who's late bass player, known as "The Quiet One" for being relatively motionless while his bandmates exhibited seemingly boundless energy. Careful listeners and those with sharp vision could often discern that Entwistle's blazing fingers always demonstrated a groundbreaking style of bass-playing that made him akin to a lead guitarist. Bruce Eder's biography for the online *All Music Guide* states that Entwistle was "probably the most influential bassist in rock music. Before Entwistle came along as a member of the Who, bassists seldom stood out for their playing and few casual listeners knew or cared what purpose the four-stringed instrument served…."

John Alec Entwistle was born October 9, 1944 and was the only child of Herbert and Queenie Maud. John was the only member of the Who to receive a formal education in music; he played brass in his school band and was later in the Middlesex Youth Orchestra. He earned the privilege of attending the Royal Academy of Music but his parents couldn't afford to enroll him. In the late 1950s he was easily the most skilled and experienced of his eventual bandmates in the Who. He and Pete Townshend were classmates at Acton County Grammar School and first played music together in a band called the **Confederates**. They were later in the **Aristocrats** and the **Scorpions** before Entwistle was persuaded by Roger Daltrey in 1961 or '62 to join the **Detours**. Entwistle soon arranged for Townshend to be a member as well. In early 1964 Entwistle saw another group use the name "Detours" on television, so Daltrey's Detours changed their name to the Who. In the spring of that year Keith Moon took over for **Doug Sandom** as the band's drummer, and one of Entwistle's strongest friendships began.

Though John showed restraint on stage he didn't seem to mind the new pop art wardrobe that the Who's new managers **Kit Lambert** and **Chris Stamp** encouraged the band to adopt. In the book *Decade of the Who* John Entwistle noted that under Lambert and Stamp the Who "really just started the whole sort of Union Jack jacket thing, we started the whole sort of pop art thing. Kit was, I suppose, far seeing enough, to see that we had to innovate something else — in fact the Who never got the credit for starting that whole craze, but we actually did.... I mean, I was the first person to wear a shirt with sergeant stripes on it, and medals and stickers ... stuff like that ... And then the mass produced Union Jack shirts came out, and garbage, like Union Jack handbags..."

Though the Who only became celebrities in early 1965, a poll that year of *New Musical Express* readers named Entwistle best bass player. Entwistle received a shared writing credit for the instrumental "The Ox," on the Who's first album, *My Generation*. He contributed the first two songs he ever wrote to their next album, *A Quick One*. In Gary Herman's biography *The Who*, Entwistle talked about his early songwriting: "The first two songs I wrote were 'Boris the Spider' and 'Whiskey Man' and they had this sort of child-like quality, even the tunes were simple and easy to remember, and our manager said to me, 'Why don't we record an LP for children?' because it seemed that my songs really appealed to kids. So I wrote about fifteen songs for this album and they all ended up as b-sides." John would also go on to have one to three of his songs on every subsequent Who album except 1973's *Quadrophenia*; presumably by coincidence, it fell to John to remix that album for the 1979 movie of the same name. Nevertheless, he grew frustrated by not being able to get more of his songs recorded during the 1960s, so he became the first member of the Who to release a solo album (in 1971).

It may have been a different kind of frustration that caused a very rare outburst by Entwistle in 1967: Pete Johnson of the *Los Angeles Times* reported that John joined in during Pete Townshend's typical end-of-concert destruction by battering and shattering his bass against the stage at a concert in Anaheim on September 8. Speaking of violence, Entwistle's first solo album was entitled *Smash Your Head Against the Wall*. He followed that up with the intentionally misspelled *Whistle Rymes* in late 1972 and *Rigor Mortis Sets in* by mid–1973. In 1975 he released *Mad Dog* but the *Flash Fearless* album he worked on with **John Alcock** that same year almost constituted another solo album for Entwistle. He didn't release another solo album until *Too Late the Hero* in 1981, on which he was helped by **Joe Walsh** and **Joe Vitale**.

Around 1985 John was supposed to join several members of **Iron**

Maiden in the supergroup Gogmagog but he ultimately did not perform on that band's lone EP. John tried to release another solo album in the mid–1980s but record company problems kept *The Rock* delayed well into the 1990s. He, **Steve Luongo**, and **Godfrey Townsend** started the John Entwistle Band in 1995, and their activities have included providing music for a syndicated science fiction show called *Van-Pires*. The series didn't last long but their soundtrack album was still released, well after the fact, in 2000. One track, "Bogey Man," includes a previously lost performance by Keith Moon. In 2001 Entwistle, Luongo, and Townsend toured with **Todd Rundgren**, **Alan Parsons**, and Ann Wilson of **Heart** in the **Beatles** tribute billed as *A Walk Down Abbey Road*. John Entwistle married long-time girlfriend Alison Wise on June 23, 1967. They had one son, Christopher, but divorced years ago. John died from an apparent heart attack. **Pino Palladino** played bass on that year's Who tour. In a survey conducted by the UK's *Guitar Magazine*, John was named best bassist of the 20th century.

The Escorts A band that Keith Moon was in prior to the **Beachcombers**. Tony Fletcher's definitive Moon biography, *Dear Boy*, shed much light on the Escorts. Members included Colin Haines on bass, Keith's good friend Gerry Evans on drums, and Tony Marsh singing under the name "Lee Stuart." The guitarists were Roger Painter and Rob Lemon; Lemon and singer Marsh would later be members of Lord Sutch's Savages. A Liverpool band also named the Escorts became popular in 1963 and released singles from 1964 to '66. Sometime after the spring of 1966 this band included Paddy Chambers of **Paddy, Klaus and Gibson**. Terry Sylvester of Liverpool's Escorts had joined the **Swinging Blue Jeans** in 1964 and was later in the Hollies.

ESP Hard rock band whose self-titled debut album in 1999 closed with a cover of the Who's "Won't Get Fooled Again." ESP includes John Corabi, who replaced Vince Neil as Mötley Crüe's vocalist, and two members with connections to Kiss: Karl Cochran, who has played with Kiss member Ace Frehley, and onetime Kiss drummer Eric Singer, who also drummed with Black Sabbath.

Essex, David Mid–1970s teen idol in his native Britain whose only real success in the U.S. was the 1974 gold single "Rock On." Around 1970 he had a role in the London production of the musical *The Fantasticks* and gained much notice as Jesus in the London production of *Godspell* that opened in late 1971. Jeff Wayne helped him launch a successful UK recording career shortly thereafter. Essex starred in the movie *That'll Be the Day* in 1973 and its sequel *Stardust* in 1975. Keith Moon appeared in both movies and performed on the latter's soundtrack. The former included **Billy Fury** singing the Who's "Long Live Rock." **Adam Faith** portrayed David's sidekick in *Stardust,* which also featured **Larry Hagman**. On December 13, 1973, Essex took part in the second live benefit performance of **Lou Reizner**'s production of *Tommy*. Ken Russell wanted Essex to have a role in the *Tommy* movie, but he had to decline because he was committed to working on *Stardust*. After 1984 Essex rarely recorded for about a decade though his acting career continued. In the 1990s he spent over two years in Africa for the Voluntary Service Overseas organization and then started releasing albums again.

Eurythmics   Name for the popular rock duo consisting of Annie Lennox and Dave Stewart, whose song "Somebody Told Me" was performed by Roger Daltrey on his 1984 solo LP, *Parting Should Be Painless*. Stewart, who had been in a band called Longdancer, met Lennox in the late 1970s and persuaded her to join a newly formed band, the Tourists. They had a top five hit in the UK with a version of Dusty Springfield's "I Only Want to Be with You" but Lennox and Stewart, who had developed a romantic relationship, soon left to become the Eurythmics. Their hits included "Sweet Dreams (Are Made of This)," "Here Comes the Rain Again," and "Would I Lie to You?" Stewart and Lennox stopped collaborating around 1990. Around that time Stewart provided the score for the movie *Lily Was Here* and the title track became an instrumental hit for sax player Candy Dulfer. Stewart and ex–**Pretenders** drummer Martin Chambers formed the band Spiritual Cowboys and issued albums in 1990 and '91 but neither sold particularly well. Stewart also released a solo album in 1995. Lennox was much more active and much more successful during the '90s. Her 1992 album *Diva* yielded the top 40 hits "Walking on Broken Glass" and "Why," and her 1995 collection of covers, *Medusa,* went platinum. About 10 years after they had quietly parted company, the Eurythmics released the album *Peace* in 1999. Among the musicians backing them was Pete Townshend's frequent bass player **Chucho Merchan**, who has worked Stewart and the Eurythmics on several projects since 1987.

Evans, Mal   Roadie for the **Beatles** who helped Keith Moon on his only solo album, 1975's *Two Sides of the Moon*. Evans arranged the horns on "Move Over Ms. L" and did the basic tracks production on all tracks except for "Together." Evans was the Beatles' second road manager and often participated in their recording sessions. As an executive with their Apple Records label he discovered a band called the Iveys, which later became Badfinger. He had moved to Los Angeles by 1975 and ended up living with a woman and her preschool daughter. One day in January of

1976 he was in a particularly bad mood, prompting the woman to call the police. Two officers arrived to find him waving an air pistol and thus they shot him to death.

The Everly Brothers Duo that was among the most influential early rock acts. The Who recorded their 1965 song "Man with Money" for a BBC radio show in March of 1966 and another version in August for possible use on the album *A Quick One*. It did appear on that album as a CD bonus track in 1995. The Who also performed the Everly Brothers song "Love Hurts" in concert, and the use of "Instant Party" as an alternate title for the mid-1960s Who song "Circles" was a nod to the 1962 Everly Brothers *Instant Party*. Don and Phil Everly were both under the age of 21 in 1957 when they released their second single, "Bye Bye Love," which reached #2. They closed out the '50s with other memorable hits including "Wake Up Little Susie," "All I Have to Do Is Dream" and "When Will I Be Loved." In the early '60's "Cathy's Clown" hit #1 and the brothers released two critically acclaimed albums. However, after 1962 they were unable to replicate their successes on the singles charts. The brothers refused to perform together from 1973 to 1983 and their acrimony apparently resurfaced during much of the 1990s. In 1986 they were among the first performers inducted into the Rock and Roll Hall of Fame.

The Fabulous Poodles British rock group that released four albums during its brief existence in the last half of the 1970s, including one that was produced by John Entwistle. *Mirror Stars*, which reached #61 in the U.S. in 1979, also featured some bass playing by John. The band didn't survive into the 1980s. Only two of its members continued to be particularly active in the music industry. Violinist Bobby Valentino has recorded with such artists as David Knopfler in 1983, the Style Council in 1984, Tom Petty in 1986, Mike Oldfield in 1989, the Proclaimers in 1994, **B.J. Cole** in 1995, **Big Country** in 1996 and Kristy MacColl in 1998. John Parsons has been a producer and musician, primarily for the jazz/new age band Acoustic Alchemy from 1987 to the present.

The Faces *see* Small Faces.

Fairweather-Low, Andy Leader of one of the last mod bands, Amen Corner, which had a handful of hits from 1967 to 1969. He received special thanks in the credits on Roger Daltrey's third solo album, 1977's *One of the Boys* and a year later played guitar on five songs on the *Who Are You* album, including the title track. In 1982 he played rhythm guitar on "It's Your Turn" on the Who's *It's Hard* album and in 1993 he provided guitar and vocals on Pete Townshend's *Live* video.

Faith, Adam   Pre-British Invasion UK pop star who has had a long association with Roger Daltrey. Faith, whose real name is Terry Nelhams, had been in a skiffle group called the Worried Men but left around 1958 and began a string of chart hits in 1959. In 1972 Faith was using Roger Daltrey's new East Burwash recording facilities to produce an album for **Leo Sayer**, who had been brought to his attention by Sayer's songwriting partner **David Courtney**. Courtney had drummed for Faith. Roger Daltrey was impressed with the Courtney-Sayer compositions he heard and thus Faith and Courtney ended up producing a batch of versions by Roger for his self-titled debut solo album in 1973. Courtney wrote two of that album's songs with Faith instead of Sayer, "The Way of the World" and "You And Me." In 1980 Faith had one of the main acting roles in the movie *McVicar*, which featured Daltrey in the title role. Faith had earlier acted in a 1972 British TV show called *Budgie* and then played **David Essex**'s sidekick in the movie *Stardust,* the sequel to *That'll Be the Day*. Keith Moon was in both movies. In 1993 Faith released the album *Midnight Postcards*, which included a version of the Who's "Squeeze Box." In addition, Roger Daltrey played guitar on the song "I'll Be Your Baby Tonight" and sang a duet with Faith on "Stuck in the Middle," which had been a hit for **Stealers Wheel**. That song was also released on a CD EP produced by David Courtney.

Family   Progressive rock group that was successful in its native England from the late 1960s until its farewell in 1973. In 1969 **Johnny Weider** joined the band to play bass and violin but left within two years. In 1972 **Tony Ashton** replaced John "Poli" Palmer in Family for the band's final year. Also joining around then was Jim Cregan, formerly of **Julian Covey** and the Machine. Two of Family's founding members, Roger Chapman and Charlie Whitney, went on to form **Streetwalkers**. "Poli" Palmer, who played percussion, flute, and piano, went on to be the percussion tuner on Pete Townshend's 1982 solo album, *All the Best Cowboys Have Chinese Eyes*.

Fanny   All-female American band in the first half of the 1970s that backed Keith Moon on one song on his only solo album, 1975's *Two Sides of the Moon*. It was the song "Solid Gold," which was written by Fanny's keyboard player, Nickey Barclay, who played piano on it. Other Fanny members who performed on the track were bass player Jean Millington, drummer Cam Davis, and guitarist Patti Quatro (whose sister Suzi had some chart success). A year earlier Moon was thanked fervently on the back cover of what turned out to be Fanny's final album, *Rock and Roll Survivors*. Around the time of their 1970 debut album they also backed **Barbra**

Streisand in the studio. Also around that time Nickey performed with Joe Cocker and Jesse Ed Davis. Their fourth album, 1973's *Mother's Pride*, was produced by **Todd Rundgren**. In 1975 Jean backed **David Bowie** on his hit "Fame" and in 1976 Nickey released a solo album. After the 1970s, however, most of the band's members maintained relatively low profiles. In the late 1990s Jean and her sister June, Fanny's original guitarist, were in a band called Slammin Babes.

Fatboy Slim   "Brit hop" producer who transformed **Yvonne Elliman**'s version of the Who's "I Can't Explain" into the popular instrumental single "Going Out of My Head" in 1997. The man behind Fatboy Slim is Norman Cook, who in his early twenties played bass for the pop group the Housemartins in 1986 for their final year. He soon became part of the trio Pizzaman, which had a few Top 40 hits in the UK around 1990. A year after "Going Out of My Head" was released came the second Fatboy Slim album, *You've Come a Long Way, Baby*, which went platinum in the U.S. and earned two Grammy nominations.

Fender, Freddy   Tex-Mex singer and guitarist who covered the Who's "Squeeze Box" on a 45 in 1979. The song also appeared on his *Texas Balladeer* album. Fender, born Baldemar Huerta in 1937 in Texas, recorded the original version of "Wasted Days and Wasted Nights" in 1959 and waited until 1975 for an even bigger hit, "Before the Next Teardrop Falls."

Fenn, Sherilyn   American actress who was nominated for an Emmy for her role in David Lynch's critically acclaimed TV series *Twin Peaks* and who began the new century as the star of the series *Rude Awakening* on cable TV's Showtime network. Roger Daltrey's character Nobby Clegg, a substance-abusing rock star, has made repeat appearances. One of Fenn's earliest film credits was a memorable cameo in Lynch's *Wild at Heart*, which was named best picture at the 1991 Cannes Film Festival. In 1993 she appeared in *Three of Hearts* with Billy Baldwin and Kelly Lynch and in *Boxing Helena*. She has also appeared in *Of Mice and Men* with John Malkovich and Gary Sinise and in *Diary of a Hit Man*.

Fenton, Shane   Leader of a band that rejected Keith Moon after he auditioned for them in 1962. According to Tony Fletcher's Moon biography, *Dear Boy*, the 16-year-old drummer wasn't nervous about auditioning, despite the fact that Shane Fenton and the Fentones had released six hit singles at that point. Keith's relatively young age was apparently the determining factor. Shane Fenton and the Fentones was one of several bands that the **Detours** supported a number of times before becoming the Who. **Richard Barnes** said that as a relatively unknown band, the Detours would "play a first set for an hour or so, then after the main band had played their set, return and play for the rest of the evening." on December 3, 1965, the Who made the last of many appearances at the Goldhawk Club in Shepherd's Bush, London, and only performances by **Adam Faith** and Shane Fenton came close to causing as huge a queue as the Who did that night.

Ferguson, Jay *see* Jo Jo Gunne.

Ferrer, Miguel Actor among the cast of the NBC drama *Crossing Jordan* who in 1975 played drums on "Don't Worry Baby" on Keith Moon's only solo album, *Two Sides of the Moon*. His father was the late actor Jose Ferrer and his mother singer Rosemary Clooney. On the *Tonight Show* with Jay Leno in April of 1998 his connection to Moon came up very briefly at the end of their chat.

Ferry, Bryan Leader of the art rock band Roxy Music, which thrived in the 1970s and early 1980s. Ferry also started to regularly release solo albums within a couple of years of the band's formation. Ferry wrote the song "Going Strong," which Roger Daltrey recorded for his 1984 solo album, *Parting Should Be Painless*.

Fishof, David *see* The British Rock Symphony.

The Flamin' Groovies Long-running San Francisco pop band that was formed in the mid–1960s and has maintained a following despite a lack of chart success. They have recorded covers of Who songs, "Call Me Lightning" and "I Can't Explain."

Flo and Eddie Singers who were among the founding members of the California group the Turtles, which had its biggest hit in 1967 with "Happy Together." However, the desire to make more profound music led Howard Kaylan and Mark Volman to soon leave the band and perform under the name "the Phlorescent Leech and Eddie." Flo and Eddie backed **Frank Zappa** during the early '70s. On Keith Moon's only solo album, 1975's *Two Sides of the Moon,* they provided backing vocals on "One Night Stand," "The Kids Are Alright," "Back Door Sally" and "Don't Worry Baby." Starting in 1986 "The Turtles featuring Flo & Eddie" included bass player Don Kisselbach, who played and contributed songs for a project entitled "The Man on the Moon Takes a Night Off," which was designed for Roger Daltrey by Bob Hinkle, a producer of records for children. Flo and Eddie recently spent about a year as disc jockeys on New York's WXRK-FM.

Fontaine, Dick British filmmaker who uses music prominently and often applies experimental techniques. Pete Townshend's tapes for the songs "Don't Know Myself" and "Pile Driver" were used in his 1970 art film *Double Pisces, Scorpio Rising*, which was shown at that year's New York Film Festival. In recent years he has served as head of the Documentary Department at the National Film & Television School.

Foster, David   Exceedingly successful record producer known for powerful ballads. He started out primarily as a session musician in the 1970s and recorded with a variety of well known performers, such as **Rod Stewart** in 1976 and '77. Just before those albums he played piano on "Move Over Ms. L" on Keith Moon's only solo album, *Two Sides of the Moon*. Starting in the early 1980s Foster tended to focus on producing, and helped **Chicago**, Whitney Houston and Celine Dion land huge hits. He and **Jack Blades** wrote "The Price of Love" on Roger Daltrey's 1987 solo album, *Can't Wait to See the Movie*. Foster also played keyboards on the song and produced it. The song was also used on the soundtrack of *Secret of My Success*, a Michael J. Fox movie which Foster scored.

Foster, Gina   Singer who has backed Pete Townshend and other well known performers. In 1986 she was of five backing vocalists in Pete's **Deep End** band and in 1989 was in the chorus on his *Iron Man* album, a musical adaptation of the **Ted Hughes** tale. From April of 1992 to October of 1993 she backed up **Eric Clapton**, and has also worked with Stevie Wonder, Billy Ocean, **Pink Floyd**'s David Gilmour, Maxi Priest, and the reformed Culture Club.

4" Be 2"   *see* The Sex Pistols.

The Fourmost   *see* The Naturals.

Frampton, Peter   Guitarist and singer with teen idol good looks who achieved great solo success in the mid–1970s, enough to land him a starring role with the **Bee Gees** in the movie version of the **Beatles**' *Sgt Pepper* album. Frampton had been in the band Herd and then formed **Humble Pie** in 1969 with former **Small Faces** frontman Steve Marriott. In late 1971 he left to start his solo career and soon fronted the short-lived Frampton's Camel. He played lead guitar on half the songs on John Entwistle's second solo album, 1972's *Whistle Rymes*. In 1974 Frampton, Keith Moon and **Led Zeppelin**'s John Bonham made cameos in **Harry Nilsson**'s movie *Son of Dracula*, which starred Nilsson and ex–Beatle Ringo Starr. Most recently, Frampton has appeared with the **British Rock Symphony**.

Franklin, Juanita "Honey"   Lead vocalist, along with the **Chanter**

Sisters, on John Entwistle's song "Mad Dog" in 1975. The three singers also provided backing vocals on the rest of the *Mad Dog* album, John's fourth solo release. Despite the obviously feminine vocals on "Mad Dog" Entwistle was asked by a French television show to mime the song for a broadcast. He declined. Franklin's few recording credits are bunched from 1973 to 1975, including one **David Bowie** album.

Free *see* Bad Company.

The Full Metal Rackets *see* McEnroe, John.

Fury, Billy   Major pop star in England beginning in the late 1950s, prior to the British Invasion of America. After 1965 he had less chart success, but by then he had enjoyed well over a dozen hits in the UK. In 1973 he sang the Pete Townshend composition "Long Live Rock" in the movie *That'll Be the Day*, which starred **David Essex** and in which Keith Moon also appeared. The Who recorded their version of the song on June 5, 1972, but it wasn't released until the fall of 1974. Fury, whose real name was Ronald Wycherly, died of heart disease in 1983.

Gallagher and Lyle   Scottish guitar duo that wrote a couple of Top 10 UK hits in the early 1970s for the band McGuinness Flint and had a couple of their own in 1976. In between Benny Gallagher and Graham Lyle were both in **Ronnie Lane**'s Slim Chance and played on that band's first album in 1974. A year earlier Pete Townshend had played harmonica on their own *Willie & the Lapdog* album, which was produced by **Glyn Johns**. Gallagher played accordion and Lyle 12-string acoustic guitar on the song "Annie" on the 1977 Townshend/Lane collaboration, *Rough Mix*. The duo parted in 1980 and reteamed temporarily in 1988 before once again heading down separate musical paths. Most notably, Lyle and Terry Britton wrote the 1984 Grammy-winning hit "What's Love Got to Do with It" for **Tina Turner**.

Gallagher, Mickey   Keyboard/synthesizer player on Roger Daltrey's 1984 solo LP, *Parting Should Be Painless*. From 1965 to 1971 Gallagher teamed with **Graham Bell** a few times, in Chosen Few, Skip Bifferty and Bell and Arc. Gallagher's other bands included Cochise and **Frampton**'s Camel. In the late 1970s he was in Ian Dury and the Blockheads, as was **Norman Watt-Roy**, who also played on Daltrey's 1984 album. He also played with the **Clash** around that time. Gallagher and Dury wrote a musical called *Apples* that debuted in 1989, and Gallagher backed Dury on an album in 1993. Most recently he has been managing his son's band, called Little Mothers.

Garrett, Leif   Mid–1970s teen idol who had as much success on TV as he did as a recording artist. He released his first album in 1977, focusing on rock oldies, and his fourth album was 1980's *Can't Explain*, which featured a cover of the Who's early single "I Can't Explain." Garrett made his movie debut at the age of eight. His rise and fall was the subject of a VH1 show about 20 years after the peak of his fame.

Gay, John   British playwright and poet who was best known for the *Beggar's Opera*, which debuted in 1728. In a 1983 BBC production Roger Daltrey played the pivotal role of Macheath, a character reminiscent of Robin Hood. That production also starred **Bob Hoskins**. The *Beggar's Opera* was intended to satirize society and the fixation with Italian opera through the thieves and prostitutes who served as its main characters, and its sequel a year later, *Polly*, was the subject of government censorship. Gay died three years later at the age of 47. He had been a friend of such famous writers as Jonathan Swift and Alexander Pope. Two hundred years after the *Beggar's Opera* debuted it served as the basis of the *Threepenny Opera*, by **Bertolt Brecht** and **Kurt Weill**, which in turn was the basis for the 1989 movie *Mack the Knife*, featuring Roger Daltrey as the Street Singer and which also starred **Raul Julia** and **Richard Harris**.

Gaye, Marvin   Celebrated soul singer who was among the Who's early influences. Gaye was born in Washington, DC, in 1939, and started recording with various performers in the late 1950s after serving in the Air Force. He signed with the Motown label in 1961 and started landing hits in the Top 40 in 1963. His Top 40 single "Baby Don't You Do It," a **Holland/Dozier/Holland** composition released in September of 1964 and used in the movie *Quadrophenia* in 1979, was covered by the Who on a variety of occasions including later in 1964 as one of their few early recordings while still using the name the **High Numbers**. In March of 1965 Pete Townshend told *Melody Maker* that Gaye was quite possibly the Who's favorite performer at the time. Late that year the Who played "Baby Don't You Do It" during one of their earliest TV appearances. In 1971 the Who recorded "Baby Don't You Do It" with assistance from **Al Kooper** and **Leslie West** and a live version from late in 1971 became the B-side of the "Join Together" 45 the next year.

Gaye co-wrote "Dancing in the Street," which was a hit for **Martha and the Vandellas** in the summer of '64. The Who recorded this song for a radio show in March of 1966. They also played it live in Philadelphia in late 1979 and this performance turned up in mid–1988 on a 12" single of "Won't Get Fooled Again." Gaye had already scored a bunch of Top 10 hits before his "I Heard It Through the Grapevine" reached #1 in 1968.

Different styles in the 1970s produced the top five hits "What's Going On" and "Mercy Mercy Me (the Ecology)" in 1971 and the #1 hit "Let's Get It On" in 1973. In 1982, shortly after leaving Motown, he won a Grammy Award for the hit "Sexual Healing." Gaye was 45 years old when he was shot to death by his own father in 1984. Marvin Gaye was inducted into the Rock and Roll Hall of Fame in 1987.

Geldof, Bob Leader of the rock group the Boomtown Rats and one of popular music's leading humanitarians. In 1977 the Boomtown Rats had the first New Wave hit to be played by the BBC, "Looking After No. 1," which charted at #11 in the UK in the summer of 1977. They are best known in the U.S. for the modest 1980 hit "I Don't Like Mondays." In 1981 Geldof played the lead role in the film version of **Pink Floyd**'s *The Wall*. Geldof spearheaded the Live Aid benefit in 1985 and coaxed the Who to reunite for it. Pete Townshend helped hoist Geldof into the air during the "Let It Be" chorus finale. Geldof was subsequently nominated for a Nobel Prize and was knighted. The Boomtown Rats disbanded in 1986 and Geldof pursued a solo career. In the summer of 1998 London radio station Xfm hired Geldof as a disc jockey.

Genesis One of the leading groups during the development of the "progressive rock" subgenre. The band was formed in the UK in 1966 but it was the lineup in place by 1971 that really made Genesis hit its stride. However, Peter Gabriel left in the mid–1970s for a successful solo career and guitarist Steve Hackett left by 1978. That left the trio of Phil Collins, Mike Rutherford, and Tony Banks. Their 1978 album *And Then There Were Three* went gold and beginning in 1980 they had a string of big hits. After Keith Moon's death in the autumn of 1978 Collins was among the drummers who reportedly had some interest in replacing him. On May 2, 1979, Collins was among the celebrities who attended **Kenney Jones**'s first concert with the Who, at the Rainbow Theatre in North London. Collins did end up replacing Keith Moon in a manner of speaking when he portrayed Uncle Ernie during the Who's charitable performance of *Tommy* in Los Angeles in 1989. This concert was released on video. In 1990 the Genesis contribution to the live compilation *Knebworth the Album* was a medley that included the Who's "Pinball Wizard." The next year Pete Townshend played guitar and Collins drums on ex-**Beatle** Paul McCartney's *Press to Play* album, on the track "Angry." In a 1997 issue of the UK fan publication *Naked Eye* Roger Daltrey said somewhat cryptically that, "I wasn't interested in solo gigs; I could see the Phil Collins syndrome and I would only end up doing what the Who should be doing." All three remaining members of Genesis have had respectable solo careers (e.g., Rutherford with Mike + the Mechanics) but Collins's has been much more commercially successful.

Gerson, Gregg Drummer who received "special thanks" on Roger Daltrey's 1992 solo album, *Rocks in the Head*. According to an interview conducted by and posted on rogerdaltrey.net by Dave Van Staveren, **Gerard McMahon** wanted a few of the album's drum tracks redone and picked Gerson for the job. Gerson was the drummer on **Billy Idol**'s most successful album, 1983's *Rebel Yell*, and later drummed on the tour that resulted in Idol's live *White Wedding* album. His other noteworthy credits include playing flute on albums for Ronnie Spector in 1980 and Gloria Estefan in 1994. In the late 1990s Gerson backed Daltrey and others as part of the **British Rock Symphony**.

Gibb, Barry *see* The Bee Gees.

Gibbons, Steve Musician who got his big break by opening for the Who at a couple of German concerts in November of 1975 as well as at several UK venues that year. John Entwistle produced the Ramport mix of their 1976 *Any Road Up* album, and Pete Townshend was thanked on the back cover of 1977's *Rollin' On*. Gibbons wrote "One of the Boys," the title track of Roger Daltrey's third solo LP, which was released in the spring of 1977. Roger's recording of that song also appeared as the B-side of a U.S. promotional 12" record that had one of the Gibbons Band's own tracks, "Please Don't Say Goodbye" from *Rollin' On*, as the A-side. On one side of the record's cover Gibbons wrote: "My association with the Who, especially Pete Townshend and Roger Daltrey, marked the turning point in my career, which included the opportunity to debut the Steve Gibbons Band in the U.S. while touring with the Who in 1976. So, when Roger asked me to write a song for his new album, I felt it had to be about him: 'One of the Boys'." on the flip side of the cover Roger wrote: "I first saw Steve Gibbons in a small club in London over a year ago. I experienced that rare feeling one has when confronted with a star. The charisma of his on-stage performance, coupled with superb writing talent, make him a certainty for worldwide success." For awhile the Steve Gibbons Band was being managed by **Peter Meaden** and **Bill Curbishley**. On July 13, 1979, Townshend formed his first band outside of the Who for the "Rock Against Racism" concerts and Gibbons joined him, **Kenney Jones**, **Tony Butler**, **John "Rabbit" Bundrick** and **Peter Hope-Evans** for a couple of numbers. The Steve Gibbons Band was among several bands on the bill headlined by the Who at Nuremberg on September 1, 1979. Gibbons recorded off and on through the 1990s.

Gilmour, David *see* Pink Floyd.

Glennie-Smith, Nick   Keyboard player on two of Roger Daltrey's solo albums, 1985's *Under a Raging Moon* and 1987's *Can't Wait to See the Movie*. Among Glennie-Smith's earliest recording credits were on albums for Duane Eddy in 1979 and **Leo Sayer** in 1980. Other credits in the 1980s include playing on albums with Katrina & the Waves from 1983 to '85, ex–**Beatle** Paul McCartney in 1986, and Julio Iglesias in 1988. He also played on a few albums each for **Tina Turner** from 1984 to '93 and **Pink Floyd**'s Roger Waters from 1987 to '93. Glennie-Smith has also worked on a number of soundtracks, including serving as conductor and choir master/arranger on the *Lion King* in 1994.

Glitter, Gary   British glam rock pioneer in the early 1970s who had the role of the Godfather during the 1996 leg of the Who's Quadrophenia tour. Glitter, born Paul Gadd, recorded ballads in the early 1960s under the name "Paul Raven" and finished the decade singing in German clubs under the name "Paul Monday." In 1972 he had adopted his most famous identity and had a bit hit with "Rock and Roll Part II." By 1980, however, he was mired in bankruptcy court. He has publicly retired several times over the years. While preparing with the Who for the *Quadrophenia* performance at London's Hyde Park, Glitter flung a microphone stand that hit Roger Daltrey in the eye. Daltrey needed to wear a patch over the eye for awhile but magnanimously allowed Glitter to continue throughout the 1996 leg of the tour. Roger later told the UK fan publication *Naked Eye* that Glitter did a great job but he preferred **P. J. Proby** in the role because "people didn't know who he was" and that this was better from a purely theatrical standpoint. In November of 1997 Glitter was arrested for violating child pornography laws. He eventually served two months of a four-month prison sentence and was released in January 2000.

Gogmagog *see* Iron Maiden.

Goldberg, Whoopi   American comedienne and movie star who portrayed the Grand Banshee in "The Magical Legend of the Leprechauns," a four-hour TV special on NBC in 1999 that also starred Roger Daltrey as King Boric.

Gordon, Coral *see* Chyna.

Gorman, Tim   American keyboard player for the Who on their 1982 album *It's Hard*. Gorman, who released two albums with a band called Lazy Racer in 1979 and 1980, was discovered by *It's Hard* producer **Glyn Johns**. From 1985 to '87 Gorman played with the KBC Band, which featured three

Jefferson Airplane/Starship members. In 1988 Gorman was the keyboardist on the 1988 tour that followed the recording of John Entwistle's long-delayed solo album *The Rock*, which wasn't released until 1996. In 1991 Gorman was a member of Airplane/Starship guitarist Paul Kantner's new band Wooden Ships. From 1992 to mid–1995 Gorman was a member of Kantner's new Jefferson Starship lineup, which released the live album *Deep Space/Virgin Sky* in '95. In 1996 he released the solo album *Classical Daydreams*.

The Grateful Dead   San Francisco band formed in the mid–1960s that sustained a massive cult following into the 1990s. They covered the Who's "Baba O'Riley" live in the early 1980s, including at a Washington, DC concert with guest Steve Miller. The Dead, as they were often called for short, performed at the legendary Monterey Pop Festival in mid–1967, as did the Who. According to Dave Marsh in his book *Before I Get Old*, Pete Townshend characterized the Dead at the time as "terrible." The Who and the Dead had equal billing at two Oakland concerts in October of 1976. Townshend's opinion of the Dead must have changed over time because after the Who played on German television on March 28, 1981, Townshend joined the Dead during their subsequent set. The Dead remained a popular live attraction until the death of member Jerry Garcia in 1995.

Groening, Matt   Creator of the long-running prime time animated TV series *The Simpsons*. In the fall of 2000 the first episode of the show's twelfth season featured the Who prominently, though Roger Daltrey and John Entwistle were joined in the recording session by **Paul Townshend** instead of his brother Pete.

Gunne, Jo Jo   *see* Jo Jo Gunne.

Hadley, Tony   *see* Spandau Ballet.

Hagar, Sammy   Hard rock singer who established a name for himself with several successful albums and who replaced David Lee Roth as the lead singer of **Van Halen**. While fronting his own band a concert of his was shown on MTV in the early to mid–1980s which included a version of the Who's "Baba O'Riley." with Van Halen in 1993 he recorded a live version of that other famous anthem from *Who's Next*, "Won't Get Fooled Again."

Hagman, Larry   American actor known for lead roles in two popular television series, *I Dream of Jeannie* and *Dallas*. He and Keith Moon became very good friends as a result of appearing in the movie *Stardust*, which starred **David Essex**.

Hain, Kit Songwriter whose compositions have turned up on three of Roger Daltrey's solo albums. She wrote "Looking for You" and "Parting Would Be Painless" on 1984's *Parting Should Be Painless*, "Fallen Angel" on 1985's *Under a Raging Moon,* and "Ready for Love" on 1987's *Can't Wait to See the Movie.* Hain released a few albums as a solo artist or as part of a duo prior to 1984. In 1985 she sang backup on a Morris Day album and has provided backing vocals for a few other artists since then. Besides Daltrey, well known artists who have recorded her songs include Cher, **Heart**, Kiki Dee, and Peter Cetera and Chaka Khan (a duet). Selena, the very popular Latino singer, recorded one of her songs several days before she was murdered in 1995.

Halpin, Scott Audience member who volunteered to fill in for an ailing Keith Moon part of the way through a concert at San Francisco's Cow Palace on November 20, 1973. Halpin, from Muscatine, Iowa, was 19 years old at the time. After playing songs from *Quadrophenia* the band launched into "Won't Get Fooled Again" but Moon slumped over his drums moments later. Attempts to revive him were barely successful, so Pete Townshend asked if there was a good drummer in the audience. Halpin, who was sitting toward the front, struggled to get onto the stage and promoter Bill Graham escorted him to the drum kit. With Halpin the Who played a medley of **Howlin' Wolf** songs, "Smokestack Lightning" and "Spoonful," and finished with "Naked Eye." Halpin then got to hang out backstage with the band. Roger Daltrey said Halpin's drumming was good, but Halpin told *Rolling Stone* magazine that he hadn't drummed in six months; it was his familiarity with the songs that saved him. Moon, it was later determined, was under the influence of the animal tranquilizer PCP. Several years later the *San Francisco Examiner* tried to track Halpin down but said in an article that he couldn't be found. The paper, however, thought it was looking for someone named "Sandy Scott" and thought that the concert was in 1975, but the Who didn't perform in California that year.

Hancock, Herbie Chicago-born keyboard player known for fusing funk and jazz in the 1970s. Hancock's first of many solo albums was released in 1963, the same year he joined a quintet formed by **Miles Davis**. He was part of that quintet until 1968 and also shared keyboard duties on Davis's 1969 album *In a Silent Way.* In 1968, however, he had also provided the score for Michelangelo Antonioni's movie *Blow Up.* His 1973 album *Headhunters* was the one that clearly established him as a leader in the fusion genre. Around 1975 he provided the soundtracks for the movie *Death Wish* and the Bill Cosby animated TV special *Fat Albert Rotunda.*

In the late 1980s he became the host of the Showtime cable network's music series *Showtime Coast to Coast*, and toward the end of 1990 Pete Townshend performed several songs on the show, including "Magic Bus" with Hancock.

Handel, George Frideric Eighteenth-century German-born baroque composer whose oratorio the *Messiah* was given a modern arrangement and sung by various popular music stars in December of 1999, including Roger Daltrey (whose acting career began by portraying Tommy, the New Messiah). At this performance in Dublin, the city where the *Messiah* was first presented in 1742, Daltrey sang "Every Valley Shall Be Exalted," an update of the familiar Hallelujah chorus often heard around Christmas time. Other singers included Gladys Knight and Chaka Khan. Starting in 1712, when he moved to England at the age of 27 after four years in Italy, Handel presented numerous operas in London. A Handel landmark figured in Pete Townshend's speech in September of 1997 at the London ceremony unveiling a Blue Plaque in honor of **Jimi Hendrix**: "There's been a lot of talk about whether [a Hendrix plaque] deserves to be on a building next door to George Frideric Handel. I think he does."

Harper, Roy English guitarist known for his eccentric folk songs. His performances in London clubs starting in 1964 made him a familiar face to a couple of the members of **Led Zeppelin,** who put the tribute song "Hats Off to Harper" on their third album in 1970. Keith Moon is credited with drumming on Harper's two 1974 albums, *Valentine* and *Flashes from the Archives of Oblivion*. In 1975 Harper sang lead on the song "Have a Cigar" on **Pink Floyd**'s *Wish You Were Here* album. He continued to release albums throughout the 1980s and 1990s.

Harpo, Slim Louisiana blues artist whose songs were often performed by the **Detours.** Harpo, whose real name was James Moore, played guitar and harp in addition to singing and writing songs. He had a 20-year association with guitarist Lightnin' Slim, who played on Harpo's 1961 hit "Rainin' in My Heart" and on "I'm a King Bee," a song covered by the **Rolling Stones** in their early days. Pete Townshend became familiar with Harpo's music thanks to the impressive collection of his friend **Tom Wright**. After the Detours became the Who and then temporarily the **High Numbers,** Harpo's "Got Love If You Want It" was transformed by publicist **Peter Meaden** into "I'm the Face" for the High Numbers' only released 45. In 1966 Harpo had a #1 R&B hit with "Baby, Scratch My Back." He died of a heart attack in 1970 at the age of 43.

Harris, Richard Familiar movie actor who also had a big hit as a singer with "MacArthur Park" in 1968. In 1972 Harris was the Doctor on **Lou Reizner**'s orchestral *Tommy* album. However, **Peter Sellers** took over the role when Reizner's production was performed live for charity. Harris, who was born in Ireland in 1930, started appearing in movies in 1958. It was his performance as King Arthur in the 1967 movie musical *Camelot* that led to his recording career. After "MacArthur Park" reached #2 in the U.S. he continued to record music for awhile but with far less success. Harris had top billing or prominent roles in several successful movies in the 1970s. He withdrew during most of the 1980s to overcome self-inflicted health problems, though in 1989 Harris appeared in the movie *Mack the Knife* with Roger Daltrey. In the early 1990s he starred in the *Field*, a dramatic movie that earned him an Academy Award nomination. He passed away on October 25, 2002, at the age of 72.

Harris, Steve *see* Iron Maiden.

Havens, Richie African-American folksinger whose fame peaked in the late 1960s thanks to appearances at such events as the Monterey Jazz Festival in 1967 and Woodstock in 1969. The Who appeared at the latter. Havens covered the Who's "See Me, Feel Me" on his 1971 album *The Great Blind Degree*, the same year that his cover of the **Beatles** song "Here Comes the Sun" provided him with his only real chart success by reaching the top 20. In 1972 Havens played the Hawker in **Lou Reizner**'s all-star stage version of *Tommy*. His version of "Eyesight to the Blind" was released as a single, with the B-side consisting of "Underture" as performed by the **London Symphony Orchestra** and English Chamber Choir. Havens has appeared in movies, such as Richard Pryor's *Greased Lightning* in 1977. By the end of the 1970s he had given up on studio recording, but starting in 1987 he released several more albums.

Hawkins, Screamin' Jay Showman known more for his wild wardrobe and onstage antics than for his singing or musicianship. Jalacy Hawkins was a top-ranked boxer in the 1940s but turned to a career in music in 1952. Two years later he toured with Fats Domino and began solo work in 1955. He was part of rock pioneer Alan Freed's circuit, and quickly made a name for himself by being carried offstage in a burning coffin. In 1956 he wrote "I Put a Spell on You," which Pete Townshend covered with his band **Deep End** on their 1986 live album. Townshend also performed the song on TV in late 1990 with backing from **Pat Metheny**. Other bands that covered this song included the Crazy World of **Arthur Brown** and **Creedence Clearwater Revival**. He had few other hits but recorded extensively for a variety of top labels. He was also prolific in another respect, reportedly fathering over 50 children. He died in 2000 at the age of 70.

Heart Seattle hard rock band that rose to prominence in the mid–1970s with a lineup that was rare at the time: It was fronted by two women. Years later one of them recorded a duet with Roger Daltrey. In 1970 Ann Wilson joined the all-male group White Heart, which dated back to 1963. In 1974 the band shortened its name to Heart and Ann was joined by her sister Nancy. The band's debut album in 1976, *Dreamboat Annie*, sold well in excess of two million copies over time thanks to the title track, the Top 40 single "Crazy on You" and the Top 10 hit "Magic Man." In 1977 their second album's single "Barracuda" also came near the Top 10. Ann tended to be the lead vocalist though she also plays flute and guitar; Nancy plays guitar regularly in addition to singing. In the early 1980s the band slumped but roared back in 1985 with a self-titled album that sold more than five million copies and included four Top 10 hits: "What About Love?," "Never," "These Dreams" (#1) and "Nothin' at All." They had a couple of hits from their next album and then in 1990 their song "All I Want to Do Is Make Love to You" reached #2 on the charts. Ann and Roger Daltrey sang the **Led Zeppelin** song "Kashmir" on the **British Rock Symphony** CD in 1999. Ann's profile in the CD's liner notes states that Heart has sold over 30 million records and has 21 top 40 hits. In 2001 John Entwistle, **Steve Luongo**, and **Godfrey Townsend** of the John Entwistle Band toured with Ann, **Todd Rundgren**, and **Alan Parsons** in the **Beatles** tribute billed as *A Walk Down Abbey Road*.

Heath, Frederick *see* Kidd, Johnny.

Helm, Levon Drummer and mandolin player in the Band, a group that had a long association with Bob Dylan. Helm recently narrated a special on the Who on cable TV's VH1. Helm was born in Arkansas in 1942 and was the only non–Canadian in the Band. He and the other members had all been one of rockabilly singer Ronnie Hawkins' Hawks at some point in the late 1950s and early 1960s. In 1963 they started working on their own under several names, including Levon and the Hawks. Helm and fellow Band founder Robbie Robertson had backed Dylan at his famous Forest Hills concert on August 28, 1965. Over the next 11 years they collaborated with Dylan often, except for a lull between 1969 and 1973. They released their first album in 1968, the critically-acclaimed *Songs from Big Pink*. They released several more before calling it quits on Thanksgiving Day in 1976 at a star-studded farewell performance that was filmed by

Martin Scorsese and released under the title *The Last Waltz*. Helm continued to record with various performers over the years, and made his film debut in *Coal Miner's Daughter* in 1980.

Hendrix, Jimi   Legendary African-American 1960s rock guitarist. On March 23, 1967, the Jimi Hendrix Experience's second single, "Purple Haze," was the debut single for Track Records, the British label founded by the Who's managers, **Kit Lambert** and **Chris Stamp** ("Hey Joe" had been released on Polydor in December of 1966). In September of 1966 Lambert saw Hendrix perform at a London night club and was disappointed to learn that manager Chas Chandler, the former **Animals** bassist, was already negotiating with Decca. When that deal fell through, Lambert was able to convince Polydor that his brash idea of forming a new label would be viable with Hendrix in addition to the Who. The Experience's drummer was Mitch Mitchell, who was auditioned by the Who to replace **Doug Sandom** before Keith Moon entered the picture.

The Who and the Jimi Hendrix Experience shared a bill in January of 1967 at Epstein's Saville Theatre in London, which created a rivalry between the two bands, and both made many Americans sit up and take notice at the Monterey Pop Festival in mid–June of that year. In *Before I Get Old* Dave Marsh said that Pete Townshend got into an argument with Hendrix backstage and this resulted in the Who playing with even more energy than usual, assuring that Hendrix would not be the only performer remembered from that day when he later set his guitar on fire. During an America Online chat in February of 2000, Roger Daltrey discussed the reason Pete confronted Jimi: "A lot of Jimi's act was stolen from the Who. He came to England and was signed by our record company. He used to watch us. A lot of his feedback and stuff, the guitar stuff, was stolen from Pete. Pete was doing it a long time before Jimi. It built up a lot of—not animosity, because Pete obviously admired Jimi's talent. We were blown away by the guy. He didn't need what we were doing. Just the way he played was enough. But a lot of the stuff, the banging of the amps and all that, was stolen from Pete. So obviously, when we got to hear that Jimi was literally on before us or after us, we thought, well, he's going to just do our show—and I think Pete had a few words with us. It was no more than that. Of course, he didn't do our show, but he did very similar. He burned his guitar, which was a masterstroke. Jimi was far too quiet. He was a quiet guy."

In mid–August of 1969 Hendrix and the Who both cemented their reputations as legends at the famous Woodstock festival, parts of which were released on albums and in a documentary. In an interview that appeared in Gary Herman's book *The Who*, Roger Daltrey said "Pete could go up on stage with two strings stuck over a piece of wood with a microphone under it and make it work. He didn't need a guitar to do it. Which is the difference between him and Hendrix who used the same sort of feedback, but he uses it with technical things which completely changes it. But basically it's the same."

Hendrix last performed live at the Isle of Wight Festival in August of 1970, which was also the setting of one of the first complete Who performances captured on film and sold commercially (over two decades later). About a month later Hendrix died of a drug overdose at the age of 27. One of the most sought after German albums that was released around this time was the compilation *The Who & the Jimi Hendrix Experience*; each band had a disc in this double album. A similar album released in Japan in 1971 was called *Battle of the Who and Jimi Hendrix* but Japanese fans were also treated to *Battle of the Who and Jimi Hendrix Live*, which paired the Who's *Live at Leeds* with Hendrix's *Band of Gypsies*. Roger Daltrey told the UK fan publication *Naked Eye* that "Jimi was a really nice, humble, down to earth, quiet guy who would turn into this different person once he got on stage." In September of 1997 Pete Townshend gave one of the speeches at the London ceremony unveiling a Blue Plaque in honor of Jimi Hendrix. Townshend said that Jimi "was up there with **Miles Davis** and Charlie Parker as a virtuoso, an innovator...."

Henley, Don *see* The Eagles.

Henrit, Bob *see* Argent.

Henson, Jim Creator of the Muppets on American public TV's *Sesame Street*. They proved so popular that in 1976 the *Muppet Show* began a successful run on TV and attracted many big name guest starts. It has been assumed by many that the show's maniacal drummer, Animal, was modeled after Keith Moon. Henson died in May of 1990.

Herman's Hermits British Invasion group that the Who backed on its first U.S. tour, in the summer of 1967. As a child actor using the name Peter Novack in the late 1950s, Peter "Herman" Noone was in a popular prime-time UK soap opera called *Coronation Street*. He also started a band that attracted the attention of producer Mickie Most in early 1964. It was either Noone's bandmates or Most who gave Noone his new alias, reportedly based on his resemblance to the "Sherman" character in the Mr. Peabody segments of the *Rocky and Bullwinkle* cartoon series. Later in 1964 the band's first single, "I'm Into Something Good," reached the top 20. Herman's Hermits had a whopping 10 Top 10 hits in 1965 and 1966, including two that reached #1: "Mrs. Brown You've Got a Lovely Daughter" and "I'm Henry the Eighth, I Am." Herman's Hermits, the Who, and many other artists performed at what **Richard Barnes** called "the pop event of 1966," a concert that included many of the UK artists who ranked high in a *New Musical Express* poll from 1965. The last big hit for Herman's Hermits, "There's a Kind of Hush," peaked in early 1967. The band's American agent was **Frank Barsalona** of Premier Talent, who also became the Who's American agent. During the 1967 tour Herman's Hermits and the Blues Magoos reportedly helped pay for damage Keith Moon caused to a Holiday Inn. In *Dear Boy* Tony Fletcher indicated they did so because they actually caused a fair amount of the damage for which Keith was blamed (or for which he took credit). The band broke up in 1970 but has reformed in recent times without Noone to play on the oldies circuit, which Noone sometimes does as well.

Heron, Mike Co-founder in 1965 of the Incredible String Band, a Scottish folk group that developed a cult following in the U.S. over the next decade. In November of 1966 they performed for the first time outside of Scotland, at London's Royal Albert Hall. They shared the bill with American performers Judy Collins and Tom Paxton, who spread the word about the ISB upon returning to the U.S. They issued roughly an album a year, each tending to be increasingly ambitious. In 1971 Heron released a solo album, *Smiling Men with Bad Reputations*, and on the song "Warm Heart Pastry" he was backed by performers credited as "Tommy and the Bijoux." This reportedly was Pete Townshend, Keith Moon, John Cale of the Velvet Underground on electric viola, and either **Ronnie Lane** or John Entwistle on bass. Several years later a "**Bijou Drains**" was credited on the Townshend/Lane album *Rough Mix*. After releasing a self-titled album in 1980 Heron maintained a low profile until 1996, when he released the well-received *Where the Mystics Swim*.

The High Numbers The Who's name for roughly four months during the second half of 1964, when the band's first 45 was released. By the beginning of July of that year Who publicist and de facto manager **Peter Meaden** had persuaded the members of the Who to adopt the mod lifestyle, at least publicly, and to become the High Numbers because the name fit with mod slang. By this time Meaden had also managed to get a 45 recorded and released for the High Numbers with assistance from **Jack Baverstock**. Though Pete Townshend had already written at least one song by this point, called "It Was You," Meaden decided to change **Slim Harpo**'s "Got Love If You Want It" into "I'm the Face" for one side of the 45 and the 1961 song "Country Fool" by a group called the Showmen into "Zoot

Suit." Around the time that the 45 was released **Richard Barnes** encountered **Kit Lambert** at a concert. Lambert said he was looking for a pop group to appear in a film, and Barnes brought Peter Meaden to meet him. This proved to be the beginning of the end for Meaden and nominal manager Helmut Gorden. By mid–August Meaden and Gorden had largely been pushed out of the picture by Lambert and **Chris Stamp**. As the High Numbers the band had its first encounters with some noteworthy bands by playing support for them, such as the **Kinks** on July 31 and the **Beatles** on August 16. According to Barnes, Lambert grew concerned that housewives might see an ad for an evening with "the High Numbers" and show up expecting to play bingo. Conversely, he thought "The Who" was a catchy, intriguing, and unforgettable name. By early November Kit had persuaded the band to become the Who again, and this time the name stuck.

Hilfiger, Tommy   Wealthy and popular clothes designer who sponsored Pete Townshend's *Psychoderelict* concerts in 1993.

Hoffman, Abbie   Prominent American activist and author. In August of 1969 Pete Townshend swatted Hoffman off the stage with his guitar during the famous Woodstock concert. The Who had stayed up all night, not knowing when they would perform, and went on around dawn only to see someone jump onstage and grab a microphone. Hoffman yelled, "I think this is a pile of shit while John Sinclair rots in prison!" Sinclair was founder of the radical White Panther Party and was serving 10 years in prison for being caught with two marijuana cigarettes. After knocking Hoffman off the stage, Townshend said, "I can dig it" and then warned: "The next fucking person who walks across this stage is going to get fucking killed! You can laugh. I mean it!" Townshend had already kicked movie director Michael Wadleigh off the stage just before the Who started performing. John Lennon of the **Beatles** eventually performed a concert on Sinclair's behalf, in late 1971.

Hoffman was one of the seven leaders of a protest against the Vietnam War who were tried as the "Chicago Seven" on charges of conspiring to start a riot during the 1968 Democratic National Convention in Chicago. The trial began a few weeks after Woodstock and concluded with convictions in early 1970. However, on appeal they were ultimately overturned. Hoffman was born in 1936 and died in 1989. In the late 1990s Sinclair, who had been very close to the band MC5 around the time of that fateful Democratic Convention, was in a band and working on radio in New Orleans. In the book that came with the Who's 1994 boxed set *30 Years of Maximum R&B* Townshend reflected on his encounter with

Hoffman: "What Abbie was saying was politically correct in many ways—the people at Woodstock really were a bunch of hypocrites claiming cosmic revolution simply because they took over a field, broke down some fences, imbibed bad acid and then tried to run out without paying the band. All while John Sinclair rotted in jail after a trumped-up drug bust. My response was reflexive rather than considered. Later I realized his humiliation on that occasion was fatal to his [Hoffman's] political credibility."

Hoffs, Susanna   Lead singer of the Bangles, a very successful all-female band in the 1980s. John Entwistle played bass on the song "Boys Keep Swinging" on Hoffs's 1991 solo album, *When You're a Boy*. That album generated a Top 40 hit, "My Side of the Bed."

Hogan, Paul   Australian actor known for the Crocodile Dundee movies. He shared some screen time with Roger Daltrey in the movie *Lightning Jack*, which also starred Cuba Gooding, Jr., and Beverly D'Angelo.

Holland/Dozier/Holland   Prolific and very successful Motown songwriting and production team, usually for other artists. The Who covered four of their songs. Brian and Eddie Holland and Lamont Dozier were all born in Detroit before 1942. Dozier was signed by Berry Gordy, Jr. As a singer in the late 1950s as he was laying the foundation for Motown. By 1961 Dozier started to focus on songwriting and was paired with Brian Holland, and they were eventually joined by Brian's brother Eddie, who sang the Top 40 hit "Jamie" in 1962. Eddie also released the song "Leaving Here" under his own name in late 1963, and the **High Numbers** recorded it twice in 1964 before switching their name to the Who. One version was first released in 1985 on the U.S. Album *Who's Missing* and the other appeared as a bonus track on the *Odds and Sods* CD in 1998. Holland/Dozier/Holland also wrote **Marvin Gaye**'s September 1964 single "Baby Don't You Do It," which was covered by the Who on a variety of occasions, including later in 1964 during one of the aforementioned High Numbers recording sessions. In late 1965 the Who played it during one of their earliest TV appearances. In 1971 the Who recorded it with assistance from **Al Kooper** and **Leslie West**, and a live version from late in 1971 became the B-side of the "Join Together" 45 the next year.

The Who also covered two Holland/Dozier/Holland compositions that **Martha and the Vandellas** first recorded, 1963's "Heat Wave" and 1965's "Motoring." The former was covered on the Who's *A Quick One* album in 1966 though it was replaced on the U.S. album to make room for the hit

"Happy Jack." A longer recording of "Heat Wave" had been made in March of 1965 but didn't turn up until the album *Two's Missing* was released in the U.S. in 1987. That album also included the long overdue appearance of the Who's version of "Motoring," which was recorded only a month or so after Martha and the Vandellas debuted it. Holland/Dozier/Holland had over two dozen Top 10 hits from 1963 to '66 but after one too many squabbles with Gordy they left Motown in 1968 to form their own label, which enjoyed its first #1 hit in 1971 with "Want Ads" by Honey Cone. Holland, Dozier, and Holland were inducted into the Rock and Roll Hall of Fame in 1990, the same year as the Who. On February 15, 1998, the ABC network aired a Motown birthday special that included a segment about non-Motown bands performing Motown tunes, and among the clips was video footage of the Who performing "Heat Wave" on the 1960s show the *Beat Club*.

Hooker, John Lee Blues singer whose electric guitar work had a big influence on Pete Townshend. Hooker was born in Mississippi in 1917 and began recording in the late 1940s, several years after taking up residence in Detroit. His first single, "Boogie Chillun," was quite successful, and "I'm in the Mood" sold a million copies in 1951. He released his first album in 1959 and in the early 1960s he toured Europe, where he developed quite a following. His songs have been covered by such artists as the **Animals**, Canned Heat, and the **Spencer Davis** Group. Pete Townshend was exposed to Hooker's records thanks to the impressive collection of his friend **Tom Wright**. Geoffrey Giuliano's 1996 Townshend biography quoted Pete about those days: "It was amazing to hear his first electric guitar recordings, which were some of the wildest you'd ever heard and done straight onto disk. It gives you a certain depth in your perception of the artist." Sometimes Townshend would discover a gem that Hooker recorded but that had been originally done by another performer, such as "Driftin' Blues," which was originally sung by **Charles Brown**. Hooker appeared in the *Blues Brothers* movie in 1980. Hooker's distinctly deep singing was featured on "Over the Top" and "I Eat Heavy Metal" on Pete Townshend's 1989 *Iron Man* album, his musical adaptation of the **Ted Hughes** tale. Giuliano quoted Hooker about this experience: "I never thought I could do that. I never dreamed … that was so far out of my territory in music. The lyrics he wrote for me to do, I never heard such lyrics. 'I'm the Iron Man, I eat barbed wire,' something like that. I said, 'I can't do that Pete,' He said, 'Yes, you can. You've been my idol all my life; now you tell me you ain't gonna do it?' Now I never say I can't do it anymore." In 1991 Hooker was inducted into the Rock and Roll Hall of Fame, a year after the Who. He died in 2001.

Hope-Evans, Peter Harmonica player on most of Pete Townshend's solo albums. From 1968 to 1976 he was at the core of the band Medicine Head, which was heavily promoted by British disk jockey John Peel. By the time the group disbanded Hope-Evans had become a devotee of **Meher Baba** and his composition "Contact" appeared on the 1976 tribute album *With Love*, a collection which also featured Townshend. A year later Hope-Evans played on "Nowhere to Run" and "Misunderstood" on the Pete Townshend/**Ronnie Lane** collaboration, *Rough Mix*. On July 13, 1979, Townshend formed his first band outside of the Who for the "Rock Against Racism" concerts, consisting of Hope-Evans, **Kenney Jones**, **Tony Butler**, and **John "Rabbit" Bundrick**. Work on other Townshend solo projects followed in the 1980s: *Empty Glass* in 1980, *All the Best Cowboys Have Chinese Eyes* in 1982, *White City* in 1985, and the **Deep End** concerts in 1986. In 1987 he played on **Jon Astley**'s *Everyone Loves the Pilot (Except the Crew)* album and in 1989 on Tears for Fears' *Seeds of Love* album. In 1993 he played on Townshend's *Psychoderelict* album and the subsequent *Live* video. In November of 1998 he and **Chucho Merchan** backed Townshend at London's Vibe Bar for VH1's *Storytellers* series but the performance didn't air and a March, 2000 performance was arranged instead. He also backed Townshend in Chicago for 1999's *Live* CD. Two songs on which he backed Townshend at the Shepherds Bush Empire in 1998, "Won't Get Fooled Again" and "Who Are You," turned up on Townshend's six-disc *Lifehouse Chronicles* boxed set in early 2000.

Hopkins, Nicky Much in-demand session pianist who was among the Who's earliest studio collaborators. At the start of his career Hopkins played with Lord Sutch and British bluesman Cyril Davies before producer **Shel Talmy** recruited him for early **Kinks** and Who albums. On the Who's *My Generation* album in 1965 the instrumental "The Ox" was credited to Townshend, Entwistle, Moon, and Hopkins. Other mid–1960s Who recordings on which he played include "Anyway Anyhow Anywhere," "Anytime You Want Me," "I Don't Mind," "I'm a Man," "It's Not True," "La-La-La Lies," "A Legal Matter," "Lubie Come Back Home," "Motoring," "Much Too Much," "Please Please Please," and "Heat Wave." In the early 1970s he played on "The Song Is Over," "Getting in Tune," "Let's See Action," "When I Was a Boy," and "Too Much of Anything." Hopkins told *Melody Maker* in 1971 that Pete Townshend had offered him a permanent spot in the Who earlier that year but he declined. In 1975 he was credited on two Who projects, *The Who by Numbers* album and the *Tommy* movie soundtrack. On the former he contributed to "Slip Kid," "Imagine a Man," "They Are All in Love," and "How Many Friends." On the movie soundtrack he played piano on "1951/What About the Boy," "Amazing Journey," "Christmas," "Acid Queen," "Go to the Mirror," "I'm Free," "Sensation," "Sally Simpson," "We're Not Gonna Take It," "Listening to You"/"See Me, Feel Me," "Tommy Can You Hear Me?" and "Do You Think It's Alright?" Hopkins seemingly worked with every major rock band at some point, including the **Rolling Stones** and the **Beatles**. Hopkins also recorded three solo albums. Often in ill health, he died in 1994 at the age of 50.

Hoskins, Bob   Actor who has had quite a varied and successful career since the 1970s, with his strongest connections to popular music probably being roles in the movie version of **Pink Floyd**'s *The Wall* in 1981 and in the Spice Girls' *Spice World* in 1998. In 1983 he and Roger Daltrey appeared in a BBC production of **John Gay**'s *The Beggar's Opera* and Hoskins received an Oscar nomination as best actor for the movie *Mona Lisa*. Other movies in which Hoskins has appeared include *Zulu Dawn* in 1979, *Othello* in 1981, *The Cotton Club* in 1984, *Brazil* in 1985, *Who Framed Roger Rabbit?* in 1988, *Mermaids* in 1990, *Super Mario Brothers* in 1993, *Nixon* and the animated *Balto* in 1995, and *Michael* in 1996.

Houston, Thelma   American disco singer who hit #1 with "Don't Leave Me This Way" in 1977. The song earned her a Grammy Award for best R&B female vocal performance. She was in the gospel group the Art Reynolds Singers before starting her solo career in the late 1960s. Though she never came close to repeating her success with "Don't Leave Me This Way" she has performed and recorded regularly. Her music has been used in such movies as *Looking for Mr. Goodbar* and *Thank God It's Friday*. In 1999 she sang the **Beatles** song "Let It Be" with Roger Daltrey on the **British Rock Symphony** CD.

Howlin' Wolf   Influential American blues performer whose creative peak came in the 1950s in time to shape rock & roll, and whose recordings Pete Townshend could find in the impressive collection of his friend **Tom Wright**. When the **High Numbers** auditioned for EMI Records around October of 1964 (shortly before switching to "The Who" permanently), John Atkins's book *The Who on Record* states that the only song known to have been recorded was their version of Wolf's 1956 single "Smokestack Lightning."

Wolf was born Chester Arthur Burnett in Mississippi in 1910. He formed his first band in Memphis in the late 1940s. His first R&B hit, "Moanin' at Midnight," came in 1957, five years after he moved to Chicago. His other hits from that era included 1960's "Spoonful," which was written by

Willie Dixon, whose material he frequently recorded. Dixon also wrote hits for **Muddy Waters**, including "I Just Want to Make Love to You," which was covered by the Who live. The Who played "Spoonful" as part of a medley with **Johnny Kidd**'s "Shakin' All Over" at 1970's Isle of Wight Festival, though this music wasn't commercially released until 1996. The Who also played a medley of "Smokestack Lightning" and "Spoonful" in late 1973 when audience member **Scott Halpin** filled in for an ailing Keith Moon toward the end of a concert in San Francisco. Wolf's songs have been covered by such noted artists as the **Grateful Dead**, **Jeff Beck**, the **Doors**, Cream, **Led Zeppelin**, and the **Rolling Stones**. He appeared on TV with the latter group in 1965 and had help from a couple of Stones in the early 1970s for his album *The London Sessions*, which was engineered by **Glyn Johns**. He received an honorary doctoral degree from Chicago's Columbia College that same year but lived the next few years on that city's poverty-stricken South Side before his death in early 1976. He was inducted into the Rock and Roll Hall of Fame in 1991 and Willie Dixon followed in 1994. In the UK fan publication *Naked Eye* around 1997 Roger Daltrey compared himself to Howlin' Wolf in the time before the Who had hit records that required a different vocal style. "If you listen to the Marquee tapes I sound more like Howling Wolf than Howling Wolf does!"

Hughes, Graham   Award-winning photographer for his cover of cousin Roger Daltrey's 1975 solo album *Ride a Rock Horse*, on which Roger appeared as a half-man half-horse centaur. In 1971 Hughes did the photography for the Who's *Meaty, Beaty, Big & Bouncy* album. That same year he and John Entwistle conceived of the album cover for John's first solo album, *Smash Your Head Against the Wall*. Graham also provided photos and helped with the design. From that he moved on to helping out Pete Townshend with the cover of *Who Came First*, on which Pete appeared to be standing on eggs. Ira Robbins's 1992 liner notes for a deluxe CD reissue of *Who Came First* quoted Townshend about the album's cover: "The idea and title came from a brainstorm with Graham. They were real eggs and, so they wouldn't break, I was hung in a Peter Pan truss. I was so distorted by this that the photo had to be retouched in any case, so it could have been done equally well with a cut-up." Hughes provided photos for most of Roger's solo albums, including *Daltrey* in 1973, *Best Bits* in 1982, *Parting Should Be Painless* in 1984, *Under a Raging Moon* in 1985, *Can't Wait to See the Movie* in 1987, and *Rocks in the Head* in 1992. His photo for the cover of *Daltrey* was the basis for Sally Simpson's wallpaper in the 1975 *Tommy* movie. Also in 1975 "Cousin Graham" was mentioned in John Entwistle's solo song "Cell Number Seven" on his *Mad Dog* album.

The song was about the Who and a number of associates being jailed briefly for some post-concert hotel destruction in Montreal on December 2, 1973.

Hughes, Ted   Late British poet laureate who was married to author Sylvia Plath of the *Bell Jar* fame. Hughes's much-loved children's story *The Iron Man* was the basis of Pete Townshend's 1989 solo album of the same name and the critically-acclaimed movie *The Iron Giant* a decade later, for which Townshend served as Executive Producer.

Humble Pie   Hard rock band formed in 1969 by Steve Marriott of the **Small Faces** and **Peter Frampton**. Drummer Jerry Shirley of Humble Pie played for John Entwistle on his first solo album, 1971's *Smash Your Head Against the Wall*. In Jud Cost's 1997 liner notes for the U.S. release of the album on compact disc, Cy Langston said that he, John and Jerry would get drunk at least once a week around the time the album was recorded and that during one session "Shirley nodded out on us right in the middle of 'Heaven And Hell,' while he was playing the drums. But we wound up doing the album in next to no time." Frampton left in late 1971 and played on Entwistle's second solo album and served as an opening act for Humble Pie. Frampton's replacement in Humble Pie was Dave "Clem" Clempson, formerly of the British jazz-rock fusion band Colosseum. Humble Pie broke up for the first time in 1975. That year Clempson played the guitar solo on "Feeling" on Roger Daltrey's 1975 solo album, *Ride a Rock Horse*. Clempson was not a member when Marriott and Shirley reformed the band in 1980. Clempson instead worked with Cozy Powell briefly and joined the Jack Bruce Band in 1980. In late 1985 Clempson joined **Russ Ballard**, **Alan Shacklock**, and a few other performers on a Roger Daltrey mini-tour. In 1987 he played on Daltrey's solo album *Can't Wait to See the Movie*. In the late 1980s **Eric Clapton** asked Clempson to record Clapton's hit "Layla" for an automobile commercial. In 1993 he played acoustic guitar on the **Adam Faith**/Roger Daltrey duet "Stuck in the Middle."

Idol, Billy   White-haired British singer with a tough guy image who had several big hits during the 1980s and who subsequently took part in live performances of *Tommy* and *Quadrophenia* with the Who. Idol, who was born William Broad in 1955, was a founder of the moderately successful punk band Generation X in the 1970s. They broke up in 1981 and a year later Idol's self-titled solo album sold very well on the strength of such hits as "White Wedding." His 1983 album *Rebel Yell* was even more successful, selling two million copies and giving him hits with the ballad "Eyes without a Face" and the more characteristic title track. When the

Who performed *Tommy* for charity in Los Angeles in 1989, Idol sang "Cousin Kevin." This concert was released on video. The next year Idol had another big hit with the song "Cradle of Love" but since then hasn't been able to replicate the chart success he enjoyed in the '80s. Idol performed on a regular basis with the Who on their 1996 leg of the *Quadrophenia* tour as the character Ace Face. In the UK fan publication *Naked Eye* Roger Daltrey said that although Idol did a great job, from a theatrical standpoint Idol's fame got in the way: "You start to watch Billy Idol *and not* the Ace Face."

The Incredible String Band *see* Heron, Mike.

Innes, Neil *see* The Bonzo Dog Doo-Dah Band.

Iron Maiden Heavy metal band that burst onto the scene in 1980. Around 1985 Jonathan King, early producer for **Genesis** and the original backer and producer of the *Rocky Horror Picture Show*, was attempting to assemble a heavy metal supergroup to be called Gogmagog. John Entwistle was supposed to join with Iron Maiden guitarist Janick Gers, original Iron Maiden vocalist Paul Di'Anno, and Def Leppard guitarist Pete Willis. For awhile it looked like Cozy Powell, who had just left Whitesnake, would be Gogmagog's drummer instead of King's first choice, Clive Burr of Iron Maiden. However, Cozy quickly received and accepted an offer to transform **Emerson, Lake and Palmer** into Emerson, Lake and Powell. When the band eventually recorded its only release, a 1985 EP that included a song written by **Russ Ballard**, the lineup included Whitesnake bassist Neil Murray and Burr instead of Entwistle and Powell. (Twelve years later Entwistle and Powell would play on the same track on an album by Glenn Tipton of **Judas Priest** fame.) In 1991 Iron Maiden's founder, Steve Harris, and its drummer, Nicko McBrain, teamed with Roger Daltrey as the Full Metal Rackets to perform with tennis players **John McEnroe** and Pat Cash on a charitable recording of the **Led Zeppelin** song "Rock And Roll." Five years later Iron Maiden released a version of the Who's "My Generation," which appears on their "Lord of the Flies" CD EP. (That release's third track is called "Doctor, Doctor" but it isn't the 1960s John Entwistle composition.) Prior to joining Iron Maiden, McBrain had been in **Streetwalkers**.

The Ivy League Trio of singers that backed the Who on several early tracks, most notably the Who's first hits, "I Can't Explain" and "Anyway Anyhow Anywhere." Jimmy Page, later of **Led Zeppelin**, was present when the former was recorded. The latter became the theme song for the TV show *Ready Steady Go*. The Ivy League also sang on the latter single's

B-side, "Anytime You Want Me." In *The Who on Record* John Atkins said that it also sounds like the Ivy League on the *My Generation* track "Out in the Street (You're Gonna Know Me)." John Carter and Ken Lewis had a minor hit in 1963 as the Carter-Lewis Duo but after adding Perry Ford and becoming the Ivy League they had more success in 1965 with the song "Funny How Love Can Be." However, the original duo grew to despise each other and Carter left at the beginning of 1966. He went on to collaborate with Ivy League manager Terry Kennedy but without chart success. His replacement was Tony Burrows, who would sing lead on the 1970 top five hit "Love Grows (Where My Rosemary Goes)" for one-hit wonders Edison Lighthouse. However, Lewis didn't stay much longer in the Ivy League either, prompting Ford to find another replacement in 1967 and record as the Flowerpot Men.

Jagger, Mick *see* The Rolling Stones.

The Jam Mod band that helped usher in a revival of that fashion and lifestyle beginning in 1976. They were sometimes referred to as "the new Who" and, fittingly, covered two Who songs during their successful career. In the August 12, 1978 issue of *Melody Maker* Jam leader Paul Weller said that he respected the Who but didn't enjoy being compared to them, nor did he like much of their music. However, just after Keith Moon's death in September the Jam recorded "So Sad About Us" in the same studio where *Who Are You* was recorded. It appeared as the flip side to their song "Down in the Tube Station at Midnight" and the 45's picture sleeve had a photo of Moon on the back. Weller and Pete Townshend met for the first time for a joint *Melody Maker* interview that ran in their issue of October 11, 1980. The two musicians compared their music and contrasted their attitudes toward American audiences. The next year a version of the Who's "Disguises" was the B-side for the Jam's "Funeral Pyre" 45. In March of 1982 a piece by Pete Townshend about the Jam appeared in *Time Out* magazine. That fall Weller announced the group's dissolution. "Disguises" and "So Sad About Us" both appear on the 1992 CDs *Jam Covers* and *Extras*. In 2001 the CD entitled *Substitute: The Songs of the Who* included a version of "Circles" by Weller.

The James Gang Hard rocking American band of the early 1970s that released several popular albums despite a lack of hit singles. Pete Townshend wrote the song "Sheraton Gibson" after a very pleasant barbecue with this Cleveland band. In Pittsburgh the next day Townshend found himself not only homesick for London but also yearning to be back in Cleveland. However, it was a Cincinnati hotel, not one in Pittsburgh, that provided the title of the song, which appeared on Pete's solo effort *Who Came First* in 1972. Not only did the James Gang prompt a Townshend composition, but he also arranged for them to open for the Who in Europe in 1971. The James Gang, which was formed in Cleveland in 1966, featured **Joe Walsh** from 1969 to 1971 and future Deep Purple guitarist Tommy Bolin in 1973 and 1974. The group then disbanded, reunited with a different lineup for two more albums, and disbanded again in 1976. Their song "Walk Away" has proven to be a classic rock radio staple.

Jason   Co-author, along with Keith Moon and Towser, of the "Pinball Wizard" B-side "Dogs Part Two." Jason and Towser were dogs belonging to John Entwistle and Pete Townshend, respectively and thus are the only non-humans to have entries in this book. They were credited on the UK 45 but omitted in the U.S.

Jefferson Airplane/Starship   Band which has undergone numerous lineup changes as well as name modifications since becoming one of San Francisco's biggest acts of the '60s. Their early hits "Somebody to Love" and "White Rabbit" from 1967 remain staples on oldies and classic rock radio stations in the U.S. That same year a drummer named Joey Covington would release his only single, which featured a cover of the Who's "Boris the Spider." Covington was a member of Jefferson Airplane in the early 1970s and also played with one of that band's spin-offs, Hot Tuna. Before fading from the music scene he teamed with Marty Balin to co-write "With Your Love," a top 20 hit for Jefferson Starship in 1976. By the end of the 1970s Balin left the band and his replacement was Mickey Thomas, who had sung lead on Elvin Bishop's big 1976 "Fooled Around and Fell in Love." Jefferson Starship (which eventually dropped the "Jefferson") would do quite well with Thomas in front, especially when singer Grace Slick rejoined the band. The two sang on the band's number one singles "We Built This City" and "Sara" in 1985 and "Nothing's Gonna Stop Us Now" in 1987. During a subsequent period of inactivity on the part of Starship, Thomas performed live on a limited basis with John Entwistle and **Jeff "Skunk" Baxter**. Jefferson Airplane was inducted into the Rock and Roll Hall of Fame in 1996.

Jett, Joan   Successful rock performer of the 1980s who led the Blackhearts. Jett, who was born in Philadelphia in 1960, was in the female teen hard rock band the Runaways in the late 1970s. After some effort she secured a record contract in America for her 1981 solo debut, *Bad Reputation*. In 1982, her album *I Love Rock 'n' Roll* was a top five platinum seller and the title track was a number #1 single. She soon followed that up with other hits. Jett's longtime lead guitarist in the Blackhearts was

Ricky Byrd. When *Bad Reputation* was re-released in 1992, bonus tracks included "Summertime Blues" and a cover of the Who's "Call Me Lightning."

Jewel   Very successful American recording artist of the 1990s. A turning point for Jewel, born Jewel Kilcher in 1974, came in 1979 when she performed "Over the Rainbow" on Tom Bodet's *End of the Road Show* on Alaska Public Radio. By 1995 she had moved to California and that year she released her debut album, *Pieces of You*. Over time the album sold 10 million copies, but while it was slowly climbing the charts she appeared as Dorothy next to Roger Daltrey's Tin Man in *The Wizard of Oz in Concert: Dreams Come True*. The soundtrack for this Children's Defense Fund stage and TV benefit was released in 1996.

Jo Jo Gunne   Moderately successful California rock band in the first half of the 1970s. Several of the band's members backed Keith Moon on his only solo album, 1975's *Two Sides of the Moon*. Jay Ferguson played piano and Curly Smith drummed with Moon on "Crazy Like a Fox," "The Kids Are Alright," and "Back Door Sally." John Staehely played electric guitar on the first two but not the latter. His brother Al, who wasn't a member of Jo Jo Gunne, wrote "Crazy Like a Fox" and played acoustic guitar on it. He also played guitar on "One Night Stand," "The Kids Are Alright," and "Back Door Sally." Jo Jo Gunne was formed by Jay Ferguson and Mark Andes after they left the band Spirit at the beginning of 1971. Their new band's name was a nod to a **Chuck Berry** song. They soon had their only Top 40 hit, "Run Run Run" (which was not a version of the 1965 Who song). They recorded their last album in 1974 and Ferguson went on to have his greatest success with the Top 10 single "Thunder Island" in 1978.

Jobson, Eddie   Musician who played keyboards and/or violin on four tracks on John Entwistle's fourth solo album, *Mad Dog*. Around the same time he also played strings on the **John Alcock**/John Entwistle *Flash Fearless* album. From 1973 to '76 Jobson worked with **Bryan Ferry** in Roxy Music and in the late 1970s he was also a member of the art rock supergroup U.K. and Jethro Tull.

John, Elton   Successful performer of the 1970s, '80s and '90s whose flamboyant stage apparel helped him gain notice. His garb in the 1975 movie *Tommy* gives a hint of John's stage presence in those days. Reginald Dwight started using the name Elton John after performing with saxophonist Elton Dean and singer Long John Baldry in 1966 and '67. He then met lyricist Bernie Taupin, with whom he established a long and successful writing partnership. From 1970 onward John earned over two dozen Top 40 singles. A handful of those reached #1 as did seven of his 1970s albums, consecutively. In *Tommy* he sang "Pinball Wizard," as he did with the Who for their 1989 charitable performance of *Tommy* in Los Angeles, which was released on video. Pete Townshend played on John's 1982 album *Jump Up!* on the song "Ball & Chain" and on John's 1988 album *Reg Strikes Back* on "Town of Plenty." For the 1985 movie *The Lost Boys* Roger Daltrey covered the John/Taupin #2 hit "Don't Let the Sun Go Down on Me." For the 1991 album *Two Rooms*, on which a variety of musicians paid tribute to John and Taupin, the Who recorded "Saturday Night's Alright (for Fighting)." The song represented one of the rare instances of the Who recording music after 1982.

John's Children   Short-lived British band that had a very interesting history. Most notably, drummer **Chris Townson** filled in for an ailing Keith Moon on a few occasions in 1966 and 1967, and Marc Bolan was a member just before he co-founded Tyrannosaurus Rex (later simply T. Rex) in 1967. John's Children got its start as the Clockwork Onions around 1965 and was also called the Few. They were using the name the Silence when one of their members approached former Yardbirds manager Simon Napier-Bell. He changed their name to John's Children and during 1966 and '67 they released a handful of singles plus one album. Many of the recordings released by John's Children could be faulted for poor recording techniques, heavy doctoring, unusual overdubs of crowd noises, and/or for being too dependent on session musicians. The band reportedly didn't even play on its second 45's A-side and on the B-side relied on an overdubbed guitar track by **Jeff Beck**. To make matters worse, protests that quickly arose in the U.S. due to pre-release publicity for their album *Orgasm* resulted in it being cancelled. However, things improved when former mod Marc Bolan came on board and **Kit Lambert** signed John's Children to the Who's new Track label. Bolan had already released two singles as a solo artist, and his song "Desdemona" provided John's Children with their only real success.

In April of 1967 the band toured Germany in support of the Who. However, Bolan left the band about a month later. His band T. Rex had a big hit in the early 1970s with "Bang a Gong (Get It On)." Bolan died in a car crash in 1977. John's Children had broken up in 1968. By the end of 1970 Track included "Desdemona" on two of its compilations, *The House That Track Built* and *Backtrack 7*, both of which included three Who songs. "Desdemona" was also covered by Track artist Marsha Hunt. After John's Children disbanded Townson drummed for a London club band called

Sparks and Jook until 1975, when they split up. He then formed Jet with two other ex-members of John's Children. That band evolved into Radio Stars, which appeared on a TV show hosted by Marc Bolan. John's Children reformed in the '90s for occasional concerts.

Johns, Glyn English recording engineer and producer who helped create what many fans consider to be the two best Who albums, *Who's Next* (1971) and *Quadrophenia* (1973), and who also helped launch the successful recording careers of the Steve Miller Band and the **Eagles**. For the Who he also produced *The Who by Numbers* in 1975, *Who Are You* in 1978, and *It's Hard* in 1982. Johns was born in early 1942 and in the early 1960s sang in a band called the Presidents. About two months before becoming the Who, the **Detours** opened for the **Rolling Stones** in the London area on December 22, 1963 and January 3, 1964 and Johns helped Pete Townshend get into the Stones' dressing room, which Pete said "was like going into a sacred place after the gig." Johns was with the Presidents at the time but would go on to engineer a number of records for the Stones from 1965 to 1972.

After releasing a few 45s as a performer in the 1960s Johns shifted gears to become an apprentice recording engineer under **Shel Talmy**. Johns thus had a hand in the recording of the Who's first album, *My Generation*. However, Talmy and **Kit Lambert** were growing increasingly hostile to one another, and **Richard Barnes** said Glyn would side with Talmy because that's "who was paying his wages." Barnes said Johns and Lambert also experienced a period of "warfare" and never forgave each other, which "caused problems years later." In *Before I Get Old* Dave Marsh noted that this lingering animosity plagued the recording sessions for *Lifehouse/Who's Next* in 1971.

In 1968 Glyn helped produce the Steve Miller Band's first album and later that year he started working with studio manager George Martin on the tapes from a **Beatles** project called "Get Back" but noted American producer Phil Spector eventually took over and the result was the *Let It Be* album. In the first half of the 1970s Glyn engineered **Howlin' Wolf**'s *London Sessions* album and produced the first two albums for the Eagles. Their self-titled debut in 1972 went gold on the strength of the single "Take It Easy." Glyn has also engineered and/or produced several albums for **Eric Clapton**, beginning with *Eric Clapton's Rainbow Concert* in 1973. That same year he produced **Gallagher and Lyle**'s *Willie & the Lapdog* album, on which Pete Townshend played harmonica. In 1976 he produced *Mahoney's Last Stand* for **Ron Wood** and **Ronnie Lane** and the next year he produced *Rough Mix* for Lane and Pete Townshend. In 1978 Glyn's commitment to **Joan Armatrading** overlapped with the *Who Are You* sessions and thus provided an opportunity for **Jon Astley** to impress the Who.

Johns produced Midnight Oil's *Place Without a Postcard* album in 1981 and mixed the **Clash**'s *Combat Rock* album in 1982. He received special thanks "for advice and experimental work" on Pete Townshend's *Iron Man* album, his 1989 musical adaptation of the **Ted Hughes** tale. In the late 1990s a new hour-long documentary about *Who's Next* was released on DVD and it included comments from Johns as well as from Daltrey, Townshend and John Entwistle.

Johns, John   One of John Entwistle's early aliases. When Colin Dawson was still the fifth member of the **Detours**, a photo of the band printed this alias in its caption. The photo can be found in **Richard Barnes**'s *The Who: Maximum R&B*.

Jones, John Paul *see* Led Zeppelin.

Jones, Kelly *see* Stereophonics.

Jones, Kenney   **Small Faces** and Faces drummer who took over those chores in the Who for several years after the death of Keith Moon. However, his first recording with Daltrey, Entwistle and Townshend was on the soundtrack for the *Tommy* movie — that was the lineup, along with **Nicky Hopkins** on piano, for that album's version of "I'm Free." Kenney also teamed with Pete Townshend and/or John Entwistle on "Eyesight to the Blind," "Acid Queen," and "Smash the Mirror," among others. Around this time Kenney also played on the **John Alcock**/John Entwistle *Flash Fearless* album. In 1976 he and Townshend played on the song "Tonight's Number" on the **Ron Wood**/**Ronnie Lane** album *Mahoney's Last Stand*. That same year he also drummed on **Joan Armatrading**'s self-titled 1976 album as well as on her 1977 *Show Some Emotion* album, on which **John "Rabbit" Bundrick** also played.

Kenney was announced as the Who's new drummer in December of 1978. His first concert with the Who was at the Rainbow Theatre in North London on May 2, 1979, even though their "official" London relaunch was on August 18 in Wembley Stadium. On July 13, 1979, Townshend formed his first band outside of the Who for the "Rock Against Racism" concerts, consisting of Kenney, **Tony Butler**, John "Rabbit" Bundrick and **Peter Hope-Evans**. The issue of *Time* dated December 1, 1979, featured the Who on the cover, but this uplifting achievement was soon forgotten when 11 fans were crushed to death at a Who concert in Cincinnati. On December 28 the Who took part in the Concerts for the People of Kampuchea.

Highlights were included in a UK television broadcast in January of 1981 and the Who earned one side of the double album that followed in March. The Who were still impressive enough in 1979 with Kenney on drums to be named the year's best band by *Rolling Stone* readers. Kenney's credits in 1980 included drumming on the **McVicar** soundtrack and on "Rough Boys" on Pete Townshend's solo album *Empty Glass*. In addition to making his new Who album debut on *Face Dances* in 1981 Kenney helped John Entwistle with the demos for John's fifth solo album, *Too Late the Hero*. In addition to the Who's *It's Hard* album in 1982 Kenney played on Townshend's contribution to the *Music & Rhythm* compilation, the track "Ascension Two." In the last quarter of 1983 Kenney was part of a supergroup that performed at a benefit concert for ARMS, Artists for Research into Multiple Sclerosis. The lineup included **Ronnie Lane**, **Eric Clapton**, **Jeff Beck**, **Steve Winwood**, **Andy Fairweather-Low**, **Chris Stainton**, **Simon Phillips**, Jimmy Page of **Led Zeppelin**, and Charlie Watts and Bill Wyman from the **Rolling Stones**. Kenney was also credited with drumming on "Dirty Water" on Pete Townshend's first double album of demos, 1983's *Scoop*. On December 16 of that year Townshend announced the end of the Who. **Bob Geldof** persuaded the band to reunite for the huge Live Aid benefit on July 13, 1985.

Kenney's next and final appearance with the Who was on February 8, 1988, when the Who received a Lifetime Achievement award at a British Phonographic Industry (BPI) event. The Who performed "Substitute," "Who Are You" and "My Generation" that night. In 1991 Kenney formed half of the short-lived band called the **Law**. When "Let My Love Open the Door" from *Empty Glass* was released in 1996 on a three-track CD with the new version that was used in John Cusack's *Grosse Point Blank* movie and with "Rough Boys," the credits listed only Simon Phillips on drums.

Jones, Tom Welsh singer who made a big splash in 1965 with the hits "It's Not Unusual" and "What's New, Pussycat?" and is still a familiar name in some circles, particularly among senior citizens. Around the time that the **High Numbers** changed their name back to the Who they appeared on a concert bill headlined by Jones and Marianne Faithfull. The Who performed "Pinball Wizard" on his television show *This Is Tom Jones* on April 20, 1969, not long after the single was released.

Judas Priest British heavy metal band that started developing a following around 1976. In 1977 their major label debut album, *Sin After Sin*, featured **Simon Phillips** on drums. They netted their first gold album in the U.S. with 1982's *Screaming for Vengeance*. The next year Judas Priest became one of **Bill Curbishley**'s clients. In 1990 the band was hit with a major lawsuit in Nevada by the parents of two fans who had committed suicide, allegedly due to lyrics that could be heard when the band's 1978 *Stained Class* album was played in reverse. Judas Priest was found not guilty. In 1992 frontman Rob Halford left the band and he wasn't replaced until 1996. Judas Priest guitarist Glenn Tipton released the solo album *Baptizm of Fire* in 1997 and John Entwistle played on one track, "The Healer," with Cozy Powell on drums.

Julia, Raul Actor who had a number of movie roles, culminating in the lead role of Gomez in the two popular Addams Family movies of the early 1990s. Just before those movies he starred in *Mack the Knife*, which was based on the *Threepenny Opera* by **Bertolt Brecht** and **Kurt Weill** and which also starred **Richard Harris** and Roger Daltrey. Raul Rafael Carlos Julia y Arcelas was born on March 9, 1944 (just eight days after Daltrey) in San Juan, Puerto Rico. In 1964 Julia moved to New York City to study acting and performed in many on- and off-Broadway plays for the next decade or so. He appeared in a few movies in the 1970s, such as *The Eyes of Laura Mars* in 1978, but his list of noteworthy credits in the 1980s is much longer. They include *Pennies from Heaven* in 1981, *Kiss of the Spider Woman* in 1985, *Moon over Parador* in 1988, and *Romero* in 1989. Julia died on October 24, 1994, after suffering a stroke.

Kaufman, Murray *see* Barsalona, Frank.

Kaylan, Howard *see* Flo and Eddie.

Keene, Speedy *see* Thunderclap Newman.

Kelly, Mike Drummer on the *Tommy* movie soundtrack, on "1951/What About the Boy" and "We're Not Gonna Take It." Among his few other noteworthy credits are some drumming for Spooky Tooth and Jerry Lee Lewis and producing Yoko Ono's 1996 album *Rising Mixes*.

Kessel, Barney Respected jazz guitarist who flourished for several decades starting in the 1940s. He performed with Artie Shaw starting in 1945 and teamed with many noted musicians over his long career. In 1973 Kessel formed the group Great Guitars with **Charlie Byrd** and Herb Ellis. Pete Townshend paid tribute to him with the song "To Barney Kessell" on his first double album of demos, 1983's *Scoop*. In his liner notes, Pete wrote: "A simple guitar chord chart I worked out and dedicated to a great guitar player." Townshend wrote the song in the mid–1970s. Kessel, who was born in Oklahoma in 1923, suffered a serious stroke in 1992.

Kick Horns Saxophone and brass group that has backed Pete Townshend and the Who. At their core are sax players Simon Clarke and Tim

Sanders and trumpet player Roddy Lorimer. In 1984, a year after they were formed, they played on **Pink Floyd** guitarist David Gilmour's solo album *About Face*, for which Townshend co-wrote two songs. The next year they played on Pete's *White City* album and were part of his **Deep End** band. Performing with Clarke, Sanders and Lorimer at that point in time were Dave Plews (listed as Sanders on *White City*) on trumpet and Peter Thoms on trombone. By 1989 these two were replaced by other accomplished musicians, namely Simon Gardner and Neil Sidwell, respectively. That year they played on the **Rolling Stones** album *Steel Wheels* and backed the Who on their reunion tour. Probably borrowing from a **Monty Python's Flying Circus** sketch, Pete Townshend introduced the quintet as "Bruce, Bruce, Bruce, Bruce, and Bruce." In the 1990s they played on Pete's *Psychoderelict* album as well as on albums for **Billy Nicholls**, Blur, **Eric Clapton**, and the Spice Girls, sometimes as a trio and at other times as a quintet with two new members.

Kidd, Johnny   Leader of Johnny Kidd and the Pirates, a band that was a very big influence on the Who. Legend has it that bandleader Frederick Heath wore an eyepatch for a short while after a string on his guitar snapped and hit him in the eye, and when a young woman backstage commented about his resemblance to a pirate, Johnny Kidd and the Pirates were born. When the Who were still known as the **Detours**, Johnny Kidd and the Pirates were one of several bands that they supported a number of times. According to *The Who Concert File*, in 1963 the Detours decided to model themselves after Johnny Kidd's band by dismissing singer Gabby Connolly and becoming a quartet with Roger Daltrey shifting from guitar to vocals. **Richard Barnes** listed two Johnny Kidd numbers among the songs that the Detours frequently played, "Shakin' All Over" and "Shot of Rhythm & Blues." These were hits for Kidd in 1960 and 1963, respectively. Unlike many of the British bands they influenced, Johnny Kidd and the Pirates hadn't become big in America by the time of Kidd's death in an auto accident in 1966 at the age of 27. In late 1966 the Who recorded a version of the first hit for Johnny Kidd and the Pirates, "Please Don't Touch," which Kidd wrote (under his real name) with manager Guy Robinson in 1959. The Who's version was used on *Ready Steady Go!* just before Christmas.

Kings Road   Group of studio musicians that issued a series of albums consisting entirely of covers of recent hits. In the U.S. there were at least 10 volumes of the *Super Hits* series on the Pickwick label and in the UK at least 34 of the *Top of the Pops* series on Pickwick's Hallmark affiliate. Who songs covered by Kings Road included "Join Together" and "5.15" plus six from *Tommy* on *Excerpts from Rock Operas*.

The Kinks   British band that made it big a year before the Who with their 1964 hits "You Really Got Me" and "All Day and All of the Night." The Kinks started as the Ravens but changed their name around the time a demo tape of theirs reached record producer **Shel Talmy**. Their third single, "You Really Got Me," was written by Ray Davies and featured a solo by his brother Dave. It reached #1 in the UK and landed in the Top 10 in the U.S. Shortly after the Who temporarily adopted the name the **High Numbers** they played support for the Kinks two or three times, starting on July 31, 1964. According to **Richard Barnes**, "the simplicity and effectiveness of the guitar riff in 'You Really Got Me' was not lost on the group, particularly Pete [Townshend]." In 1971 Roger Daltrey told Gary Herman for his biography *The Who* that the Who's second single, "Anyway Anyhow Anywhere," was much more original than their first, "I Can't Explain," which he said "was a pinch from the Kinks." Late in 1964 the Kinks released their next single, "All Day and All of the Night," which gave them their second Top 10 hit in the UK and U.S. The Kinks had varying degrees of success in each country through the mid–1980s. Their hit singles included "Sunny Afternoon" in 1966, "Lola" in 1970 and "Come Dancing" in 1983. They also had some albums that sold very well during those years, though Ray Davies' more ambitious concept albums generally proved to be poor sellers. After the mid–1980s the band experienced a consistent slump in sales that eventually found them without a label. In the midst of this the Kinks were inducted into the Rock & Roll Hall of Fame in 1990. On September 14, 1997 Kinks drummer Mick Avory was among the invited guests who watched Pete Townshend give one of the speeches at the London ceremony unveiling a Blue Plaque in honor of **Jimi Hendrix**. Three days later, John Entwistle, **Steve Luongo** and **Leslie West** happened to play "You Really Got Me" at London's Shepherds Bush Empire.

Kiss   *see* ESP.

Kissoon, Katie   Singer who got her start singing with her brother Mac and who has backed many famous performers, including Pete Townshend on his 1993 album *Psychoderelict* and the follow-up *Live* video. Other artists with whom she has performed live or in the studio include **Eric Clapton**, ex–**Beatle** George Harrison, **Elton John**, **Tom Jones**, Annie Lennox of **Eurythmics**, George Michael, Van Morrison, Dusty Springfield, **Tina Turner**, Bonnie Tyler, Roger Waters of **Pink Floyd** fame, Stevie Wonder, and the Pet Shop Boys.

Kokomo   British band with four singers, three of whom provided backing vocals on Roger Daltrey's 1975 solo album, *Ride a Rock Horse*. The three, Dyan Birch, Frank Collins, and Paddy McHugh, had all been in a pop group called Arrival that released a couple of albums and six singles from 1969 to 1973, including two Top 20 hits. Kokomo also released two albums, in 1975 and 1976. The three worked together on albums periodically afterwards, including backing **Bryan Ferry** in 1977 and Alison Moyet in 1991. Birch backed **Manfred Mann** in 1979 and 1980. Another member of Kokomo, Mel Collins, played saxophone on the song "Catmelody" on the Pete Townshend/**Ronnie Lane** 1977 collaboration, *Rough Mix*. Mel's first break was as a member of the Stormsville Shakers, which included Philip Goodhand-Tait (who wrote three songs that Roger Daltrey recorded in the 1970s, "Oceans Away," "Parade," and "Leon"). By 1969 the band had changed its name to Circus and recorded a self-titled album. However, by mid–1970 he had joined King Crimson and switched to Kokomo in 1973. Mel has backed an astounding number of artists, often more than once, including **Tina Turner**, Dire Straits, the **Rolling Stones**, and many art-rock performers.

Kooper, Al Keyboard player and record producer who has had a phenomenal career despite never really becoming a "star" in his own right. Kooper gained some recognition among performers in the mid–1960s for co-writing the #1 hit "This Diamond Ring" by Gary Lewis & the Playboys and for his first recording on organ, which happened to be on Bob Dylan's classic song "Like a Rolling Stone." Kooper's two-year-old band the Blues Project was one of the acts sharing the bill with the Who when the latter band made its American debut on Murray the K's 1967 Easter show. Kooper recounted his impressions of watching the Who that day in Dave Marsh's book *Before I Get Old*. At the conclusion of the Who's short set, Kooper said his heart "was beating three times its normal speed. I figure, as a critic of that show, my electrocardiogram was the best testimonial I could have offered." In August of that year Kooper played organ on different takes of the Who's "Mary Anne with the Shaky Hands," which were first released as CD bonus tracks in 1995 and 1998. At some point that same year Kooper left the Blues Project to form Blood, Sweat & Tears, but he didn't stay with that band long, either. Kooper went to work as a producer for Columbia Records and persuaded the label to sign the **Zombies** despite the fact that this British Invasion band hadn't had a hit in awhile and were close to dissolving. The Zombies did in fact break up just two short weeks after recording "Time of the Season" and it fell to Kooper to fight to have the record released in late '68. It became a #1 hit. In 1971 he and **Leslie West** recorded several songs with the Who, including a version of the **Holland/Dozier/Holland** composition "Baby Don't You Do It." This didn't surface until bonus tracks were added to the *Who's Next* album 1995. During those sessions Kooper also backed the Who on a different version of "Getting in Tune" but that wasn't officially released until 2003. In the early 1970s Kooper also discovered the Southern rock band Lynyrd Skynyrd and produced their first three albums. Among his other producing credits is the first **Tubes** album in 1975. Kooper has been a bit less active since the dawn of the 1980s.

LaBelle, Patti Singer from Philadelphia who has enjoyed some notable success in each of the last four decades. In 1962 the song "I Sold My Heart to the Junkman" gave Patti's relatively new group the Blue Belles a top 20 hit before she was 20 years old. The Blue Belles reached the top 40 two years later with a version of "You'll Never Walk Alone," the Rodgers and Hammerstein number from the 1945 musical *Carousel*. Patti LaBelle and the Blue Belles didn't have a hit for the rest of the decade and by 1970 acquired a new manager in Vicki Wickham, who had been the producer of the 1960s British TV music show *Ready Steady Go* (which had used the Who's "Anyway Anyhow Anywhere" as its theme song). Wickham persuaded the group to shorten its name to Labelle and move its sound toward funk and rock. In his book *Dear Boy* Tony Fletcher said that shortly after the Who finished *Tommy* Keith Moon drummed on some demos for Labelle, who had just been signed by Track Records, but his rate of drumming kept accelerating. Wickham said "he was extremely good but… I know we never used the demos."

With this connection to the Who, Labelle opened for them at concerts in 1971. In 1972 Labelle covered the Who's instant classic "Won't Get Fooled Again" on their album *Moon Shadow*. In 1974 they had the distinction of being the first African-American act ever to perform at New York's Metropolitan Opera House and a year later they had a #1 single, "Lady Marmalade." However, before long Labelle disbanded and Patti began her solo career in earnest in 1977. Patti had a #1 R&B hit with "If You Only Knew" in 1983 and in 1985 had a Top 20 hit on the pop charts with "New Attitude" from the soundtrack to Eddie Murphy's hit movie *Beverly Hills Cop*. The following year she and Michael McDonald had a very successful duet with "On My Own," which helped her album *The Winner in You* go platinum. Patti was the Acid Queen when the Who performed *Tommy* for charity in Los Angeles in 1989. This concert was released on video. In 1991 she won a Grammy Award for best female R&B performance with her album *Burnin'*. In 1995 she published her autobiography.

The Ladybirds Female trio familiar to British viewers on TV's *Top of the Pops* and *the Benny Hill Show* and which provided backing vocals on John Entwistle's third solo album, 1973's *Rigor Mortis Sets In*. The Ladybirds started out as a duo consisting of Maggie Stredder and Gloria George. The duo was an outgrowth of the Vernon Girls, which began as a much larger choir and recorded without success from 1958 to 1961. The Ladybirds released three 45s in 1964 and one more in '65. That year they also provided backing vocals on a 45 by Marc Bolan, who would go on to **John's Children** and T. Rex. They also recorded with Ronnie Aldrich, who was a longtime compatriot of **Cliff Townshend** and served as music director for Benny Hill. In July of 1968 the Ladybirds backed Gene Pitney and the Mike Cotton Jazzmen during a couple of TV appearances. By the time the Ladybirds worked with Entwistle they were a trio, having added Marion Davies. They backed John on the songs "Do the Dangle," "Made in Japan" and "Roller Skate Kate." Around this time Stredder also sang on **Roger Ruskin Spear**'s *Unusual* album. Subsequent recording credits for the Ladybirds included **Sandy Denny**'s *Rendezvous* album in 1977. "The Maggie Stredder Singers" were credited on "Best of" collections for Benny Hill in 1992 and **Jimi Hendrix** in 1998. In 1999 Stredder had gone full circle by performing as one of the Vernon Girls on the "Solid Gold Rock 'n' Roll Tour" with Eden Kane and others.

Lambert, Dave Guitarist with the British progressive rock band the Strawbs who released a solo album produced by John Entwistle. Entwistle also played bass on this 1979 album, which was called *Framed*. Lambert joined the Strawbs in 1972, just after **Rick Wakeman**'s three-year stint in the band. The Strawbs broke up by the end of the 1970s. Though they reformed in 1983 and have worked periodically since then, Lambert maintained a low profile for two decades before touring with the Strawbs in 1999.

Lambert, Kit Manager of the Who with **Chris Stamp** from 1964 into the 1970s. Christopher "Kit" Lambert was the son of famous English composer Constant Lambert. In the early 1960s Kit was an assistant director on such movies as *From Russia with Love* and *The Guns of Navarone*. In 1963 he and another assistant director, Stamp, decided to tap into Britain's pop music craze. They spent at least four months hunting for a relatively unknown group to showcase on camera. In the last half of 1964, not long after the Who temporarily became the **High Numbers**, **Richard Barnes** encountered Lambert at a concert. Lambert said he and **Mike Shaw** were looking for a pop group to appear in a film, and Barnes brought **Peter Meaden** over to meet him. This proved to be the beginning of the end for Meaden and nominal manager Helmut Gorden. Though Meaden had arranged for the band's first 45 and obtained some valuable publicity for them, it appeared that the band was starting to stall. Two to three weeks after Lambert and Shaw first saw the High Numbers Stamp saw them for the first time, and by mid–August Meaden and Gorden had largely been pushed out of the picture.

Early in Pete Townshend's development as a songwriter, Kit persuaded him to move into the spare room of Kit's flat in Belgravia. Kit would play Pete many classical recordings unearthed by Kit's father Constant, and several classical composers would thus exert some influence on Townshend over the years. By November the High Numbers had reverted to their previous name, the Who. When Lambert and Stamp created their New Action company, the only other people involved were Shaw and Kit's friend **Anya Butler**. Anya helped bring **Shel Talmy** in to produce records for the Who. Despite the success of the 45s released with Talmy in 1965, Lambert and Talmy could not get along. This also meant a sour relationship between Lambert and Talmy's assistant, **Glyn Johns**, which led to clashes during recording sessions in 1971.

Throughout their tenure with the Who Lambert and Stamp encouraged the band to be creative visually as well as encouraging Pete Townshend to be creative musically. In the book *Decade of the Who* John Entwistle noted that under Lambert and Stamp the Who "really just started the whole sort of Union Jack jacket thing, we started the whole sort of pop art thing. Kit was, I suppose, far seeing enough, to see that we had to innovate something else — in fact the Who never got the credit for starting that whole craze, but we actually did.... I mean, I was the first person to wear a shirt with sergeant stripes on it, and medals and stickers ... stuff like that ... And then the mass produced Union Jack shirts came out, and garbage, like Union Jack handbags...."

When Roger Daltrey was temporarily kicked out of the Who in late 1965, Lambert and Townshend considered merging the Who with **Paddy, Klaus and Gibson**. 1966 was marked by the Who's jump to **Robert Stigwood**'s new Reaction label and the resulting legal battles with Talmy, but Stamp and Lambert also became the managers of the **Merseys**. That group then released a version of the Pete Townshend composition "So Sad About Us" in July, before the Who released its own version. In September of 1966 Lambert saw **Jimi Hendrix** perform at a London night club and was disappointed to learn that manager Chas Chandler, the former **Animals** bassist, was already negotiating with Decca. When that deal fell through, Lambert was able to convince Polydor Records (which released Hendrix's "Hey Joe" in December of 1966) that his brash idea of forming a new label would be viable with Hendrix in addition to the Who. Thus on March 23, 1967, the Jimi Hendrix Experience's second single, "Purple Haze," was the debut single for Lambert and Stamp's Track Records. The Who's "Pictures of Lily" became the second Track single a month later (the woman in question being vaudeville actress **Lily Bayless**).

The band **John's Children** achieved its only real chart success after Lambert signed them to the Track label in 1967, with the song "Desdemona." Track had an even more successful recruit in 1968, when the Crazy World of **Arthur Brown** scored the #2 hit "Fire" in the U.S. Lambert was credited as producer of the song and the band's eponymous album. Lambert was widely credited with prodding Townshend to create a rock opera, and in 1969 this resulted in the Who's phenomenal double album *Tommy*. When Pete Townshend and Roger Daltrey were arrested in May of 1969 for booting plainclothes New York police officer **Daniel Mulhearn** off the stage during a concert, it was Lambert's vigorous advocacy that managed to free Daltrey, though Townshend faced a court appearance nine days later for third degree assault.

By 1969 Lambert and Stamp had turned the day-to-day operations of the Who over to **John "Wiggy" Wolff**, and Wiggy and Townshend tried mightily but ultimately in vain to resist **Frank Barsalona**'s effort to recruit the Who for the now-legendary Woodstock festival. When trying to follow up *Tommy* in 1971, Townshend was hoping to get the same kind of quality guidance from Lambert for the ambitious *Lifehouse* project, but Lambert proved unreliable. The Who then gave Glyn Johns freer reign to salvage a single disc, which became the hugely successful album *Who's Next*. Due to growing animosity between Roger Daltrey on the one hand and Lambert and Stamp on the other, Daltrey anointed **Bill Curbishley** as his personal manager for his 1973 debut solo album, *Daltrey*. Roger then snapped when an investigation revealed just how much of the Who's money was unaccounted for and soon insisted that Lambert and Stamp turn over managing responsibilities of the Who to Curbishley. Curbishley became the manager around the summer of 1974, and then many months were spent disentangling the Who contractually from New Action and Track Records. *Quadrophenia* was thus the last new Who album on which Lambert and Stamp were credited, as executive producers. However, in 1975 Stamp received credit as executive producer of the *Tommy* movie though there was no credit for Kit, who not only had pushed Townshend to develop a rock opera but was also among the earliest proponents of turning *Tommy* into a movie. Lambert then issued a press release threatening legal action against the movie's producer, the aforementioned Stigwood, and took swipes at the Who as well as his most loyal ally, Stamp.

This tirade may have been the result of Lambert's addiction to heroin, which also limited the amount of time he spent in the 1970s producing some early punk rock bands.

In the spring of 1978 *Melody Maker* reported one final nail in the coffin: Track Records had been liquidated (though it had essentially been dead for two years). In May of 1979 Lambert saw the Who with new drummer **Kenney Jones** twice in France and gave Townshend a critique after the first concert. One month after the new Who lineup released *Face Dances* in 1981, Kit died at the age of 45 from a brain hemorrhage after falling down a flight of stairs after having moved back in with his mother. On the Who's 1987 U.S. album *Two's Missing* their version of **Bo Diddley**'s "I'm a Man" from 1965 was incorrectly attributed to Lambert and Stamp.

Lamm, Robert *see* Chicago.

Lane, Nathan Popular Broadway actor who has also become a familiar face on television as well as in movies, such as *The Birdcage* (1996) and *Mousehunt* (1997). In the mid–1990s he appeared as the Cowardly Lion alongside Roger Daltrey's Tin Man on stage in *The Wizard of Oz in Concert: Dreams Come True*. The soundtrack for this Children's Defense Fund stage and TV benefit was released in 1996.

Lane, Ronnie Bassist for the **Small Faces** and **Meher Baba** follower with whom Pete Townshend collaborated with during the 1970s. Ronnie "Plonk" Lane re-recorded his song "Stone" from the Faces' 1970 album *First Step* and retitled it "Evolution" for the album *Happy Birthday*, a compilation devoted to Baba released that same year. That version was over six minutes long and was trimmed for Townshend's commercially-released spin-off, *Who Came First*, in 1972. Townshend confessed in the June 24, 1972 issue of *Sounds* that he took Lane's song and "edited out all the important verses." In 1973 Lane recut the song yet again for his first solo album. In 1975 Lane's mobile unit was used to record tracks for *The Who by Numbers*. With producer **Glyn Johns**, Lane and **Ron Wood** released the *Mahoney's Last Stand* album in 1976, around the time that Wood was jumping from the Faces to the **Rolling Stones**. Guests included Townshend and **Kenney Jones**. Pete and Kenney played on "Tonight's Number" and Pete supplied percussion on "Car Radio." Pete produced the single "Kuschty Rye" though not its B-side, "One Step." In 1977 Ronnie and Pete concluded their closest collaboration when the album *Rough Mix* was released to critical acclaim. In 1983 Lane was part of a supergroup that performed at a benefit concert for ARMS, Artists for Research into Multiple Sclerosis. The lineup, which was featured on a *Rolling Stone* cover, included Kenney Jones, **Eric Clapton**, **Jeff Beck**, **Steve Winwood**,

Andy Fairweather-Low, **Chris Stainton, Simon Phillips,** Jimmy Page of **Led Zeppelin,** and Charlie Watts and Bill Wyman from the **Rolling Stones.** Ronnie Lane died at the age of 51 in June of 1997 after battling MS.

Larden, Dennis *see* Nelson, Rick.

Lasley, David   American singer whose 1982 album *Missin' Twenty Grand* included Pete Townshend on guitar on the song "Roommate." **Jody Linscott** also performed on the album. Lasley released three albums from 1982 to '90 but has had much more success getting his songs on albums by other artists and as a prolific backing vocalist. In the 1970s he backed such artists as Bonnie Raitt, Melissa Manchester, ex–**Beatle** Ringo Starr, **Bette Midler,** Linda Ronstadt, Ace Frehley of Kiss, and Whitney Houston's mother, Cissy. During the 1980s he backed Aretha Franklin and Jimmy Buffett. He recorded with several of the aforementioned performers in the 1990s as well. Lasley has backed James Taylor several times from 1979 to the present and Luther Vandross from 1983 to the present. His songs have appeared on albums recorded by Vandross, Raitt, Aretha, and **Patti LaBelle,** among others.

The Law   Duo consisting of Paul Rodgers on vocals and **Kenney Jones** on drums that produced a self-titled album in 1991. This was Kenney's first band after leaving the Who. Rodgers had been in Free and **Bad Company** and recorded with **Led Zeppelin**'s Jimmy Page in the Firm prior to hooking up with Kenney. **Bryan Adams, Pink Floyd**'s David Gilmour, and Chris Rea were among the album's guitarists, each playing on one track. Keyboards and programming were credited to Steve Pigott and **Jon Astley** and **Pino Palladino** played bass.

Led Zeppelin   Leading heavy metal band of the 1970s that was named by a member of the Who. Zeppelin guitarist Jimmy Page had been a session musician in the mid–1960s and was present when the Who recorded "I Can't Explain" in 1965. Page did play on at least one version, but **Richard Barnes** said that Pete Townshend thinks the version that was released only featured Pete. Page did play on the flipside, "Bald Headed Woman," because he wouldn't let Townshend use his fuzzbox for the guitar solo. Page soon joined the Yardbirds but then **Jeff Beck** left. On May 16 and 17, 1966, Beck arranged a recording session involving Page, Keith Moon, **Nicky Hopkins** and future Zeppelin member John Paul Jones. Most sources indicate that this session was in June or July of 1967 but the new chronology *Jeff's Book* set the record straight. The primary result of this session was the song "Beck's Bolero," which surfaced on Jeff's album *Truth* in 1968. Timpani drumming was credited to "You Know Who."

Led Zeppelin

When the Yardbirds were dissolving in mid–1968, Page formed the New Yardbirds to fulfill contractual obligations and then changed the name to Led Zeppelin. Some sources indicate that Keith Moon came up with the name "Lead Zeppelin" while others attribute it to John Entwistle. "Lead" had become "Led" to assure the intended pronunciation. Entwistle and Moon had talked with **Richard Cole** at least once about quitting the Who and forming a new group with other top performers. Cole, who was the Who's driver for several months, later suggested the name to Jimmy Page while Page was in the Yardbirds and Cole was working for him. There is also disagreement regarding when this occurred. Some sources, most notably John Entwistle himself, indicate that he came up with the name in early 1966 just before Cole left the Who's employment. Others, such as Tony Fletcher in his Moon biography *Dear Boy*, state that Entwistle or Moon mentioned the name to Cole in August of 1968 when the Who duo bumped into Cole in New York City. It's possible that Cole did hear the name in 1966 and was merely reminded of it in 1968. In either case, Page wasn't present. Entwistle's claim was made most clearly in a *Rolling Stone* article that appeared on December 5, 1974. He even said he had designed an album cover much like the one used for Led Zeppelin's first album. Also around this time, in the book *Decade of the Who*, Entwistle seemed glad that he hadn't joined Page's band: "I'm not really into heavy heavy music — like heavy riffs and stuff like that. I don't possess any Deep Purple or Led Zeppelin records at all. Never have done."

Led Zeppelin opened for the Who in Maryland on May 24, 1969, with reserved seats priced under six dollars. In his introduction to Eddie McSquare's book *Led Zeppelin: Good Times, Bad Times*, John Paul Jones wrote: "We were no different from any other rock 'n' roll band around at the time — pretty raucous. But we didn't do anything particularly unusual in those days, and meeting the Who on the road we felt positively tame!" Led Zeppelin had a number of hit albums and very popular songs in the 1970s, most notably "Stairway to Heaven," but they disbanded after drummer John Bonham died in 1980.

Page and singer Robert Plant continue to be popular artists. On September 14, 1997 John Paul Jones was among the invited guests who watched Pete Townshend give one of the speeches at the London ceremony unveiling a Blue Plaque in honor of **Jimi Hendrix**. In 1999 Ann Wilson of **Heart** and Roger Daltrey sang Led Zeppelin's "Kashmir" on the **British Rock Symphony** CD. In 2000 **Bill Curbishley** arranged for the Who and another client, Jimmy Page and the Black Crowes, to minimize tour expenses by often playing in the same venue on consecutive nights. Robert Plant opened for the Who on tour in 2002.

Lee, Spike Acclaimed director of such movies as *Do the Right Thing* in 1989 and *Mo' Better Blues*, *Jungle Fever*, and *Malcolm X* in the 1990s. Lee's 1999 movie *Summer of Sam*, which was set in 1977, made prominent use of two Who classics from 1971, "Baba O'Riley" and "Won't Get Fooled Again."

Lennon, John *see* The Beatles.

Lennox, Annie *see* Eurythmics.

Liberace Flamboyant American pianist who amassed two Emmy Awards and six gold albums. "Mr. Showmanship" was known for candelabras and ornately decorated pianos. Part of his success was due to his television series, which began in 1952. Liberace's *Love & Music Festival—Live* album in 1971 included his version of the Who's "Overture from Tommy." In the book *Before I Get Old* Dave Marsh noted that Keith Moon "liked theater and theatrical music, even listing Liberace among his favorites." Born Wladziu Valentino Liberace in the Milwaukee suburb of West Allis in 1919, he died in 1987.

The Lightning Seeds Pop act that serves as a performing vehicle for producer Ian Broudie. Broudie was born in 1958 in Liverpool and by the time he was 25 years old he had produced the first two Echo and the Bunnymen albums. Other production work has followed regularly, such as Alison Moyet's 1994 album *Essex*. Under the Lightning Seeds name Broudie had a hit with the single "Pure" in the late 1980s and followed it immediately with an album. The second Lightning Seeds album was released in 1992 and synthesizer programmer Simon Rogers became Broudie's partner. Rogers had been in the Fall, for whom Broudie produced albums in the later 1980s. Broudie and Rogers did the synthesizer programming on the track "**Meher Baba** M4 (Signal Box)" on Pete Townshend's 1993 *Psychoderelict* album.

Lily *see* Bayless, Lily.

Lind, Jon Songwriter and singer who has co-written songs with **Billy Nicholls** for two Who-related projects. In between, Lind co-wrote Vanessa Williams's 1991 Grammy-nominated song "Save the Best for Last." Among Lind's earlier credits as a singer was backing **John Sebastian** on his 1976 album *Welcome Back*. His other notable singing credits were on two of Cher's albums in the late 1980s. Lind helped Nicholls write "White City Lights," which appeared on the soundtrack of Roger Daltrey's ***McVicar*** movie in 1980. With Nicholls and **Jon Astley**, Lind composed the music for "Fake It" on Pete Townshend's 1993 album *Psychoderelict*; Pete wrote the lyrics. Lind also co-wrote "Psycho Montage" and an alternate version of "Early Morning Dreams" with Townshend and Nicholls; the two songs were bonus tracks on European CD singles of "English Boy," Pete's first single from *Psychoderelict*. Other songs by Lind appear on the two albums by Cher and two by Aaron Neville as well as on multiple albums by Earth, Wind & Fire and by Madonna.

Linscott, Jody   American percussionist who has been among the few women besides vocalists to back members of the Who. Jody hails from the Boston area. Her earliest credits include albums with **Kokomo** in 1975, Robert Palmer in 1976, and **David Sanborn** in 1976 and 1979. She has recorded and toured with many other very well known artists; her recording credits in the 1980s include albums with ex–**Beatle** Paul McCartney in 1984 and **Elton John** in 1986. Early in the 1980s she played on Pete Townshend's solo album *All the Best Cowboys Have Chinese Eyes* and was a member of his **Deep End** band in 1985 and '86. Jody backed the Who on its 1989 reunion tour. In 1992 she played on Roger Daltrey's solo album *Rocks in the Head,* backed Pete on his *Psychoderelict* album the next year, and the year after that returned to working with Roger for his 1994 CD *A Celebration — The Music of Pete Townshend and the Who*. She was among the musicians who performed with the London Philharmonic Orchestra on the 1998 album *Who's Serious* and she can be heard on Pete Townshend's 1999 *Live* CD.

Liszt, Franz   Hungarian composer who lived in the 1800s and who was portrayed by Roger Daltrey in the 1975 movie *Lisztomania*. This over-the-top film was Ken Russell's follow-up to *Tommy* and was Daltrey's second starring vehicle. **Rick Wakeman** and Roger Daltrey dominated the movie's soundtrack, and Daltrey teamed with **Jonathan Benson** to add lyrics to several melodies. Liszt, who was considered the greatest pianist of his time, influenced Richard Wagner and Richard Strauss while also teaching most of the major pianists of the generation following his.

Little, Carlo   Drummer who discretely gave Keith Moon lessons in the early 1960s, when Keith was a member of the **Escorts**. Moon always claimed to be self-taught, but Little's instruction was one of several big revelations in Tony Fletcher's Moon biography *Dear Boy*. Little formed a band called the Savages in 1960, and about a year later he would use the name as one of Lord Sutch's backing musicians. Keith saw them on June 25, 1962, and approached Little about tutoring him. Around 1963 Little joined Cyril Davies' All-Stars but the group disbanded at the beginning of 1964 when Davies died. In 1970 Keith shared Carlo's drum kit onstage during a concert by Screaming Lord Sutch and the Savages, which was the basis for their *Hands of Jack the Ripper* album. Carlo soon left the band and it was renamed Screaming Lord Sutch and His Whole Lotta Shakin'. Little did a little session work in the 1970s and picked up the pace from 1982 to '86 as a drummer or producer. However, none of these performers were particularly well known. He then disappeared from the music scene. *Salon* magazine reported in 1999 that instead of becoming the **Rolling Stones'** permanent drummer in the early 1960s, as he reportedly had a chance to be, the 60-year-old Little was a food vendor in London outside a Stones concert. Little said he declined to stick with the Stones because they couldn't promise him many gigs or much money, but he added, "I have no regrets, even though I could have become a millionaire, but then I remember that I'm alive and happy."

Little Steven *see* Van Zandt, "Little Steven."

Lloyd Webber, Andrew   Collaborator with **Tim Rice** on such popular musicals as *Joseph and the Amazing Technicolor Dreamcoat*, *Jesus Christ Superstar*, and *Evita*. Another huge success for Lloyd Webber has been the musical *Cats*. In a 1996 BBC radio production of *Jesus Christ Superstar* Roger Daltrey was Judas and former **Spandau Ballet** lead singer Tony Hadley had the title role. Around the same time Daltrey was interviewed for the UK fan publication *Naked Eye*. Although Roger has not been enamored of Pete Townshend's interest in staging *Tommy* and other Who works on Broadway, Roger did say, "When you see things like Prats, sorry Cats, which possibly has one good song … And has been on stage forever, I just feel Pete's been cheated."

The London Symphony Orchestra   Famous musical ensemble that has performed Who music on occasion, as well as other rock songs. The LSO was instrumental in making **Lou Reizner**'s orchestral version of *Tommy* a reality in 1972. Pete Townshend and **Raphael Rudd** worked with the LSO late in the decade to augment the soundtrack for the movie *Quadrophenia*. In 1978 the LSO included a new version of "Pinball Wizard" with minimal vocals by Townshend on its album *The Second Movement*. This piece reappeared on the 1997 album *Symphonic Rock-The British Invasion Volume 1*. *Volume 2* the next year included a performance of the Who's "Pictures of Lily." In 1984 the LSO was featured when **Lewis Carroll**'s epic nonsense poem "The Hunting of the Snark" was transformed into a musical by **Mike Batt**. Roger Daltrey portrayed the Barrister and sang lead on "The Pig Must Die." It was the London Philharmonic Orchestra and not the LSO that was featured on the 1998 album *Who's Serious*.

Lord Sutch *see* Little, Carlo.

Love Critically acclaimed Los Angeles band for whom Keith Moon drummed in 1974, on their *Reel to Real* album. Love was formed in 1965 and led by singer/guitarist Arthur Lee. They proved popular with music critics from their self-titled debut album in 1966 through several lineup overhauls. By 1976 Lee had largely turned his back on show business to paint houses in LA but he reconvened the original Love lineup for an album in 1978. Subsequently Lee was rarely heard from until 1989 when he revived the Love name again. Lee remained active until the fall of 1996 when he was sentenced to eight years in prison for illegal possession of a firearm.

Love, Darlene Singer who performed "Let It Be" with Roger Daltrey on the 1999 **British Rock Symphony** and whose recording career dates back to the 1950s. In 1957 she was a founding member of an influential girl-group, the Blossoms. In addition to enjoying an extensive recording career, the Blossoms were one of the resident groups on the U.S. television show *Shindig*. The Who appeared on the show three times. In the Who movie *The Kids Are Alright* the Blossoms and the Wellingtons were mentioned briefly during one old clip from the show. Due to her association with producer Phil Spector, Love sang lead vocals on the Crystals' "He's a Rebel." Love released six 45s under her own name and reached the top 30 in the U.S. with "Wait Til My Bobby Gets Home" in 1963. In the 1980s she appeared in the first two *Lethal Weapon* movies with Mel Gibson and Danny Glover as well as in a Royal **Shakespeare** Company production of Stephen King's horror novel *Carrie*. In 1996 she teamed with **Merry Clayton** and Marianne Faithfull to perform a cabaret billed as "20th Century Pop." Regarding the British Rock Symphony performance, Love said Daltrey was the only singer who memorized his lyrics early and that she and the other singers taped theirs to the floor while trying to memorize them. Roger would wander around during rehearsals just to walk all over the pieces of paper.

The Lovin' Spoonful *see* Sebastian, John.

Luongo, Steve The John Entwistle Band's drummer and musical director. Steve met John in 1987, in Chicago. Entwistle soon found himself performing several Who songs at the Vic Theater with Luongo's band, Rat Race Choir. This led to a joint tour later that year. John recorded an album with **Zak Starkey** around that time and when he decided to tour in 1988, Steve stepped in for Zak. In 1989 he backed **Leslie West** in the studio and then on tour. He has also been a songwriter, including for movie soundtracks, and appeared briefly in an episode of NBC's long-running drama *Law & Order*. Luongo and **Godfrey Townsend** played with the John Entwistle Band since its formation in 1995. One side project for Steve was playing drums on Leslie West's 1999 album *As Phat as It Gets*. Steve's wife Laurie helps run the agency that coordinates activities for the John Entwistle Band, Bitsa Talent of Lake Peekskill, New York. Bitsa also handles bookings for Steve Luongo & Friends, which Bitsa describes as an "ever changing group of musicians that perform at a variety of events. Steve started inviting his fellow musicians to take part in jam sessions during the winter holiday season. The idea was to collect coats for the homeless, toys for underprivileged or hospitalized children and even towels and food for the Humane Society. These jam sessions became more frequent and the list of superstar friends got longer." In 2001 Entwistle, Luongo, and Townsend toured with **Todd Rundgren**, **Alan Parsons**, and Ann Wilson of **Heart** in the **Beatles** tribute billed as a *Walk Down Abbey Road*.

Lyle, Graham *see* Gallagher and Lyle.

Lynch, John   Star of the movie *Best*, which also featured Roger Daltrey. Lynch portrayed soccer star **George Best**. Lynch, born in Northern Ireland in 1961, has been in a movie or two most years since 1990. He also played Drew Carey's brother Steve in a 1997 episode of the ABC television comedy the *Drew Carey Show*.

Lynn, Vera   Popular British singer of the 1940s and '50s who was called "The Forces' Sweetheart" during World War II. The musical career of Pete Townshend's eventual father-in-law, **Ted Astley**, got an early big boost when she recorded a song he co-wrote. Pete Townshend characterized his own singing on the song "Content" on his *Who Came First* album as similar to that of Dame Vera.

The Machine *see* Covey, Julian.

Mancini, Henry   American composer, arranger and conductor who received 20 Grammy Awards, which remained the all-time record for a pop artist throughout his lifetime. His 1971 album *Mancini Concert* included "Overture from 'Tommy' (A Rock Opera)" and this cover of the Who's instrumental reappeared on Mancini's 1993's *Moon River* album, a greatest hits collection. Mancini died the following year. He was born in 1924 and had a career in film and TV that spanned four decades. His earliest successes included film scores for such movies as the *Glenn Miller Story* (1954) and the *Benny Goodman Story* (1956). He wrote theme songs for several TV series, including *Peter Gunn* and *Newhart*. The former theme earned him two of his Grammy Awards. He also won four Oscars, two for 1961's *Breakfast at Tiffany's*. That soundtrack also netted five Grammy Awards. It included "Moon River," for which Johnny Mercer provided lyrics. Mercer did the same for another hit of Mancini's, "Days of Wine and Roses." That song added an Oscar and two more Grammy Awards to Mancini's totals. His other notable songs include "Dear Heart." He also had a #1 hit and won yet another Grammy for Nino Rota's "Love Theme from Romeo and Juliet." He also provided the memorable theme for the *Pink Panther* and reeled in three more Grammy Awards.

Mann, Manfred   The name of both a successful British group of the 1960s and the stage name of one of its members. Keyboard player Michael Lubowitz, who had studied at New York's renowned Julliard School of Music, adopted the name Manfred Mann and he and drummer Mike Hugg formed the Mann-Hugg Blues Brothers in 1962. About a year later the group became simply Manfred Mann. Their third single, "5-4-3-2-1," brought them some chart success; it was used in the movie *Quadrophenia* in 1979. What really established them was their #1 hit in 1964, "Do Wah Diddy Diddy." Manfred Mann soon covered the Who's "My Generation" on a couple of discs released in the UK. Later in the 1960s they would again have a memorable hit with a cover of Bob Dylan's "Mighty Quinn." Mann and Hugg recruited a new lineup under the name Manfred Mann's Chapter Three for albums in 1969 and 1970. Mann and Hugg then parted company and in 1971 Mann formed Manfred Mann's Earth Band. Guitarist Chris Thompson joined in time for their very successful cover of Bruce Springsteen's "Blinded by the Light" in 1976.

In 1983 Manfred Mann's Earth Band became the first western rock band to work in then-communist Hungary. Thompson, who had released the first of several solo albums in 1983, was principal writer of the song "Move Better in the Night" on Roger Daltrey's 1985 album *Under a Raging Moon*. Playing on that album was Thompson's frequent bandmate **Robbie McIntosh**. In 1986 Thompson's song "It's Not Over" from his third solo album appeared on the soundtrack of the movie *Playing for Keeps,* which also featured a new Pete Townshend song, "Life to Life." In 1992 Thompson played an important behind-the-scenes roll for **Queen**'s Freddie Mercury Tribute Concert held at Wembley Stadium. He thus worked with Roger Daltrey again. Thompson performed on **Alan Parsons** Project albums in 1993 and 1995 and on the Manfred Mann's Earth Band album *Soft Vengeance* in 1996.

Markee, Dave   Bass player who performed on numerous albums during the 1970s, 1980s, and 1990s, including the Pete Townshend/**Ron-**

nie Lane *Rough Mix* album in 1977 and the *McVicar* soundtrack in 1980. He also played on at least two albums for Alan Price, **Leo Sayer**, Cleo Laine, **Joan Armatrading**, and **Eric Clapton**.

Marsh, Rodney   Soccer player portrayed by Roger Daltrey in the movie *Best*, the story of Manchester United soccer legend **George Best**. In 1976 the Tampa Bay Rowdies of the North American Soccer League spent $80,000 to acquire Marsh from the British team Queens Park Rangers.

Martha and the Vandellas   One of the most successful "girl groups" of the 1960s and the pinnacle as far as the Who were concerned. Martha Reeves and two high school classmates had recorded once as the Del-Phis before Reeves was hired for a secretarial job at Motown in 1960. There are differing stories about how the name "Vandellas" originated but their chart success using that name began in 1963 and quickly hit it very big with "Heat Wave" and "Dancing in the Street," both top five hits in 1964. The latter, co-written by **Marvin Gaye**, was recorded by the Who for a radio show in March of 1966. They also played it live in Philadelphia in late 1979 and this performance turned up in mid–1988 on a 12" single of "Won't Get Fooled Again." "Heat Wave" was one of two **Holland/Dozier/Holland** compositions that Martha and the Vandellas first recorded and which the Who covered; the second was 1965's "Motoring." The Who's version of "Heat Wave" appeared on their *A Quick One* album in 1966 though it was replaced on the U.S. Album to make room for the hit "Happy Jack." The Who had recorded a longer version of "Heat Wave" in March of 1965 but it didn't turn up until the album *Two's Missing* was released in the U.S. in 1987. That album also included the Who's version of "Motoring" for the first time though it was recorded only a month or so after Martha and the Vandellas debuted it.

Martha and the Vandellas had more Top 10 hits from 1965 to '67 but then were unable to achieve much more success. They gave a farewell performance in Detroit just before Christmas in 1972. Martha Reeves continued as a solo performer on other major labels but still without commercial success. Martha and the Vandellas were inducted into the Rock and Roll Hall of Fame in 1995. On February 15, 1998, the ABC network aired a Motown birthday special that included a segment about non–Motown bands performing Motown tunes, and among the clips was video footage of the Who performing "Heat Wave" on the 1960s show *The Beat Club*.

Marvin, Hank *see* The Shadows.

McAnuff, Des Director who won a 1993 Tony Award for the Broadway musical *The Who's Tommy*. McAnuff worked in theater in his native Canada during the 1970s and became artistic director of California's La Jolla Playhouse in 1983. During his 11 years there the Playhouse won more than 200 awards, including the 1993 Tony Award for Outstanding Regional Theatre. McAnuff has also directed movies, beginning with *Cousin Bette*, an adaptation of the Honore de Balzac novel. He co-produced the critically acclaimed 1999 animated movie *The Iron Giant*, for which Pete Townshend received credit as executive producer. The movie was based on the story by **Ted Hughes**, as was Pete's 1989 *Iron Man* album. In 2000 McAnuff directed *Rocky and Bullwinkle*.

McArdle, Andrea American singer and actress most known for portraying Little Orphan Annie on Broadway starting in 1977. She was 13. A few years earlier she made her acting debut on the soap opera *Search for Tomorrow* and she maintained that job until *Annie* came along. In 1978 she portrayed Judy Garland in the TV movie *Rainbow*. She appeared in a few other Broadway productions in the 1980s. In 1995 she released a CD titled *On Broadway* and it included a version of the Who's "Pinball Wizard." The next year she starred in a Broadway production of Rodgers & Hammerstein's *State Fair*.

McBrain, Nicko *see* Iron Maiden.

McCallum, Val Singer for whom the **High Numbers** served as a backing band in 1964. McCallum was just starting out but was considered a more promising act than the High Numbers, whose reward for backing her was a 15-minute spot of their own on the bill. According to **Richard Barnes**, the High Numbers backed her at a concert headlined by the **Beatles** (August 16), by Dusty Springfield (August 23), and by Lulu and the Luvvers and Dave Berry & the Cruisers (September 4 in Glasgow). Barnes said the High Numbers didn't enjoy backing McCallum, which Keith Moon ultimately demonstrated by playing a toy cymbal during one of her songs. She saw to it that they would no longer be her backing band, which they didn't mind. About two months later the High Numbers became the Who for good.

McCartney, Paul *see* The Beatles.

McCulloch, Jimmy *see* Thunderclap Newman.

McEnroe, John Petulant tennis star and occasional guitarist who, along with lesser known tennis player Pat Cash, recorded three versions of **Led Zeppelin**'s "Rock and Roll" for Rock Aid Armenia in 1991, to benefit that region in Asia Minor in the wake of a 1988 earthquake. They were backed by the Full Metal Rackets, which included Roger Daltrey on vocals and **Iron Maiden**'s Steve Harris and Nicko McBrain on bass and drums, respectively. The session also included **Andy Barnett** on slide guitar.

McHugh, Paddy *see* Kokomo.

McInnerney, Mike Artist who introduced his friend Pete Townshend to the teachings of **Meher Baba** and created the cover of the *Tommy* album. McInnerney also provided seven pages of paintings for the booklet that came with the double LP. He and Katie, his wife at the time, hosted gatherings of Baba followers at their Victorian villa. A few years later he produced the poster that came with Pete's album *Who Came First*. His main source of income, however, was as a painter working primarily for glossy magazines.

McIntosh, Robbie Guitarist on all songs on Roger Daltrey's 1985 album *Under a Raging Moon*. However, in the video for "Let Me Down Easy," one of the singles from that album, **Bryan Adams**, the song's author, is quite noticeable on guitar. McIntosh helped Chris Thompson of **Manfred Mann**'s Earth Band write the song "Move Better in the Night" on the album. McIntosh played with a number of smaller bands during the '70s, before he was offered a part in the group Night, which was fronted by Thompson. McIntosh also played in Thompson's Islands before joining the **Pretenders** for five years in the mid–1980s. From 1989 to 1993 he appeared on several albums by ex–**Beatle** Paul McCartney. In 1997 he was credited on Celine Dion's hugely successful *Let's Talk About Love* album.

McMahon, Gerard Songwriter and musician who has collaborated with Roger Daltrey. For Roger's 1992 solo album *Rocks in the Head* Gerard served as producer, guitarist, keyboardist, backing vocalist, and songwriter. He wrote "Who's Gonna Walk on Water," "Mirror Mirror" and "Perfect World" and co-wrote all but one of the other songs on the album with David Katz, **Ricky Byrd**, and/or Daltrey. McMahon had a few vocal credits on some minor albums in the 1970s and during the next decade found more success as a songwriter. For example, he landed songs on an album for Kiss in 1980, the *Fast Times at Ridgemont High* soundtrack in 1982, and Carly Simon's *Coming Around Again* in 1987. In the 1990s songs of his appeared on **Chicago**'s twenty-first album in 1991 and Chicago keyboard player Robert Lamm's solo albums in 1995 and 1999. Most recently, Roger Daltrey has reported that he and McMahon have written songs with an eye toward the first all-new Who album since *It's Hard* in 1982. Roger sang one song they wrote on the *Banger Sisters* soundtrack in 2002.

McVicar, John Convicted bank robber and famous escapee who was portrayed in the 1980 movie *McVicar* by Roger Daltrey. A meeting between Roger Daltrey and McVicar had earlier provided the inspiration for Daltrey to work with **David Courtney** on the song "The Prisoner," which appeared on Roger's 1977 solo album *One of the Boys*. While McVicar was loose he had gained even more notoriety by getting messages printed by newspapers in which he taunted the police. When he was recaptured he proved to be a very persuasive critic of the British penal system, in part by publishing an autobiography. McVicar thus earned an early release. **Bill Curbishley** spent three years raising funds for the movie and produced it with **Roy Baird**. **Adam Faith** had one of the supporting roles. **Richard Barnes** noted that despite many bad reviews in England the movie "was still a number one box office success." The soundtrack also yielded two hits for Roger, **Russ Ballard**'s powerful song "Free Me" and **Billy Nicholls**' ballad "Without Your Love." The soundtrack LP reached #22 in the U.S. and #39 in the UK. "Free Me" hit #53 in the U.S. but managed to slip into the top 40 in the UK. "Without Your Love" reached #55 in the UK but climbed to #20 in the U.S. John McVicar earned a college degree while in prison and went straight upon his release, eventually becoming a professional writer and a broadcaster. As part of an article in a 1998 issue of the British periodical *Punch*, McVicar discussed Curbishley's experience as someone wrongfully convicted of a crime.

Meaden, Peter Publicist who spent just a few months with the Who and their alter ego the **High Numbers** in 1964 but who had a significant effect on them. Meaden had worked with **Rolling Stones** manager Andrew Loog Oldham and according to Dave Marsh in *Before I Get Old* claimed to have lived with Mick Jagger and Keith Richards. Meaden learned of the Who and how to contact their manager Helmut Gorden through their mutual barber. Because he knew more about the music business than Gorden and was a bundle of energy, for all intents and purposes Meaden quickly became the Who's co-manager. During Meaden's tenure with the Who Keith Moon replaced **Doug Sandom** as drummer. In the November 17, 1979 issue of *New Musical Express* several interviews with Meaden were strung together and included Meaden's claim that he had been responsible for bringing Keith Moon in to audition for the band, which was contrary to all other accounts of Moon's debut.

By the beginning of July Meaden had persuaded the members of the Who to adopt the mod lifestyle, at least publicly, and to change the band's name to the High Numbers because the name fit with mod slang. Embracing mod ways helped to build the band's fan base, so much so that almost a decade later Pete Townshend devoted the entire double album *Quadrophenia* to this brief era in the band's history. At this time Meaden was able to get a 45 recorded and released for the High Numbers with assistance from **Jack Baverstock**. Though Pete Townshend had already written at least one song by this point, called "It Was You," Meaden decided to change **Slim Harpo**'s "Got Love If You Want It" into "I'm the Face" for one side of the 45 and the 1961 song "Country Fool" by a group called the Showmen into "Zoot Suit." To promote the 45 Meaden drafted a press release which concluded by calling the High Numbers "about the most potentially exciting and powerful group in the field of beat music today. The things expressed on this, their first record, cause an immediate rapport between them and thousands of young people like themselves. In a nutshell—they are of the people."

Around the time of the 45 and press release **Richard Barnes** encountered **Kit Lambert** at a concert. Lambert said he was looking for a pop group to appear in a film, and Barnes brought Meaden over to speak with Kit. This proved to be the beginning of the end for Meaden and nominal manager Gorden. By mid–August Meaden and Gorden had largely been pushed out of the picture by Lambert and **Chris Stamp**. Around this time the High Numbers had its first encounters with some noteworthy bands by playing support for them, such as the **Kinks** on July 31 and the **Beatles** on August 16. These gigs should probably be credited to Meaden. In the October 11, 1975 issue of *New Musical Express* Meaden talked about his new job managing the **Steve Gibbons** Band, which he did with **Bill Curbishley** until shortly before committing suicide by overdosing on drugs on August 7, 1978, one month prior to Keith Moon's death.

Meaney, Colm   Acclaimed character actor who has had supporting roles in a number of movies but who is perhaps best known as Chief Miles O'Brien on *Star Trek: Deep Space Nine* as well as the early years of *Star Trek: The Next Generation*. Meaney portrayed Seamus Muldoon in "The Magical Legend of the Leprechauns," a four-hour TV special on NBC in 1999 that also starred Roger Daltrey as King Boric.

Meat Loaf   Stocky American singer who had an enormously successful album in 1977, *Bat Out of Hell*, which eventually went platinum on the strength of songs like "Two Out of Three Ain't Bad." Meat Loaf, who was born Marvin Lee Aday in 1947, moved from Texas to California by 1966 and formed bands alternately known as Meat Loaf Soul and Popcorn Blizzard. By the time of his band's split in 1969 they had opened for the Who, **Ted Nugent**, Iggy Pop and the Stooges, and the Winter brothers. In the 1970s Meat Loaf appeared in a traveling production of the musical *Hair,* sang lead on one side of Nugent's gold album *Free for All,* and appeared in the cult movie *The Rocky Horror Picture Show* before *Bat Out of Hell* started its climb up the charts. Meat Loaf's 1984 album *Bad Attitude* included a duet with Roger Daltrey on the title track. This album and others have failed to approach the success of *Bat Out of Hell*.

Meehan, Tony see The Shadows.

Meg see Patterson, Meg.

Merchan, Chucho   Colombian bass player who has worked with Pete Townshend and with the **Eurythmics** on a number of occasions. Among his earliest notable credits was playing on Pete's 1985 album *White City*. This led to a few live performances as part of Pete's **Deep End** band around the end of the year. Soon thereafter, on February 9, 1986, Chucho organized a special concert in England to help victims of a volcano eruption in his homeland, and the lineup included Chrissie Hynde of the **Pretenders**, Dave Gilmour of **Pink Floyd**, and Annie Lennox of the Eurythmics. **Emma Townshend** made her stage debut with father Pete. Within two years Chucho performed on the next Pretenders album and played live with the Eurythmics. He would go on to play on Eurythmics albums in 1989 and 1999 and two of Dave Stewart's solo projects in between. Chucho played bass on the song "Cat Snatch," which appeared on Pete's 1987 album *Another Scoop*. Two years later he played bass on all but the two Who songs on Pete's *Iron Man* album, his musical adaptation of the **Ted Hughes** tale. Chucho also served as the orchestral arranger. That same year he served as assistant musical director to **Billy Nicholls** for the Who's reunion tour.

In 1990 Chucho joined a few other names familiar to Who fans on Nicholls' album *Under One Banner*. On December 4, 1992, he played with Roger Daltrey, Gilmour, and Phil Manzanera at the ECOMUNDO Conference in Colombia. In mid–1996 Pete Townshend was interviewed on Jools Holland's BBC TV show and then Pete performed three songs, "Let My Love Open the Door," "English Boy," and "Magic Bus," the latter two with Chucho. In 1998 he made several appearances with Pete, including live in Boston in August. However, on the 9th the *Boston Globe* said the bass player would be "Sherman Sean," which has to be one of the worst typographical errors ever. Two songs which Chucho helped Pete perform at the Shepherds Bush Empire in 1998, "Won't Get Fooled Again" and "Who Are You," turned up later on Pete's *Lifehouse Chronicles*. In addition, Chucho performed with Pete at London's Vibe Bar on November 16 for the VH1 *Storytellers* series on cable TV. Chucho also played bass with

Townshend's band for the Maryville Academy in Chicago, which led to Pete's 1999 *Live* CD with "mystery guest" Eddie Vedder of **Pearl Jam**.

Mercury, Freddie *see* Queen.

The Merseys Group that released a version of the Pete Townshend composition "So Sad About Us" before the Who did. After having some chart success as the Merseybeats from 1963 through 1965, thanks in part to **Jack Baverstock**, this British band dissolved into a duo, shortened their name, picked up a backing band called the Fruit-Eating Bears, and took on **Kit Lambert** and **Chris Stamp** as their management. John Entwistle and Keith Moon assisted the Bears live on February 24, 1966. They released "So Sad About Us" as a 45 A-side in July of 1966. The Who's version debuted on their album *A Quick One* in December. The Merseys faded from view about a year later. "Wishin' & Hopin'" by the Merseybeats was used in the movie *Quadrophenia* in 1979.

Metheny, Pat Acclaimed guitarist who played with Pete Townshend toward the end of 1990 on the Showtime cable network's music series *Showtime Coast to Coast*, including on the songs "I Put a Spell on You" and "Magic Bus." The latter also featured the show's host, **Herbie Hancock**, with whom Metheny toured that year. In 1991 Pete guested with the Pat Metheny Group at the Fridge in Brixton, London. Metheny has been known for being very creative, original, and risky from fairly early in his career. Metheny, whose older brother Mike is a noted trumpeter, was 20 when he took part in his recordings in 1974. In 1978 he formed his group, which quickly established itself as a top jazz act.

Midler, Bette Popular American singer and movie star who appeared as Mrs. Walker in the Seattle Opera Association's 1971 production of *Tommy* early in her career. Later in that decade, after she'd made it big, Pete Townshend wrote two songs intended for her. One appeared on his 1980 album *Empty Glass* and another a few years later on his first compilation of demos, *Scoop*. In the latter album's liner notes for the song "You're So Clever" he wrote: "I first put the lyric together at the same time as 'And I Moved' for submission to Bette Midler. Neither song ever reached her." In 1996 the CD-ROM "Pete Townshend Presents *Tommy*: The Interactive Adventure Then & Now" was released, and one of the pull-down menus leads to some racy photos of Midler during her 1971 performance in Seattle. In 2000 Midler starred in a new weekly TV series.

Miller, Pamela *see* Des Barres, Pamela.

Millington, Jean *see* Fanny.

The Miracles *see* Robinson, Smokey.

Mitchell, Mitch *see* Hendrix, Jimi.

Monty Python's Flying Circus   Very popular British comedy troupe that jumped in the 1970s from a successful TV series to a string of popular movies. In **Dennis Wholey**'s 1984 book *The Courage to Change: Hope and Help for Alcoholics and Their Families* Monty Python's Graham Chapman was quoted briefly about his friend Keith Moon (the book also shines a spotlight on Pete Townshend in three chapters). Chapman and Moon became friends after the 1974 release of *Monty Python and the Holy Grail*, the troupe's first original movie. Keith later provided seed money for Chapman's movie *The Odd Job*. In 1977 Chapman, a heavy drinker like Moon, somehow managed to survive quitting cold turkey and made a sincere commitment to do whatever it took to help Keith quit as well. Keith showed some signs of making progress but Who fans know the sad outcome of the story all too well.

Members of Monty Python were on the same bill as Pete Townshend when he performed solo at the Secret Policeman's Ball for Amnesty International on June 30, 1979. At the end of 1985 Pete and his wife Karen presided over a charitable event at which Monty Python's Michael Palin was among the celebrities who appeared. Over the years the members of Monty Python have been successful working alone or in pairs. For example, Palin and John Cleese teamed up for the hit comedy *A Fish Called Wanda* and troupe animator Terry Gilliam directed the movies *Time Bandits*, *Brazil*, and *The Adventures of Baron Munchausen*. Graham Chapman died of cancer on October 4, 1989 but it wasn't until 1997 that the book *Graham Crackers* was published. This book, which was compiled from various sources, contained two brief chapters about Keith Moon in Chapman's own words.

The Moody Blues   British band that firmly established itself by combining pop songs with classical music on its 1967 album *Days of Future Passed*. However, it took until 1970 for the album to go gold, and its primary single, "Nights in White Satin," peaked in the top five in the U.S. in 1972. Their new album that year, *Seventh Sojourn*, reached #1 in the U.S. but the band shifted into neutral from then until 1978 so its members could pursue outside projects. One of those was the Justin Hayward/John Lodge band Blue Jays. In 1975 Justin played on the **John Alcock**/John Entwistle *Flash Fearless* album, as did Blue Jays Kirk Duncan and **Graham Deakin**. The Moody Blues' 1981 album *Long Distance Voyager* was another #1 album for the band, and they've continued to release albums and tour at regular intervals ever since.

Moon, Keith   Astoundingly fast drummer for the Who. Keith Moon was born to Alf and Kitty Moon on August 23, 1946 and died on September 8, 1978. He had two sisters, Linda and Leslie. **Doug Sandom** had been the drummer in the Who until roughly late April of 1964, when a tirade by Pete Townshend pushed him out of the band. One drummer who auditioned to join the Who was Mitch Mitchell, who would later drum for **Jimi Hendrix**. Moon performed an amazing unsolicited audition about 10 days after Doug left and instantly had the job.

Moon's pre–Who bands included the **Escorts** and then the **Beachcombers**. While in the former band he secretly took drumming lessons from **Carlo Little**. According to John Schollar of the **Beachcombers**, Alf Moon accompanied young Keith on his first few outings as a member of that band "to see that he didn't get up to mischief." Over the years Keith demonstrated that he had quite a flair for mischief, particularly at parties. One thing he did not excel at, however, was singing. That was one reason why he only recorded one solo album, 1975's *Two Sides of the Moon*.

Keith wanted to be active in movies but his list of credits isn't very long. In addition to *Tommy* it includes *200 Motels*, *Son of Dracula*, *That'll Be the Day*, *Stardust*, and *Sextette*. Moon was named best drummer in a 1975 poll of *Creem* readers. Upon Moon's death Greil Marcus wrote in *Rolling Stone* that Moon was the best drummer in rock history. Twenty-two years later, listeners of Chicago classic rock station WXCD voted Moon best drummer of the century. Keith and Patsy "Kim" Kerrigan had one daughter, Mandy. When the Who were inducted into the Rock and Roll Hall of Fame at the ceremony in January of 1990, Mandy represented her father. Kim is now married to noted session musician Ian McLagan, who had joined the **Small Faces** before Keith's death.

Moon has been profiled in three books: *Keith Moon: The Life and Death of a Rock Legend* by Ivan Waterman in 1979, *Moon the Loon* (also known as *Full Moon*) by **Dougal Butler** in 1981, and *Dear Boy* by Tony Fletcher in 1998. The latter dispels many myths and untruths, such as noting that contrary to all of the Who's biographies, Keith was born in 1946, not 1947.

The Motors   British band that had some UK chart success in the late 1970s with the singles "Dancing the Night Away" and "Airport." The band was formed in 1977 by its two songwriters, Nick Garvey and Andy McMaster, and after these two hits they fired the other two band members, ex–Snakes drummer Ricky Slaughter and guitarist Bram Tchaikovsky. Garvey and McMaster recruited other musicians for a final album under the Motors name in 1980. The picture sleeve of a 45 from that album, "That's What John Said," included photos of John Entwistle,

Elton John, Olivia Newton-John, and other noted "Johns." McMaster maintained a low profile after he and Garvey performed on Tchaikovsky's 1981 album *Funland,* and Garvey also faded from the music scene after recording with ex–**Beatle** Paul McCartney in July of 1987.

Mountain *see* West, Leslie.

Mulhearn, Daniel Plainclothes New York police officer whom Pete Townshend and Roger Daltrey booted from the stage on May 16, 1969, thinking he was a crazed fan for trying to seize a microphone. According to *The Who Concert File,* a fire had broken out at a supermarket next to the Fillmore East and promoter Bill Graham was preparing to make a low-key announcement but Mulhearn attempted to beat him to the punch halfway through the Who's set. The concert was completed without anyone announcing the fire. After vigorous advocacy by **Kit Lambert,** Daltrey was ultimately released without charge but Townshend faced a court appearance nine days later for third degree assault. He received a fine.

Murray the K *see* Barsalona, Frank.

The Naturals British band that recorded as the Blue Beats in 1962–63 and was also known as the Cossacks. Their only chart success was in mid–1964 as the Naturals—they hit #24 with a cover of the **Beatles** song "I Should Have Known Better." Their follow-up on the Parlophone label in November was a version of Pete Townshend's first published song, "It Was You." Townshend and the rest of the **Detours** recorded the song in 1963 but it has never surfaced. "It Was You" did later appear on a 45 by Chaos & Co. in Australia. The song was also reportedly released as a B-side by the British band the Fourmost, which recorded 45s in 1963 and '64 that featured songs by John Lennon and Paul McCartney of the Beatles, the second written just for the Fourmost. However, extensive research hasn't turned up a Fourmost 45 with a B-side by Townshend.

Nelson, Rick 1950s teen heartthrob who shared vocals on "One Night Stand" with Keith Moon on Keith's only solo album, *Two Sides of the Moon.* Two members of his backing group, the Stone Canyon Band, also helped Moon out. Dennis Larden wrote "One Night Stand" and provided background vocals on it; he also provided background vocals on "Teenage Idol." Jay White also provided background vocals on both songs. Larden had also been in Every Mother's Son. In 1952 Eric "Ricky" Nelson began appearing as himself on his parents' long-running TV series, *The Adventures of Ozzie and Harriet.* He first sang on the show in 1957, when he was 17 years old. He quickly began to amass top 10 45s, including the

#1 hits "Poor Little Fool" in 1958 and "Travelin' Man" and "Hello Mary Lou" in 1961. However, for most of the 1960s his records didn't sell particularly well. By 1969 he had switched from "Ricky" to "Rick" and formed the Stone Canyon Band, with whom he had the Top 40 hit "She Belongs to Me," a Bob Dylan composition. In 1971 Nelson again reached the top 10 with the million-seller "Garden Party." Nelson died in a plane crash in 1985 at the age of 45. He was inducted into the Rock and Roll Hall of Fame in 1987.

Newman, Andy *see* Thunderclap Newman.

Newman, Margo One of the two nurses singing during "It's a Boy" in the *Tommy* movie. She also sang on a couple of **Olivia Newton-John** albums around this time, as did her fellow nurse, **Vicki Brown**.

Newman, Tony Drummer on the *Tommy* movie soundtrack, on "Amazing Journey," "Cousin Kevin" and "Sensation." His earliest work included drumming on **Jeff Beck**'s *Beckola* album, and he recorded with **David Bowie** on a number of occasions. He also drummed on **Bonzo Dog Band** member Roger Ruskin Spear's *Electric Shocks* album. After Keith Moon's death, Newman was reportedly among the drummers who offered to fill in on a temporary basis.

Newton-John, Olivia Extremely popular singer of the 1970s who had more than 10 Top Five hit singles. Olivia was born in England in 1948 but was raised in Australia. She started having hits in 1971 as a country and western singer around the time that she was appearing on **Cliff Richard**'s TV series in the UK. Though the 1973 Top 10 hit "Let Me Be There" earned her a Grammy Award as best country female vocalist, she started moving away from country music in 1974. In the June 7, 1975 issue of *Melody Maker* there was a report of a British stage production of the Who's *Tommy* featuring **Leo Sayer** in the title role and Olivia and Cliff among his co-stars.

Olivia was named Best Female Singer in 1976 by the Country Music Association despite strong protests from some members. She began to pursue an acting career in 1978 and met with quick success in the movie musical *Grease*. Not only was it a box office success but it also provided Olivia with the hit songs "Hopelessly Devoted to You" and "You're the One That I Want," the latter a duet with co-star John Travolta. In 1980 the quirky British rock band the **Motors** released the single "That's What John Said," which came in a picture sleeve that featured photos of Olivia, John Entwistle, **Elton John**, and other famous "Johns." Her 1980 movie *Xanadu* failed at the box office but provided Olivia with another hit song, "Magic."

In 1981 her single "Physical" gave her another #1 hit. In 1983 she temporarily returned to Australia to avoid a stalker, and upon his capture she returned the U.S. to open a chain of clothing stores that ultimately went bankrupt in the early 1990s. In 1984 she and Roger Daltrey were members of the chorus that backed Barry Gibb of the **Bee Gees** on his album *Now Voyager*, on the song "Fine Line." In 1992 Olivia learned she had breast cancer, and after her treatment she became an advocate of early detection.

Nicholas, Paul   Singer and actor with two distinct links to the Who. He sang a Pete Townshend composition that wasn't released by the Who, "Join My Gang," on a 1966 single. This 45 was attributed to Oscar and was released on **Robert Stigwood**'s Reaction label. The Who were supported by Oscar at gigs on May 28 and September 16, 1966. Not quite a decade later Nicholas portrayed Cousin Kevin in the movie version of *Tommy*. He also appeared with Roger Daltrey in Ken Russell's follow-up movie, *Lisztomania,* and sang "Excelsior Song" on the soundtrack. In 1978 he appeared in Stigwood's movie version of the **Beatles'** *Sgt. Pepper's* album, which bombed despite the popularity of its stars, **Peter Frampton** and the **Bee Gees**. Around this time Nicholas achieved some chart success recording under his own name with "Heaven on the 7th Floor." In the 1990s his most prominent work was starring in London productions of other rock operas, *Jesus Christ Superstar* and *Hair*, recordings of which were released on compact disc.

Nicholls, Billy   British singer/songwriter who might very well have the strongest association with the Who among all of the performers who have collaborated with the band over the years. Nicholls, whose surname has sometimes been spelled "Nichols" on albums, was still in his teens when he was signed to the Immediate label and wrote songs for another Immediate performer, Del Shannon, while working toward records of his own. Shannon recorded three Nicholls compositions in early 1967 and Nicholls' own 45 "Would You Believe"/"Daytime Girl" came out almost a year later. For reasons that are unclear, an album he recorded around this time remained largely shelved until emerging on compact disc many years later. Over the years Nicholls recorded and released a few more solo albums. According to Billy's website, www.nicholls.co.uk, he has also written songs for such performers as **Leo Sayer**, the Outlaws, Kiki Dee, Marilyn Martin, **Jon Astley**, and Justin Hayward of the **Moody Blues**. He met Pete Townshend through their common devotion to **Meher Baba**. On Townshend's 1972 album *Who Came First* Nicholls composed the music for "Forever's No Time at All" and **Mike McInnerney**'s wife Katie wrote the lyrics. The only 45 from this album in the UK (there wasn't one in the

U.S.) featured that song as the A-side and another Nicholls track, "This Song Is Green," which was on the Baba tribute album *I Am* but not on *Who Came First*. These songs seemed like odd choices because Townshend's role on both was minimal, consisting of engineering the former and playing synthesized flute on the latter. However, Pete viewed *Who Came First* as just another Baba tribute album even though Townshend's name was the only one on the album cover.

In 1975 Nicholls was one of many backing vocalists recruited to sing on the *Tommy* film soundtrack. In 1977 he provided vocal help on "Till the Rivers All Run Dry" on the Townshend/**Ronnie Lane** collaboration *Rough Mix*. A song that Nicholls contributed to the 1976 Baba tribute album *With Love*, called "Without Your Love," was performed by Roger Daltrey on the ***McVicar*** soundtrack in 1980. The song was released as a single and reached #20 in the U.S. On that soundtrack Nicholls also wrote "Waiting for a Friend" and the title track, and co-wrote "White City Lights" with **Jon Lind**. Nicholls also played guitar on the album. A year later he provided backing vocals on John Entwistle's fifth solo album, *Too Late the Hero*. Nicholls provided backing vocals on Daltrey's 1984 solo LP, *Parting Should Be Painless*.

In late 1985 and early '86 Nicholls served as musical director for Townshend's **Deep End** band and was one of that ensemble's five backing vocalists. He played a similar role on Townshend's *Iron Man* album, the 1989 musical adaptation of the **Ted Hughes** tale. That year Nicholls also sang backup on the Who's 1989 reunion tour and co-produced the subsequent live album, called *Join Together*. In 1991 he produced the Who's cover of "Saturday Night's Alright (for Fighting)" for *Two Rooms*, the album that paid tribute to **Elton John** and Bernie Taupin. In 1992 it was back to backing vocals, this time on Daltrey's solo album, *Rocks in the Head*. The next year Billy took on additional roles on Townshend's *Psychoderelict* album. Nicholls co-composed the music for "Fake It" with Jon Astley and the aforementioned Jon Lind; Townshend wrote the lyrics. Nicholls also co-wrote "Psycho Montage" and an alternate version of "Early Morning Dreams" with Townshend and Lind. These were bonus tracks on Townshend's "English Boy" CD singles in Europe. This led to Nicholls providing backing vocals on Townshend's 1993 *Live* video. He appeared on camera as a background vocalist again in 1994 during Roger Daltrey's pay-per-view concert at New York's Carnegie Hall. Some of the music from this event was released on CD as *A Celebration — The Music of Pete Townshend And the Who*.

In 1998 Nicholls was the musical director on the two tracks of the album *Who's Serious* that featured a regular rock band instead of the London

Philharmonic Orchestra. He also served as Jon Astley's co-producer and was in the chorus that backed the London Philharmonic on "I Can See for Miles," "My Generation," and "Who Are You." Nicholls also did some production work for Pete Townshend's six-CD *Lifehouse Chronicles*, which was released in 2000. Later that year his son Morgan released his first album, called *Organized*. Morgan spent nine years playing bass in a punkish band called Senseless Things. Helping out in some fashion were Morgan's mother Annie, his brother William, his sister Amy, and his cousin Rose. Pete Townshend is Morgan's godfather.

Nicholson, Jack Well known actor who appeared in the movie version of *Tommy* and thus had to sing a little, on "Go to the Mirror." He received his first Oscar nomination, for Best Supporting Actor, for *Easy Rider* in 1969. Nicholson won an Oscar for Best Actor in 1975 for the movie *One Flew Over the Cuckoo's Nest* and won an Oscar for Best Supporting Actor for 1983's *Terms of Endearment*. He was nominated for an Oscar in several other years from 1970 to the present.

Night Ranger *see* Blades, Jack.

Nilsson, Harry Grammy-winning American singer who could count Keith Moon among his celebrity friends. In 1967 his song "Cuddly Toy" was a modest hit for the Monkees and Nilsson released his first solo album. He earned his first Grammy Award for singing Fred Neil's "Everybody's Talkin'," a 1969 Top 10 hit from the movie *Midnight Cowboy*. In 1971 he earned his second Grammy for his biggest hit, a #1 version of Badfinger's "Without You." In 1974 Keith Moon made a cameo with **Peter Frampton** and **Led Zeppelin**'s John Bonham in Nilsson's movie *Son of Dracula*, which starred Nilsson and ex–**Beatle** Ringo Starr. That year Nilsson also released the album *Pussy Cats,* which ex–Beatle John Lennon produced. On two tracks Ringo, Keith and popular session drummer Jim Keltner played *simultaneously*. Nilsson wrote the song "Together" and sang it with Keith in 1975 on Moon's only solo album, *Two Sides of the Moon*. After John Lennon was shot to death in late 1980 Nilsson traveled the U.S. advocating stricter handgun laws. He died in 1994 of a heart attack at the age of 52.

Nirvana Very popular 1990s "grunge" band out of Seattle that performed "Baba O'Riley" live. The band was short-lived due to the suicide of singer Kurt Cobain.

Nugent, Ted Detroit guitarist known as the "Motor City Madman" who founded the Amboy Dukes in 1965 and had success under his own name starting in the mid–1970s. The Amboy Dukes covered the Who's

"It's Not True" on one of their albums. Their only noteworthy hit came in 1968 when "Journey to the Center of Your Mind" reached the Top 20. They became known as Ted Nugent and the Amboy Dukes in 1972 and then Nugent went solo in 1975. His 1977 album *Cat Scratch Fever* went platinum and helped his previous two solo albums go gold. His 1978 album *Weekend Warriors* also went platinum. Sales of subsequent albums fell far short. Nugent returned to the spotlight in the group Damn Yankees, which also included Tommy Shaw of **Styx** and **Jack Blades** of Night Ranger. They released albums in 1990 and 1992. In 1999 Nugent took part in the "Rock Never Stops" tour but had to be replaced for one evening, and this provided the John Entwistle Band with a prime showcase. Previewing this July 1999 event, *Detroit Free Press* pop music writer Brian McCollum wrote: "Some kind of confusing contractual stuff kept homeboy and unretired rocker Ted Nugent from appearing on this bill for its Michigan stop, as he does throughout the rest of the country. Instead we get Who bassist John Entwistle, who tries to salvage a night that includes Quiet Riot, Slaughter and Firehouse. Gulp." Nugent remains a zealous advocate of hunting and of the National Rifle Association.

Oasis Very popular British pop band of the 1990s that had big hits in 1995 with "Champagne Supernova" and "Wonderwall." On the cover of their third album, 1998's *Be Here Now*, a Rolls Royce appears submerged in a swimming pool, a nod to the legend that Keith Moon celebrated his birthday in 1967 by driving a Lincoln Continental into the pool at a Holiday Inn in Flint, Michigan. (This tale was told in *The Who Concert File* in 1997 but in 1998 Tony Fletcher declared it to be a myth in his definitive Moon biography, *Dear Boy.*) Another tribute to Moon was his appearance on the picture sleeve for their single "Roll with It." Among Oasis's more recent releases was a cover of the Who's "My Generation," and in **Bob Pridden**'s liner notes for the CD *Substitute: The Songs of the Who* he mentioned that Oasis member Noel Gallagher performed with the Who during a November 27, 2000, concert to benefit the Teenage Cancer Trust. On that CD, which was released in mid–2001, Noel provided backing vocals for **Stereophonics**' version of "Who Are You."

Omartian, Michael Performer, producer and songwriter who has worked with a number of well known singers and musicians. In the early 1970s he was a well-regarded session keyboard player with such acts as the Four Tops and Loggins and Messina. He released solo albums from 1974 to '77, two more in the early '80s, and then none until the 1990s. The year before his first solo LP he released a 45 covering the Who's "Pinball Wizard." He began working with Steely Dan in 1975, around the time of

"Skunk" **Baxter**'s departure. That year he also helped form the studio group Rhythm Heritage, which soon recorded popular TV theme songs for the series *S.W.A.T.* and *Baretta*. Omartian also spearheaded Alan O'Day's 1977 hit "Undercover Angel," as well as Christopher Cross's early 1980s hits. He later produced sessions for **Rod Stewart** but in recent years has focused on Christian music.

Oscar *see* Nicholas, Paul.

Paddy, Klaus and Gibson Musical trio that Pete Townshend and **Kit Lambert** contemplated merging with the Who in the mid–1960s. When Roger Daltrey was temporarily kicked out of the Who in late 1965, for about a week Pete and Kit considered a "double group" consisting of two guitarists, two bassists and two drummers. However, the success of the Who's "My Generation" 45 prompted Daltrey's readmission. Guitarist Paddy Chambers, bass player Klaus Voormann, and drummer Gibson Kemp united in 1965 but disbanded on June 13, 1966. According to Bill Harry's 1997 *Encyclopedia of Beatles People*, Chambers joined the Liverpool band the Escorts (not Keith Moon's early band; see their entry) before managing small clubs. Kemp became a record company executive with Polygram. Voormann played with **Manfred Mann** in 1967 and joined John Lennon's Plastic Ono Band in 1969. In 1975 he played bass on "Together" on Keith Moon's only solo album, *Two Sides of the Moon*. Voormann also played on the three **Steve Cropper** songs that finally surfaced as bonus tracks when Moon's album was released on compact disc in the 1990s. In 1979 he moved back to his native Germany and became a record producer. In 1995 he stepped in to design the cover for the *Beatles Anthology* after **Peter Blake** declined. Voormann was an appropriate choice, having designed the award-winning cover for the **Beatles**' *Revolver* album back in the 1960s.

Page, Jimmy *see* Led Zeppelin.

Palladino, Pino. Welsh bass player on the Who's 2002 tour in place of John Entwistle, who had just passed away. Among his earliest studio credits is playing on Pete Townshend's 1985 album *White City*. He also backed Pete in concert in 1993 and Roger Daltrey in 1994. A very long list of musicians with whom he has worked, such as **Eric Clapton** and **Elton John**, can be found on Pino's website, pinopalladino.com.

Palmer, Carl *see* Emerson, Lake and Palmer.

Palmer, John "Poli" *see* Family.

The Palpitations *see* Clapton, Eric.

Parker, Robert Singer/saxophonist whose 1966 hit, "Barefootin'," was covered by Pete Townshend on his 1986 album ***Deep End Live!*** though the credits show his surname as "Barker." Parker, who was born in New Orleans in 1930, performed with artists such as Professor Longhair, Fats Domino and Joe Tex before "Barefootin'" reached #7 in the *Billboard* pop charts and #2 in the R&B charts in the summer of 1966. This prompted him to quit his full-time job as a hospital orderly, but he only managed one other chart success, with "Tip Toe" the following year. Still, he has remained popular in the New Orleans area.

Parr, John Singer known for the 1985 hit "St. Elmo's Fire (Man in Motion)," which was produced and co-written by **David Foster**. That same year Parr and Julia Downes wrote the title track of Roger Daltrey's solo album *Under a Raging Moon*. Parr also provided background vocals on the song. He sang on **Meat Loaf**'s *Blind Before I Stop* album in 1986 but since then his name has shown up on few album credits.

Parsons, Alan Producer and engineer whose Alan Parsons Project has released a number of conceptual albums since its formation in 1975. In 1969 Parsons had a hand in the **Beatles**' *Abbey Road* album and continued to work with Paul McCartney for several years. He also worked for other performers such as Al Stewart, Cockney Rebel, and Pilot. Performers with the Alan Parsons Project would later include **Stuart Elliott** of Cockney Rebel and **Stuart Tosh** of Pilot, among many others of various tenures. Parsons solidified his reputation by working on **Pink Floyd**'s hugely successful 1973 album *Dark Side of the Moon* and soon formed the Alan Parsons Project with songwriter and lyricist Eric Woolfson. Their biggest chart success came in 1982 when *Eye in the Sky* went platinum and the title track landed in the Top 10 on the singles charts. In 2001 John Entwistle, **Steve Luongo**, and **Godfrey Townsend** of the John Entwistle Band toured with Parsons, **Todd Rundgren**, and Ann Wilson of **Heart** in the Beatles tribute billed as *A Walk Down Abbey Road*.

Parsons, Tony *see* Burchill, Julie.

Patterson, Meg Scottish physician to whom Pete Townshend dedicated his 1982 solo album, *All the Best Cowboys Have Chinese Eyes*. In the early 1970s Townshend saved **Eric Clapton** from a heroin addiction by introducing him to Meg's acupuncture treatment. Townshend also referred Keith Moon to Meg and in early 1982 Pete himself spent four weeks under the care of Meg and her husband George. They had moved their practice to San Diego, and two of the songs on *Chinese Eyes* referred to his time there. According to John Atkins in *The Who on Record*, in 1979 at least two unreleased Who songs were supposed to be included on an all-star charity album to benefit Patterson's field, but it never materialized.

Paul, Adrian Actor who starred in the long-running syndicated television series *Highlander*. Roger Daltrey first guest-starred as fellow immortal Hugh Fitzcairn in a May 1993 episode entitled "The Hunters" and reprised the role in one or two episodes a year from 1995 through 1998.

Pearl Jam Probably the most popular American rock band of the '90s and one that regularly covers Who songs during concerts. Frontman Eddie Vedder proclaimed early that he felt obligated to send Pete Townshend cards on Father's Day because the Who's *Quadrophenia* had such a huge effect on him. Pearl Jam released two albums in the early 1990s that made them so popular and Vedder's fondness for the Who so well known that he was asked by Roger Daltrey to appear at his 50th birthday concerts at Carnegie Hall in early 1994. Vedder insisted on not being introduced prior to performing some Townshend compositions on his own, and further proof of Vedder's popularity at the time was the large percentage of audience members who immediately recognized him.

Later in 1994 Pearl Jam charged that Ticketmaster was engaging in unfair business practices that resulted in higher ticket prices for concerts, and the band pursued legal action through the U.S. Department of Justice. In 1995, however, the DOJ decided in favor of the ticket company. Vedder, who grew up in the Chicago area, was a special guest of Pete Townshend at a benefit concert on June 14, 1997, at the Chicago House of Blues. Eddie sang on "Heart to Hang Onto," "Tattoo" and "Magic Bus." This led to Vedder being the "mystery guest" on Townshend's 1999 *Live* CD. Toward the end of 1999 Vedder and the band C Average opened for the Who at the same venue for another benefit, and he joined the Who for their encore.

Pearl Jam has been releasing albums roughly every other year since 1994, but it was a non-album track that provided their biggest hit single, a cover of the oldie "Last Kiss" in 1999. In 2000 Pearl Jam officially released dozens of live performances on CD, several of which included a version of the Who's "Baba O'Riley," namely those listed as 6-26-00 Sporthalle — Hamburg; Germany; 8-15-00 Memphis; 8-25-00 Jones Beach, New York; 9-2-00 Philadelphia; 9-5-00 Pittsburgh; and 8-10-00 West Palm Beach, Florida. In addition, "The Kids Are Alright" was part of their 8-20-00 Cincinnati show. In 2001 the CD entitled *Substitute: The Songs of the Who* also included a version of "The Kids Are Alright" by Pearl Jam.

Peck, Kathy *see* Baby Buddha.

Phillips, Simon   Drummer on several of Pete Townshend's solo albums, on the Who's 1989 tour, and on numerous albums for many famous musicians. One of Phillips's early breaks was drumming with **Judas Priest** in 1977. In 1980 he drummed on 6 of the 10 tracks on Pete Townshend's *Empty Glass*, including the hit "Let My Love Open the Door." That song climbed as high in the U.S. charts as the Who's biggest U.S. single, "I Can See for Miles," reaching the Top 10. Phillips also drummed on Townshend's 1982 solo album, *All the Best Cowboys Have Chinese Eyes* and his 1985 album *White City*. He was then part of Townshend's **Deep End** band. Just before taking part in the Who's 1989 reunion tour he drummed on most of Townshend's *Iron Man* album, his musical adaptation of the **Ted Hughes** tale. When **Mark Brzezicki** left **Big Country** for awhile in mid–1989, Simon was one of his replacements. In 1993 he was the drummer in Townshend's *Live* video and a year later he served as drummer on Roger Daltrey's 1994 CD *A Celebration — The Music of Pete Townshend and the Who*. Over the years Phillips has drummed at least twice on albums by **Rolling Stones** frontman Mick Jagger, **Jeff Beck**, Mike Oldfield, Joe Satriani, and Roxy Music's Phil Manzanera. Simon released five of his own albums from 1988 through 1999 and drummed for Toto throughout the 1990s. When "Let My Love Open the Door" was released in 1996 on a three-track CD with the new version that was used in John Cusack's *Grosse Point Blank* movie and with the *Empty Glass* track "Rough Boys," the credits listed only Phillips on drums though **Kenney Jones** was credited on "Rough Boys" on the original LP.

Phish   Band that seems to have inherited the incredibly devoted following that had characterized **Grateful Dead** concerts for many years. Phish developed a tradition of covering another group's entire album each Halloween, and in 1995 they chose the Who's *Quadrophenia*. For good measure, during that night's encore they added "My Generation." In 2001 John Entwistle and Phish keyboard player Page McConnell played on the track "Same Price" for a new album by the band Government Mule. That same year the CD entitled *Substitute: the Songs of the Who* included Phish's performance of "5.15" from that 1995 concert.

Pink Floyd   British rock band that has thrived on the strength of such hugely popular albums as *Dark Side of the Moon* and *The Wall*. Pete Townshend has been close to members of Pink Floyd since 1967, when the band played at London's U.F.O. Club, then one of Pete's favorite hangouts. On Pink Floyd guitarist David Gilmour's 1984 solo album *About*

Face Townshend wrote lyrics for two songs, "All Lovers Are Deranged" and "Love on the Air." The next year Gilmour played on Townshend's album *White City* and wrote "White City Fighting" with him. He then played in Townshend's **Deep End** band, and their version of "Love on the Air" was included on the on Deep End's Brixton, England video. On December 4, 1992 Gilmour performed at the ECOMUNDO Conference in Colombia, South America with Roger Daltrey, Phil Manzanera of Roxy Music and **Chucho Merchan**. **Jon Carin** played keyboards on six Pink Floyd albums from 1987 to 1995.

The Pioneers Relatively new band that prominently featured "guest Pioneer" John Entwistle on its self-titled debut album. Leading the Pioneers are singer/songwriters Ron Magness and Roy Michaels. Magness got his start in the group Felix, which opened for the Who in the 1960s and released four well regarded albums. He went on to serve as producer for such stars as Mick Jagger of the **Rolling Stones** and ex–**Beatle** Paul McCartney and won a Grammy Award for his production work on the soundtrack of the movie *Flashdance*. The musical career of Roy Michaels includes tours with such 1960s hitmakers as Gerry and the Pacemakers, the Searchers, **Manfred Mann**, and Peter Noone of **Herman's Hermits** fame. Magness and Entwistle were old friends, and John provided this endorsement for the band: "American country and Western has always been the genesis for English Rock and Roll. Playing the music of the Pioneers has not only given me a chance to go back to those roots, but to help create a new sound for Nashville, which I think the Pioneers have done."

Player *see* Beckett, Peter.

The Police Reggae-tinged rock trio that began its rise to prominence in the late 1970s. Around this time their lead singer, Sting, portrayed the character Ace Face in the movie version of the Who's *Quadrophenia*, a movie that retains a following to this day. Shortly after the Police splintered, drummer Stewart Copeland became one of the drum soloists who honored Keith Moon on the title track of Roger Daltrey's 1985 album *Under a Raging Moon*. At the end of 1985 Pete and Karen Townshend presided over a charitable event at which Police guitarist Andy Summers appeared, among other celebrities.

Porter, Cole American songwriter known for such musicals as 1948's *Kiss Me, Kate* and 1953's *Can-Can*. Pete Townshend's version of Porter's "Begin the Beguine," a 1935 number for the musical *Jubilee*, appeared on the **Meher Baba** tribute album *Happy Birthday* in early 1970 and on his 1987 album *Another Scoop*. The song was one of Baba's favorites.

Preston, Billy Singer and keyboard player who gained notice by backing the **Beatles** and had a few big hits in the early 1970s. At the age of 10 he briefly portrayed songwriter W. C. Handy in the 1956 biopic *St. Louis Blues*. His biggest break, however, came when Little Richard invited him to tour Europe in 1962. On that tour he met the Beatles. He became the first guest musician to be credited on a Beatles record, on the "Get Back" 45. He played on several other Beatles songs and later played on several solo albums by ex–Beatles. In late 1971 Pete Townshend and Keith Moon jammed with Preston and Charlie Starr at the Troubadour in Los Angeles. From 1972 to 1974 he had five top five hits, two of which reached #1 on the U.S. pop charts: "Will It Go Round in Circles" and "Nothing from Nothing." In 1975 he wrote Joe Cocker's huge hit "You Are So Beautiful" and toured with the **Rolling Stones**. Though his solo career waned, in 1979 his duet with Syreeta Wright, "With You I'm Born Again," was another big hit. In 1999 Preston began to work with the **British Rock Symphony**, which Roger Daltrey often headlined. In March and April of 2000 Preston headlined BRS gigs and was joined by **Darlene Love**, Nikki Lamborn, and **Simon Townshend**.

The Pretenders New wave band fronted by Chrissie Hynde that hit it big with their self-titled debut album in 1980. On May 25, 1978, Hynde was reportedly present at the UK concert that **Jeff Stein** set up for use in his movie *The Kids Are Alright*, a performance that turned out to be Keith Moon's last one with the Who. Pretenders drummer Martin Chambers was one of the drum soloists who honored Moon on the title track of Roger Daltrey's 1985 album *Under a Raging Moon*.

Pridden, Bob Soundman for the Who from December of 1966 through the band's breakup in 1983. In late 1966 he was on his way to seek a job with the Easybeats when he bumped into **John Wolff**, who thought the Who could use some extra help. He hadn't seen them perform prior to his first night on the job, and was in a state of shock after the band finished with its usual equipment destruction. According to *The Who Concert File*, Pridden indicated that Roger Daltrey didn't help matters by saying, "Bobby, get it all fixed by tomorrow!" In addition to continuing to work for the Who proper, Pridden has assisted with solo projects such as Pete Townshend's 1982 album *All the Best Cowboys Have Chinese Eyes*, for which he was rehearsal supervisor and engineer. Most recently he worked with **Steve Luongo** and John Entwistle to mix the John Entwistle Band's 1999 CD *Left for Live* and with help from Darren Westbrook he mixed and engineered the 1999 versions of "Behind Blue Eyes" and "Pure and Easy" for Pete's six-CD boxed set, *Lifehouse Chronicles*. He also reworked the latter's original early-'70s demo for that 2000 release.

Proby, P. J.   American singer who had some success in the UK in the 1960s and who performed with the Who on the 1997 leg of the *Quadrophenia* tour. Proby and the **High Numbers** had performed on the same bill, at the New Theatre, Oxford on January 17, 1965. The Texan, born James Marcus Smith, had been brought to the UK to appear in a **Beatles** TV special. According to Bill Harry's 1997 *Encyclopedia of Beatles People*, Proby's career suffered a huge setback when his trousers split on stage one night and controversy ensued. In 1997 Proby was recruited to sing the part of the Godfather on the Who's *Quadrophenia* tour. Roger Daltrey told the UK fan publication *Naked Eye* that although **Gary Glitter** did a great job in the role the year before he preferred Proby because "people didn't know who he was" and that this was better from a purely theatrical standpoint. Daltrey added that Proby has "a great voice and he gives you this Elvis type feeling—he was a Godfather and he didn't have this baggage of 'Oh there's so and so', it was just someone being 'a character.'"

Purcell, Henry   Seventeenth century English composer, widely considered to be the finest born in that country. He created an English baroque style and was a master of counterpoint, the art of weaving independent melodies together in a homogeneous fashion (as Pete Townshend sought to do with *Quadrophenia*'s two instrumentals). Early in Pete Townshend's development as a songwriter, Who manager **Kit Lambert** played him many recordings unearthed by his father, composer/arranger Constant Lambert, including some by Purcell. Purcell's "Fantasia Upon One Note" and ten selections from *The Gordion Knot Untied* were used in Townshend's radio dramatization of *Lifehouse* aired by the BBC in December of 1999. Townshend also borrowed from another famous baroque composer, **Alessandro Scarlatti**.

Quatro, Patti *see* Fanny.

Queen   British pomp rock group of the 1970s that had at least 10 gold records and saw a handful of them go platinum. Frontman Freddie Mercury attended Ealing Art School at the same time as Pete Townshend but Mercury's recording career began to flourish a decade after Townshend's. Queen was formed in 1971 and released its first album in 1973. They broke from the pack with their fourth album in 1975, *A Night at the Opera*, which yielded the hit "Bohemian Rhapsody." Through 1980 seven of their subsequent singles reached the Top 20 in the U.S., including the #1 hits "Crazy Little Thing Called Love" in 1979 and "Another One Bites the Dust" in

1980. The latter was quickly parodied by **Weird Al Yankovic** as "Another One Rides the Bus," in which the Who were mentioned. Overall the decade of the '80s was a far less successful one for the band commercially. Queen drummer Roger Taylor was one of the drum soloists who honored Keith Moon on the title track of Roger Daltrey's 1985 album *Under a Raging Moon*. Freddie Mercury died of AIDS in 1991 at the age of 45 and at the tribute concert in his honor the next year Roger Daltrey performed "I Want It All" with Queen. The surviving members have worked together on occasion since then.

Rabbit *see* Bundrick, John "Rabbit."

Rafferty, Gerry *see* Stealers Wheel.

Ralphs, Mick *see* Bad Company.

The Ramones One of the earliest American punk bands to develop a following. The Ramones were formed in 1974 and all of the group's members supposedly changed their surnames to "Ramone." They released their first of many albums in 1976. Though none have been particularly successful in their native U.S. they do have a loyal fan base and have done noticeably better in Britain. In 1993 they recorded a version of the Who's "Substitute" with help from Pete Townshend himself. It was released as a CD single and on the album *Acid Eaters*, which was comprised entirely of covers. The album was a failure commercially. The Ramones split up in 1996.

Rat Race Choir *see* Luongo, Steve.

Reed, Lou Frontman of the legendary New York rock band the Velvet Underground in the 1960s and a well regarded solo performer ever since. Though the Velvet Underground didn't sell many records, their albums with Reed are critically acclaimed. He left in the summer of 1970 and the band continued for only a few years without him. Reed has recorded using many different styles over the years with varying degrees of commercial success and praise from critics. In short order he earned his only big hit single, 1972's "Walk on the Wild Side." Reed followed that up with a Top 10 album in the UK in 1973 and one in the U.S. in 1974. In 1975 Reed's backing vocalists on "Walk on the Wild Side," billed as Thunderthighs, sang on the **John Alcock**/John Entwistle *Flash Fearless* album. According to **Richard Barnes**, Reed had been considered for role of the Acid Queen in the movie version of *Tommy*, but it was **Tina Turner** who wowed moviegoers when the film was released in 1975. Reed has continued to release albums at regular intervals and hasn't been shy about experimenting on them. When Roger Daltrey held two concerts at New York's Carnegie Hall in early 1994, Lou Reed performed Pete Townshend's "Now And Then" from Pete's 1993 *Psychoderelict* album.

Reeves, Jim   Country and western singer who had a hit with "There's a Heartache Following Me," which Pete Townshend covered on his solo album *Who Came First* in 1972. The song, written by **Ray Baker**, was a favorite of **Meher Baba**'s, as was another popular English-language song, **Cole Porter**'s "Begin the Beguine." According to Pete, "Baba said that Jim Reeves' voice was full of spiritual power and love. I listened to him sing this song and had to agree." Reeves' biggest hit, however, was his version of "He'll Have to Go," which reached #1 on the Country chart and #2 on the pop chart. In 1964 he died in a plane crash near Nashville, Tennessee shortly after his 41st birthday.

Reizner, Lou   Record producer for **Rod Stewart** and the creator of the 1972 orchestral version of *Tommy*. Reizner had produced albums for Stewart in 1969 and 1970 and reportedly wanted Stewart for the lead role of Tommy but not surprisingly it went to Roger Daltrey. Stewart sang "Pinball Wizard" instead. Other cast members who sang with the **London Symphony Orchestra** and Chamber Choir included **Steve Winwood** as the father, **Merry Clayton** as the Acid Queen, **Sandy Denny** as a nurse, Maggie Bell of **Stone the Crows** as Mrs. Walker, **Graham Bell** as her lover, **Richie Havens** as the Hawker, ex–**Beatle** Ringo Starr as Uncle Ernie, John Entwistle as Cousin Kevin, and **Richard Harris** as the doctor. Roger Daltrey ended up with a Top 20 hit when his rendition of "I'm Free" was released on a 45.

Richard Barnes expressed some surprise that this version of *Tommy* was very well received; *New Musical Express* raved at length about this "milestone in contemporary music" and called Reizner's project "the best concept album ever made." Meanwhile, **Chris Charlesworth** enthused in *Melody Maker* that "Townshend's masterpiece has finally got the treatment it deserves with an all-star cast, a full symphony orchestra and a presentation that ranks among the best in the history of rock music." Keith Moon took over for Starr and **Peter Sellers** was Harris's replacement when the album resulted in a live performance at London's Rainbow Theatre on December 9, 1972. Despite the fact that the performance was to benefit the Stars Organization for Spastics, the Royal Albert Hall had cancelled as the venue because of its management's distaste for the plot of *Tommy*. On December 13, 1973 Reizner's production was staged again. New faces this time included **David Essex**, Roy Wood, and Steve Marriott of **Small Faces** fame. In 1975 Reizner produced the album *Prestidigitation* for Ronnie

Charles, which included covers of the Who's "Love, Reign O'er Me" and **Thunderclap Newman**'s "Something in the Air" performed with the LSO and Chamber Choir. The next year he produced the soundtrack for *All This and World War II,* which included Keith Moon singing the **Beatles** "When I'm Sixty Four." In 1977 Reizner died at the age of 43.

Renaissance *see* Rudd, Raphael.

Rice, Tim Collaborator with **Andrew Lloyd Webber** on such popular musicals as *Joseph and the Amazing Technicolor Dreamcoat, Jesus Christ Superstar,* and *Evita.* Rice has also worked for Disney on projects with Alan Menken, such as *Aladdin,* and with **Elton John,** such as *The Lion King* and *The Road to El Dorado.* In a 1996 BBC radio production of *Jesus Christ Superstar* Roger Daltrey was Judas and former **Spandau Ballet** lead singer Tony Hadley had the title role.

Rich, Buddy Bandleader often called "the world's greatest drummer." Rich, who was born in 1917, spent most of 1939 with clarinetist Artie Shaw, who fronted the most popular swing band at the time. He then teamed with Tommy Dorsey through 1945. For two decades after World War II he performed with a variety of well known musicians, such as Charlie Parker, and in 1966 he assembled a popular big band that would be his focus until his death in 1987. On May 29, 1969, several days after the Who released *Tommy,* the Who's supporting acts at a Chicago concert were the Buddy Rich Orchestra and Joe Cocker and the Grease Band. On Rich's 1975 album *Big Band Machine* he included a "Tommy Medley" consisting of "Eyesight to the Blind," "Champagne," "See Me, Feel Me," "Miracle Cure," and "Listening to You."

Richard, Cliff Very popular and influential rock singer in the UK prior to the emergence of the **Beatles**. Richard, whose real name is Harry Webb, impressively totaled more than 40 Top 20 hits from 1958 to 1969. Richard's backing band was the **Shadows**, which had instrumental hits in their own right. While in the **Confederates** John Entwistle and Pete Townshend regularly performed Shadows numbers. Similarly, during the days when Colin Dawson was the lead singer of Roger Daltrey's **Detours**, they covered a number of songs sung by Richard as well as Shadows instrumentals. Dawson modeled himself after Richard. Cliff Richard and the Shadows joined with the Who and many other artists to perform at what **Richard Barnes** called "the pop event of 1966," a concert that included many of the UK artists that ranked high in a *New Musical Express* poll from 1965. In the early 1970s Richard had a BBC TV series on which **Olivia Newton-John** regularly appeared. *Melody Maker* reported in its issue of

June 7, 1975 on a British stage production of *Tommy* featuring **Leo Sayer** in the title role and Cliff and Olivia among Sayer's co-stars. A couple of Richard's pre-British Invasion singles sold well in the United States, but he had to wait until the mid–1970s for bigger and more consistent success there with such songs as the Top 10 hit "Devil Woman" plus "We Don't Talk Anymore," "Dreaming," and "A Little in Love." In 1984 Richard was the Bellman when **Lewis Carroll**'s epic nonsense poem "The Hunting of the Snark" was transformed into a musical by **Mike Batt**. Roger Daltrey portrayed the Barrister and sang lead on the song "The Pig Must Die." Richard remains quite popular in the UK to this day.

Richards, Keith *see* The Rolling Stones.

Riley, Terry Avant-garde minimalist composer from California to whom Pete Townshend paid tribute by naming one of his most famous songs "Baba O'Riley" in 1971. The first half of the title indicated once again what an influence **Meher Baba** was on Townshend, and he reportedly used an "O" with apostrophe before Riley's surname because the song's synthesizer line was reminiscent of an Irish jig. From the mid–1960s onward Riley's groundbreaking work has influenced the likes of composer Philip Glass and progressive rock groups that rose to prominence in the 1960s and '70s, such as Soft Machine, Tangerine Dream, and Curved Air. In the 1970s Riley began a collaboration with Kronos Quartet founder and leader David Harrington that has produced over a dozen musical works. They have received critical acclaim in the pages of publications like *Time* and *Newsweek* and their mid–1980s album *Salome Dances for Peace* was nominated for a Grammy Award. Riley was among the composers spotlighted on *OHM: The Early Gurus of Electronic Music, 1948–1980*, released on the Ellipsis Arts label in 2000.

Ro Ro A short-lived group formed by John Entwistle, if the short news item in the issue of *Melody Maker* dated November 18, 1972 is to be believed. That periodical said the band had performed at some colleges in England with free admission. However, by November 25, *New Musical Express* was reporting about Entwistle's band as well and correctly referred to it as Rigor Mortis. Entwistle's album *Rigor Mortis Sets in* was released in June of 1973. The confusion was understandable, because four of the six members of Ro Ro had played on Entwistle's solo album *Whistle Rymes*, which was released in November of 1972. However, Ro Ro guitarist Alan Ross was the only one to also play on *Rigor Mortis Sets In*. The other three members of Ro Ro who played on *Whistle Rymes* were drummer Rod Coombes, singer Neil Sheppard, and violin player **Johnny Weider**. Ro Ro released 45s in 1971, '72 and '73 and had one album called *Meet at the Water*. Coombes drummed for **Stealers Wheel** in 1973 and would later join the Strawbs. Neil Sheppard played on Tim Hardin's 1973 album *Painted Head* and wrote the song "Til We Meet Again" on that album. He also sang on Long John Baldry's 1976 album *Good to Be Alive*. On the *Tommy* movie soundtrack Alan Ross played acoustic guitar on "Amazing Journey," "Extra, Extra, Extra," "There's a Doctor," "Smash the Mirror," "Sensation," "Miracle Cure," "We're Not Gonna Take It," "Tommy Can You Hear Me?" and "Do You Think It's Alright?" Ross had four albums of his own from 1974 to 1978 and has done occasional session work, including on woodwinds. In addition to performing on the aforementioned Entwistle solo albums Ross was thanked but not specifically credited in the liner notes for Entwistle's fifth album, 1981's *Too Late the Hero*.

Robinson, Smokey   Frontman of the famous Detroit rock group the Miracles. The falsetto voice and songwriting talents of William "Smokey" Robinson were showcased throughout the 1960s on top five hits ranging from "Shop Around" in 1960 to "I Second That Emotion" in 1967. Their song "I Gotta Dance to Keep from Crying" was performed by the Who in 1964. Smokey Robinson and the Miracles records were among those that Pete Townshend was exposed to in the impressive collection of his friend **Tom Wright**. In the liner notes of Townshend's 1987 album *Another Scoop* Pete shed some light on the Who's hit single "Substitute," which was released in March of 1966: "Smokey Robinson sang the word 'substitute' so perfectly in 'Tracks of My Tears'— my favourite song at the time — that I decided to celebrate the word itself with a song all its own. Interesting that in eulogising two of my most important influences (and ripping off a few ideas), I should end up with one of the most succinct songs of my career." The other influence Pete was alluding to was the **Rolling Stones**. Smokey Robinson and the Miracles were among several acts on the bill of the Who's first American engagement, Murray the K's Easter radio show in 1967. Robinson also served on the "board of governors" for the Monterey Pop Festival in mid–June of 1967, at which the Who made another early impression on American audiences. In 1970 Smokey Robinson and the Miracles had their last hit together, the #1 smash "Tears of a Clown," and Robinson left in 1972. The Miracles had a few hits without him by 1977. Robinson's solo successes included his top five hits "Cruisin'" in 1979 and "Being with You" in 1981. Smokey Robinson was inducted into the Rock and Roll Hall of Fame in 1987.

The Rockin' Vicars   British band that may have been the first (of at least five) to have **Shel Talmy**'s help recording a cover of a Pete Townshend composition. Talmy and the Who were locked in a dispute around the time the Who's "Substitute" 45 was released on March 4, 1966. That same month Talmy produced a 45 for the Rockin' Vicars with an A-side entitled "It's Alright" ("And Then It's Alright" in some sources). The song was a modification of the Who song "The Kids Are Alright." However, there apparently wasn't much animosity between the two bands because the Rockin' Vicars played support for the Who at a gig on May 28. The Rockin' Vicars included Ian "Lemmy" Kilminster on guitar; he would gain fame in the 1970s as the bass player in the psychedelic rock band Hawkwind and the heavy metal band Motorhead. In *The Who Concert File* Joe McMichael and "Irish" Jack Lyons noted that "Lemmy always cited John Entwistle as rock's greatest bass player, bar none!"

Roden, Jess   Singer who backed the Who on its popular single "Magic Bus." Roden had been the lead vocalist in the **Alan Bown** Set; his replacement was Robert Palmer, who would have a successful solo career many years later. In 1970 and '71 he led a band called Bronco but it didn't experience much success. In 1974 he was in the Butts Band with former **Doors** John Densmore and Robbie Krieger and recorded his first solo album around that time. According to **Richard Barnes** and Pete Townshend's book *The Story of Tommy*, for the 1975 movie soundtrack Townshend brought Roden in to do a "wailing, soulful voice part behind Roger Daltrey's lead on 'Listening to You'." In 1980 Roden joined a band called the Rivets. After singing on Grace Jones's *Nightclubbing* album in 1981 Roden maintained a low profile until singing on the 1996 album *Floodgates* for former Mott the Hoople and Spooky Tooth guitarist Luther Grosvenor (who went by Ariel Bender once upon a time).

Rodgers, Paul   *see* Bad Company.

Rogers, Simon   *see* The Lightning Seeds.

The Rolling Stones   One of the most successful and popular British Invasion bands, often grouped in a hallowed triumvirate with the **Beatles** and the Who. By never formally disbanding, the Stones have certainly proven to be more durable than virtually every other band from the 1960s. The Stones were formed in 1962 and in the second half of 1963 the Stones had two Top 40 hits in the UK. About two months before becoming the Who, the **Detours** opened for the Rolling Stones in the London area on December 22, 1963, and January 3, 1964. It was on the first of these dates that Pete Townshend saw Stones guitarist Keith Richards rotate his arm like the hand of a clock while warming up. Townshend has acknowledged he developed his trademark "windmill" motion during concerts from seeing Richards do this, but down the road Richards didn't recall doing this nor did he mind that Pete mimicked him. That night **Glyn Johns** helped Townshend get into the Stones' dressing room (Johns, who was then singing in a band called the Presidents, went on to engineer a number of records for the Stones from 1965 to 1972 and for the Who in the 1970s). Townshend told **Richard Barnes** that "it was like going into a sacred place after the gig." The Who would soon retain the services of publicist **Peter Meaden**, who had been an associate of Stones manager Andrew Loog Oldham. In late 1965 as the Who single "My Generation" was on its way to #3 on the British charts, the Stones' other guitarist, Brian Jones, said the Who was "the only young group doing something new both visually and musically. Originality usually means success."

The *New Musical Express* annual readership poll conducted in 1965 led to a joint appearance by the Stones and the Who in mid–1966. The poll's top-rated acts performed on May 1 at what Barnes called "the pop event of 1966." The concert was broadcast on television, split over the following two Sundays. *NME*'s own review said the Who were more remarkable than the Beatles and the Stones. On July 9, 1966 a Who concert in London was filmed for broadcast on Canadian television, and it has been reported that one of the songs the Who performed was the big Stones hit "Satisfaction." This concert was aired under the title *Take 30 in London* and/or *Live in London* but *The Who Concert File* said the date of broadcast is unknown. (In *The Who on Record*, John Atkins theorized that the instrumental the Who recorded for *Live in London*, called either "Sodding About" or "Signal 30," may have been recorded as late as October of 1967.)

In an interview for Gary Herman's biography *The Who*, John Entwistle credited Stones bass player Bill Wyman with helping him to come up with the idea for what was to be only the second song he ever wrote: "…I went out and got drunk down the Scotch Club with Bill Wyman and we started talking about spiders and why they frighten people and that gave me an idea for a song. Once I had the idea, it only took me about ten minutes." The result was "Boris the Spider," a song that the Who regularly played live. In late June of 1967 the Who worked quickly in the studio to record versions of the Stones' "The Last Time" and "Under My Thumb" to demonstrate support for Richards and Stones singer Mick Jagger, who had been jailed for minor drug offenses. John Entwistle was on his honeymoon at sea so he was phoned in the middle of the night to give his permission for Pete Townshend to play bass on the 45. The Who planned to release covers of Stones songs until Richards and Jagger were freed, but this happened quicker than expected and the one 45 of Stones songs was all the Who recorded.

In December of 1968 the Who performed a blistering version of "A Quick One While He's Away" for the TV special *The Rolling Stones' Rock 'n' Roll Circus* but the entire broadcast remained unreleased for almost 30 years because the Stones were upstaged by the Who. The Who's performance alone escaped from the archives after only a decade, turning up in the movie *The Kids Are Alright*. Speaking of Who movies, in the issue of *Melody Maker* dated November 17, 1973, it was reported that Mick Jagger had turned down the role of the Acid Queen in the movie version of *Tommy*. In 1977 Stones drummer Charlie Watts drummed on "My Baby Gives It Away" and "Catmelody" on the Pete Townshend/**Ronnie Lane** collaboration *Rough Mix*. Watts was credited on the UK album but, like **Bad Company**'s Boz Burrell, not on the U.S. release. Also playing on "Catmelody" was pianist Ian Stewart, often referred to as the "sixth Stone." Stewart had actually helped to found the Stones but officially remained a non-member until his death from a heart attack at the age of 47 in 1985.

On May 2, 1979 Mick Jagger was among the celebrities who attended **Kenney Jones**'s first concert with the Who, at the Rainbow Theatre in North London. Within a few years Bill Wyman hosted a radio show called "The Lost Who Tapes." In 1981 Pete Townshend played guitar and may have sung on the Stones song "Slave" from their 1981 album *Tattoo You*. In 1985 he played on Mick Jagger's first solo album, *She's the Boss*, on "Lonely at the Top" and "Hard Woman." When the Rolling Stones were voted into the Rock and Roll Hall of Fame in 1989, Townshend gave the speech inducting them at the ceremony. Roger Daltrey has performed the Stones' "Street Fighting Man" with the **British Rock Symphony** and on the 1999 BRS CD he and **Alice Cooper** teamed up to perform their song "Start Me Up."

Ronson, Mick Multitalented musician who frequently collaborated with **David Bowie** and Mott the Hoople's Ian Hunter. Ronson received special thanks for an unspecified reason in the credits on Roger Daltrey's third solo album, 1977's *One of the Boys*. Ronson's first big break was backing Bowie on his 1969 album *Space Oddity*, and the two teamed up a number of times subsequently, such as on Bowie's 1973 album *Pinups*, which included covers of the Who's "I Can't Explain" and "Anyway Anyhow Anywhere." In 1972 Ronson briefly joined Mott the Hoople and worked on Hunter's solo recordings. He consistently worked with a variety of noted performers until dying from cancer in 1993 at the age of 47. Roger Daltrey appeared at the Mick Ronson Tribute Concert in London during the spring of 1994. He sang "Baba O'Riley" and "Summertime Blues," with **Simon Townshend** among those backing him. A CD from this concert received limited release in 1997.

Rooney, Mickey   Well known American movie star who got his start as a child actor in the first half of the 20th century. He was a guest on the **Smothers Brothers** show in September of 1967 and caught fellow guest **Bette Davis** when she fainted due to the explosion of Keith Moon's drums at the end of the Who's performance of "My Generation." This famous television moment starts the movie *The Kids Are Alright* and was ranked by the cable channel VH1 as the 10th greatest rock 'n' roll moment in history.

Ross, Alan   *see* Ro Ro.

Roxy Music   *see* Ferry, Bryan.

Rudd, Raphael   A follower of **Meher Baba** who has helped Pete Townshend on Who and solo projects. His mother Virginia, who chaired the English Department at Rutgers University, met Baba in the 1950s. As a young boy, Raphael met him as well later that decade. Virginia Rudd's relationship with Baba resulted in a recent documentary video. After graduating from the Manhattan School of Music Rudd earned an advanced degree from the Julliard School of Music. The biography on his website, raphaelrudd.com, notes that Townshend invited Rudd to arrange and conduct members of the **London Symphony Orchestra** and the Royal Philharmonic in recording music for the movie version of *Quadrophenia*. Raphael told this author that in addition to supplementing "I've Had Enough" and "Love, Reign O'er Me," which were both on the soundtrack album, they also added to "Sea And Sand," which was not released at that time. Around the end of 2000 he was interviewed for the September 2001 DVD release of the *Quadrophenia* movie by Rhino, and the augmented "Sea And Sand" was considered for inclusion. Around the same time that Rudd was helping on the soundtrack he performed several concerts with Townshend that served as demos for Pete's 1980 solo album *Empty Glass*. Rudd also arranged the horns on "Rough Boys" on that album.

More than two decades after those 1980 concerts, Rhino Records released *Pete Townshend & Raphael Rudd — The Oceanic Concerts* in October of 2001. Around 1979 Raphael was also recording his own compositions for his debut solo album, *The Awakening Chronicles*, with some help from Townshend, Phil Collins of **Genesis**, and members of the British art rock band Renaissance, in which Rudd later played keyboards for a decade. A more recent collaborator of Rudd's was **Jon Lind**. One of Rudd's main activities in the 1990s was writing music for television. Raphael Rudd died on April 1, 2002, after a car accident. He was 45. His website fittingly quotes Pete Townshend in 1996, from the back of the CD release of *The Awakening Chronicles*:

Raphael Rudd and I met because of our mutual interest in the Indian spiritual master Avatar Meher Baba. When about five years old Raphael met Meher Baba, who took the child's hands in his own and gazed into his eyes. Later, when Raphael became a musician and dedicated his work to his master, it became clear to everyone that Meher Baba had inspired the child forever. I didn't meet Meher Baba in the flesh. But I was pleased to be able to work with Raphael on this recording project that was to be dedicated to Meher Baba. At one time, searching for a theme for the collection of compositions I suggested that the album should be called *The Boy*. This was to recognize the importance to the artist of remaining young. While working on this record, I was doing a number of other things, including working on the soundtrack of the movie *Quadrophenia*. Indeed Raphael orchestrated the final scene of the film and conducted the orchestra with great authority despite being only twenty-one years old at the time. I regarded myself as Raphael's musical mentor during that period. Today, we inspire each other on a more equal footing. I am greatly influenced by Raphael's piano style—especially his modality. To this day, Raphael and I regard ourselves as fellow voyagers on the path to God—who we see manifested clearly in the perfect life and continuing compassionate spiritual presence of Avatar Meher Baba. This might seem romantic, and it is of course. But whatever we like to believe as spiritual seekers, and however lost or vain we might become in our pursuit of art and fame, we are both utterly certain that we are merely channels for the will of god.

Rundgren, Todd   A member of the Nazz in the late 1960s and leader of the progressive rock band Utopia starting in 1974. Just after Keith Moon's death in September of 1978, as a tribute Rundgren helped the **Tubes** close a concert with a Who medley consisting of "Baba O'Riley" and "The Kids Are Alright." To end a mid–1979 concert in New York he again joined the Tubes to perform those songs. In 1980 he and Utopia backed **Shaun Cassidy** on a cover of the Who's "So Sad About Us" on Cassidy's *Wasp* album. In the liner notes for Rhino's 1997 compilation *Poptopia! Power Pop Classics of the '70s*, Rundgren said that "The Who is probably the prototypical power-pop band, in that their songs were all very terse and not overly arranged. They were hooky but not in a cloying way. 'Couldn't I Just Tell You' [from his 1972 gold album *Something/Anything*] has more of a Who influence with those chiming guitar figures." In 2001 John Entwistle, **Steve Luongo**, and **Godfrey Townsend** of the John Entwistle Band toured with Rundgren, **Alan Parsons**, and Ann Wilson of **Heart** in the **Beatles** tribute billed as *A Walk Down Abbey Road*.

Ruskin Spear, Roger   *see* The Bonzo Dog Doo-Dah Band.

Sadat, Anwar al-   Egyptian president who in 1979 signed the historic Camp David accords with Israeli premier Menachem Begin. Sadat was assassinated on October 6, 1981, and Roger Daltrey told the fanzine

Who's News he recorded "Treachery" that day. "That's what I sang about." The song appeared on his *Best Bits* album and on CD many years later as a bonus track on the German release of *One of the Boys*.

St. Jon, Alan   Keyboardist in **Billy Squier**'s band who was later part of the John Entwistle Band and co-wrote several songs for the latter group's *Van-Pires* CD under his real surname, Levi. In early 1998 he released a solo album called *Sky Daddy;* none of the John Entwistle Band performed on it. At some point that year Alan was replaced in the band by Gordon Cotten. Alan has provided keyboards/synthesizers and at times backing vocals for a number of other artists, including **Queen**'s Freddie Mercury, Steve Forbert, and **Ted Nugent**.

Samuels, Fuzzy   Bass player and vocalist on several Stephen Stills albums in the 1970s who also played bass on "We're Not Gonna Take It" on the *Tommy* movie soundtrack.

Sanborn, David   One of the most well known saxophonists toward the end of the 20th century, and the featured guest performer on "5:15" at Roger Daltrey's 50th birthday "party" at New York's Carnegie Hall. This song can be found on Roger's album, *A Celebration*. Sanborn was also one of the musicians featured at the 1995 6 *Wizard of Oz* concert for the Children's Defense Fund, for which Roger Daltrey turned in a riveting performance as the Tin Man. This concert was released on compact disc and turns up on TV around the holidays.

Sandom, Doug   Original drummer in the Who and a member of their precursor, the **Detours**, when they made their first recording, an early Pete Townshend song entitled "It Was You." In July or August of 1962 at the Peckham Club in South London, Detours drummer Harry Wilson was told that Townshend's "cousin" had been promised a stint on drums, and with that Harry was out and Doug was in. With eight more years experience than the rest of the quintet, his accomplished playing gave the others a burst of confidence. Doug's sister worked at a brass foundry, and its owner, Helmut Gorden, became the Who's manager in late 1963 or early 1964. In *Before I Get Old* Dave Marsh said Sandom was a fine musician and quoted John Entwistle as saying he was "ten times better than we were."

At one important audition in Willesden, a promoter pointed to Townshend out in the hallway and said to Doug, Roger Daltrey, and John Entwistle, "Get rid of him and I'll sign you" but Doug insisted, "Either you have us as we are, or you can get stuffed." Doug was the drummer when Barry Gray helped the Detours make their only recording, "It Was

You," which was Pete Townshend's first published song. A married bricklayer 10 years older than the other band members (though one newspaper listed him as being only four years older than Roger Daltrey and another the same age), and without Townshend's and Roger Daltrey's ambitions for the group, he resigned in 1964 after an uncomfortable audition for Chris Parmeinter. Pete, with whom he'd once been on good terms and whose decisions he had supported, came to feel that Sandom's more adult image and style were holding the group back, and agreed with Parmeinter's assessment of Sandom's future with the Detours.

Richard Barnes said that what Townshend did "was necessary but the way he did it left a lot to be desired" because Pete snarled something like "Get it together. What's wrong with you? If you can't get it right then you're out of the group." In Tony Fletcher's *Dear Boy* John and Roger were characterized as being stunned by Townshend's outburst, and on the way home John offered to resign as well but Doug vetoed that. Doug had a steady style of drumming that befit his calm personality, and was musically and temperamentally dissimilar to his eventual successor, Keith Moon. He was often annoyed by the constant nitpicking that occurred among them: "It was the same old thing that was going on in bands all the time. Niggling, you know? Niggly, niggly, niggly, have a go about him while he's not there. This happens all the time in bands. Oh, God! It's terrible…I mean, Peter hated to see a singer like he (Colin Dawson) was. He'd just stand there and wiggle his bum. Peter always used to say that: 'Look at him standin' there, wigglin' his arse.' It just didn't go down. Peter didn't like that."

Ironically, Sandom briefly served as drummer for the **Beachcombers** after Keith Moon left that band to join the Who. One drummer auditioned as Sandom's replacement in the Who before Keith Moon was discovered was Mitch Mitchell, who would later drum for **Jimi Hendrix**. Around 1977, John Entwistle and Pete Townshend began discussing the possible need for a new Who drummer and about a month before Keith Moon's death in 1978, John Entwistle invited Doug to an exhibition on the Who and left him with a copy of the new *Who Are You* album on which he wrote: "To Dougie — For Fuck's Sake Man. Where's your drumkit. We're desperate!" In 1998, the UK magazine *Mojo* had an article about drummers who had been in bands that eventually became famous and included were a short interview with and photo of Doug. Later that year he was warmly received by many fans at the second Who convention in London.

Sayer, Leo Singer/songwriter who had much commercial success in the 1970s after being discovered by **David Courtney**, **Adam Faith**, and

Roger Daltrey. Prior to recording under his own name Sayer had released one failed single with a band called Patches. According to Who discographer Ed Hanel, Keith Moon was the drummer on their "Living in America" 45. In 1972 Gerard Hugh Sayer responded to an ad placed by Courtney, a budding talent agent who had been a drummer for Faith. Instead of merely representing Sayer, Courtney instead forged a writing partnership with him that lasted most of the ensuing decade. Courtney introduced Sayer to Faith and it was Faith's wife Jackie who gave him the name "Leo" because she thought his frizzy hair made him look like a lion. Faith was producing an album of Courtney-Sayer songs featuring Sayer on vocals at Roger Daltrey's new East Burwash recording facilities in 1972 and the material impressed Roger. In 1973 Roger recorded a number of their songs for his self-titled debut solo album. All but two of the songs Daltrey used were Courtney-Sayer numbers, and the other two ("The Way of the World" and "You and Me") were by Faith and Courtney, who produced the album. The single "Giving It All Away" became a top five hit for Daltrey in the UK. Courtney and Sayer also wrote "There Is Love," a non-album B-side that surfaced on CD in the 1990s as a bonus track.

The album that Sayer had recorded at Daltrey's studios was entitled *Silverbird*, and it was released shortly after *Daltrey*. *Silverbird* gave Sayer a top five hit of his own in the UK, "The Show Must Go On." Around that time Sayer talked to Jeff Ward of *Melody Maker* at length about working with Daltrey. Sayer said that during his earliest encounters with Roger, before Roger had decided to attempt his own recordings of Courtney-Sayer songs, "He was a great spiritual help, giving me advice…" Later, after Roger recorded the Courtney-Sayer material for his own solo album, Sayer said, "He really got them by the scruff of the neck and really sang them. Up to then I was singing very sheepishly, and was very sheepish about my own work. I wasn't very proud of it."

Sayer recorded at least part of his second album, *Just a Boy*, at Daltrey's facility as well and it gave him his first big hit in the U.S., "Long Tall Glasses." The issue of *Melody Maker* dated June 7, 1975 reported on a British stage production of *Tommy* that included Leo in the title role and **Olivia Newton-John** and **Cliff Richard** among his co-stars. Sayer and Courtney then tabled their partnership for a couple of years but Sayer continued to form successful collaborations as evidenced by the three big hits from his platinum album *Endless Flight*: "How Much Love," "You Make Me Feel Like Dancing," and "When I Need You." However, sales of subsequent records dropped off, and Sayer reunited with Courtney in 1978. Sayer returned again to the U.S. charts in late 1980 with a version of Bobby Vee's "More Than I Can Say." However, the early '80s were generally disappointing for Sayer and he maintained a low profile until attempting a comeback in 1990 with his first new album in six years. It was largely ignored.

The Scaffold   British band that flourished in the latter half of the 1960s thanks in part to band member Roger McGough's earlier cult status as a poet and in part to the fact that band member Mike McGear was widely known as the brother of the **Beatles'** Paul McCartney despite the surname change. Keith Moon drummed on their song "Do the Albert," which can be found on their mid–1970s album, *Singles A's & B's*. The trio, which was rounded out by John Gorman, later surfaced as members of Grimms, which also included **Bonzo Dog Doo-Dah Band** member Neil Innes among others.

Scarlatti, Alessandro   Italian baroque composer (1660–1725). His son, Giuseppe Domenico, is considered the father of modern keyboard technique. Scarlatti's "Sonata K:212" and "Sonata K:213" and pieces composed by **Henry Purcell**, another famous baroque composer, were used in Townshend's radio dramatization of *Lifehouse* aired by the BBC in December of 1999.

Scorpions   A completely different group than the Who precursor listed next; this heavy metal group was formed in Germany in 1969. The Scorpions weren't widely known during the 1970s but became one of the most successful rock bands from continental Europe thanks to hits like "No One Like You" in 1982 and "Rock You Like a Hurricane" in 1984. The Scorpions were on the bill headlined by the Who in Nuremberg on September 1, 1979, a few months before their album *Animal Magnetism* surprisingly went gold in the U.S. Almost 10 years later they covered the Who's first single, "I Can't Explain," for inclusion by the Make a Difference Foundation on the heavy metal charitable compilation album *Stairway to Heaven/Highway to Hell*. Gorky Park contributed a cover of the Who's third single, "My Generation," to this compilation. "I Can't Explain" also turned up on a cassette single and on the Scorpions album *Best of Rockers 'n' Ballads*.

The Scorpions   A Who precursor led by John Entwistle and Pete Townshend, spun off of the first band the two had formed together, the **Aristocrats**. The Scorpions also included Acton County Grammar School classmates Mick Brown and Pete Wilson. The band performed only once under this name, at the Congo Club in the Acton Congregational Church, as had the very first band Entwistle and Townshend played together in, the **Confederates**. Roger Daltrey persuaded Entwistle to jump from the

Scorpions to the **Detours**, and Entwistle soon in turn succeeded in bringing Townshend in to replace the Detours' Reg Bowen.

Scott, Sandy *see* Halpin, Scott.

Screaming Lord Sutch and the Savages *see* Little, Carlo.

Sean, Sherman *see* Merchan, Chucho.

Sebastian, John   The best known member of the short-lived but popular '60s band the Lovin' Spoonful. They had a Top 10 hit in 1965 with their first 45, "Do You Believe in Magic," and a year or so later they hit #1 with "Summer in the City." They disbanded in 1968. Sebastian performed at Woodstock in 1969, as did the Who. At a Who concert in Boston during August of 1971, the audience was told that an old friend of the Who's would be joining them on stage, and out came a man in a tie-dyed outfit who looked like Sebastian. It turned out to be Keith Moon doing an impersonation. The real John Sebastian appeared onstage and played harmonica toward the end of a Who concert in the UK on October 9 of that year. In 1975 Sebastian played guitar on Moon's sole solo album, *Two Sides of the Moon*, on "Don't Worry Baby." In 1976 he reached #1 again with "Welcome Back," the theme song from the TV series *Welcome Back, Kotter*. Sebastian still turns up on TV from time to time. In 2000 the Lovin' Spoonful were inducted into the Rock and Roll Hall of Fame.

Sellers, Peter   Actor known for starring in such movies as *The Mouse That Roared*, *Dr. Strangelove*, *Being There*, and the *Pink Panther* series. **Ted Astley** provided music for the first movie in this list. When **Lou Reizner** transformed his 1972 orchestral version of *Tommy* from an album to a live performance in London on December 9, 1972, Sellers took on the role of the Doctor. **Richard Harris** had sung the role on the album. Sellers died in 1980.

The Sex Pistols   One of the famous British punk bands of the second half of the 1970s. In the issue of *New Musical Express* dated January 29, 1977, there was an account of Pete Townshend scuffling with a photographer in London's Speakeasy Club while Pete was trying to converse with Sex Pistols drummer Paul Cook and guitarist Steve Jones. Their comments about Pete in the article were positive. It has been assumed by many that after Townshend eventually staggered home he wrote the song "Who Are You" about his evening. About a year after this incident the Sex Pistols split up. Vocalist Johnny Rotten reverted to his given name John Lydon and founded the arty band Public Image Ltd; he released albums with them through 1992. Cook and Jones continued to record, with a variety of performers, but Jones has done so more frequently and with bigger names. Sex Pistols bass player Sid Vicious died of a drug overdose in early 1979 at the age of 21. On May 2 of that year some of the Sex Pistols were among the celebrities who attended **Kenney Jones**'s first concert with the Who, at the Rainbow Theatre in North London. On Townshend's 1980 solo album *Empty Glass* he dedicated the song "Rough Boys" to the Sex Pistols and to his daughters Emma and Minta. In 1980 the single "Frustration" by the band 4" Be 2" used their version of the Who's "[I] Can't Explain" as the B-side. This group included John Lydon's brother Jimmy, who produced the latter song. The A-side production credit went to "Johnny Rotten." In the liner notes for Pete Townshend's first double album of demos, *Scoop*, he noted that the 1981 Who song "Cache, Cache" was recorded "in Soho by Chris Ludwinski between drinking bouts with John Lydon and his brother Jimmy one night." In the mid– to late 1980s a live version of the Who's "Substitute" turned up on a few releases from the Sex Pistols archives. The Sex Pistols united for 1996 with Vicious's predecessor Glen Matlock on bass.

Sha Na Na   A large group of American students from Columbia University who exhibited nostalgia for the 1950s before that became a craze in the 1970s. Their big break was performing at Woodstock in 1969, and by 1977 they were popular enough to have their own syndicated TV show. On December 28, 1971 Keith Moon served as the master of ceremonies of one of their concerts, at New York's Carnegie Hall, and wore three different costumes during the event. Among his duties that night was to introduce comedians Cheech and Chong. In late 1974 John Entwistle told *Rolling Stone*: "There's quite a lack of humor in the business and I'd like to correct that. Thank God for Sha Na Na and the late **Bonzo Dog Doo-Dah Band**."

Shacklock, Alan   Producer of Roger Daltrey's 1985 album *Under a Raging Moon* and most of his 1987 album *Can't Wait to See the Movie*. He also played a few instruments on the former and co-wrote "It Don't Satisfy Me" with Daltrey. He was the bass player in the backing band when Daltrey did some rare solo gigs in December of 1985 with **Russ Ballard** and several other performers. Shacklock got his start as a musician in a 1970s band called Babe Ruth, but during the 1980s and 1990s his emphasis was producing. In the 1980s he produced albums for the Alarm and for Dennis DeYoung of **Styx**. In 1984 he produced **Meat Loaf**'s *Bad Attitude* album, which included a duet with Daltrey on the title track. In 1991 he produced the soundtrack album for Roger Daltrey's movie *Buddy's Song*, though the soundtrack album was released by co-star Chesney Hawkes under the name *The One and Only*.

The Shadows The biggest English rock instrumental group of the 1960s which existed into the '90s, fronted by guitar great Hank Marvin. He was a big influence on Pete Townshend in the late 1950s, along with **Chuck Berry**. The Shadows were originally formed as the backing band for **Cliff Richard** but had hits in their own right. While in the **Confederates** John Entwistle and Pete Townshend regularly performed Shadows numbers. Similarly, during the days when Colin Dawson was the lead singer of Roger Daltrey's **Detours**, they covered a number of songs sung by Richard as well as Shadows instrumentals. The Shadows joined with the Who and many other artists to perform at what **Richard Barnes** called "the pop event of 1966," a concert that included many of the UK artists that ranked high in a *New Musical Express* poll from 1965. The Shadows later covered "Pinball Wizard/See Me, Feel Me" on their 1973 UK LP, *Rockin' with Curly Leads*. Back in 1962 ex–Shadows Tony Meehan and Jet Harris performed as a duo and had three top five songs in the UK, including the #1 hit "Diamonds." However, Harris experienced a car crash and Meehan soon turned to songwriting and producing. On April 4, 1964, the Who opened for the Tony Meehan Combo. The Who had changed its name from the Detours about six weeks earlier but they were erroneously billed as the Detours that night. Meehan, who had been a drummer for the Shadows, provided strings, brass, woodwind, conga, and percussion on Roger Daltrey's 1975 solo album, *Ride a Rock Horse*. In 1977 Meehan teamed with **David Courtney** to produce Daltrey's third solo album, *One of the Boys*. He also handled arrangements and brought in his old Shadows associate Hank Marvin to help arrange two tracks, "Parade" and "Leon."

Shaffer, Paul Canadian keyboardist and bandleader for American talk show legend David Letterman. Paul's band has often played Who songs (though without vocals) during commercial breaks, and they've backed Pete Townshend and Roger Daltrey when each has been a guest. He told MTV after the Who's Rock 'n' Roll Hall of Fame induction that Keith Moon was "the all time greatest rock and roll drummer… ." Paul made a guest appearance at the American debut of the **British Rock Symphony** at a sold-out New York concert on April 22, 1998. Daltrey was the featured guest performer at subsequent performances but not that night. Shaffer MC'ed a press conference convened by the Who in April of 2000 to announce tour dates.

Shakespeare, William 17th-century English poet and playwright whose play *The Comedy of Errors* was performed on television by a cast that featured Roger Daltrey as both Dromio twins, comedic acting for which Roger was acclaimed. Positive reviews of the production and of

Daltrey's performance appeared in three periodicals all dated February 20, 1984: *People* magazine, the *New York Times*, and the *Washington Post*.

The Sharks *see* Spedding, Chris.

Shatlock, Alan *see* Shacklock, Alan.

Shaw, Mike   One of the Who's early employees as a result of being **Chris Stamp**'s friend from their school days. In the last half of 1964, not long after the Who temporarily became the **High Numbers,** Mike helped **Kit Lambert** shoot 16mm footage of the band performing at the Railway Hotel in Harrow & Wealdstone. This footage formed the basis of a short film that was often used to introduce the band at gigs and was an early example of how creative and original Lambert and Stamp were in promoting the band. On August 16 the High Numbers were one of several bands supporting the **Beatles** at a concert, and Mike helped make the High Numbers stand out by seeing to it that they were the only band to control their own stage lighting. Mike would also man the door at gigs to make sure that promoters wouldn't cheat the band, and his dedication was further demonstrated by his willingness to obtain information on the music business by making inquiries on behalf of the fictional Ramrods. During a telephone conversation with **Shel Talmy**, Shaw played him the demo version of "I Can't Explain," which persuaded Talmy to become the Who's producer.

Within a couple years, when Lambert and Stamp created their New Action company, the only other people involved were Mike and Kit's friend **Anya Butler**, who served as their secretary. With a background in lighting, Mike was also production manager, and did the handheld lighting for the 16-mm promotional film of "Happy Jack." He also encouraged the group to specify their lighting effects, which was very unusual at the time. "A lot of bands never realized you could go to a lighting man and tell him what lights you wanted on. For our two numbers, there'd be lights flashing off and on, good changing colors, blackouts and everything. Suddenly, the whole stage was blowing up sound-wise and the lights were going."

Later, confined to a wheelchair after an automobile accident rendered him paraplegic, Shaw was usually limited to office work. One notable exception to his new role took place on December 2, 1973, in Montreal: He was taken to jail, wheelchair and all, after the band and roadies destroyed a hotel suite. Shaw and **Bill Curbishley** designed the cover of *Meaty, Beaty, Big and Bouncy* though the photography was handled by **Graham Hughes**. In 1974 he compiled the Track compilation *Aniseed Allsorts*, which included three Who songs. Toward the end of the 1970s he was the music coordinator for the *Quadrophenia* movie soundtrack. Mike was an appropriate choice to compile *The Who's Greatest Hits* in 1983.

Shaw, Tommy see Styx.

Shepard, Vonda   Singer who hit it big in the late 1990s by singing the theme song "Searchin' My Soul" for the popular TV series *Ally McBeal* and appearing regularly on the show as a singer in a bar. Shepard, who was born in New York City in 1963, toured as a backup singer with **Jackson Browne** in the 1980s. Shepard has also appeared in commercials for the Hardee's chain of fast food restaurants. In an *Ally McBeal* episode that debuted in January of 2000 Shepard's character sang the Who's "See Me, Feel Me/Listening to You" as part of a dream sequence.

Sheppard, Neil see Ro Ro.

Shirley, Jerry see Humble Pie.

Siegler, John   Bass player on two of Roger Daltrey's solo albums, *Under a Raging Moon* in 1985 and *Can't Wait to See the Movie* in 1987. On the former, however, it was **Tony Butler** who handled that chore on the single "After the Fire." Earlier in his career Siegler was part of the band backing Hall & Oates during that duo's most successful period.

Simon, Paul   Half of the famous American duo Simon and Garfunkel, who performed at the Monterey Pop Festival in mid–June of 1967, as did the Who. Simon went on to a very successful solo career. Simon and Garfunkel were inducted into the Rock and Roll Hall of Fame in 1990, the same year as the Who. In September of 1995 Paul Simon and Pete Townshend were among the performers at a benefit concert in New York City for the Children's Health Fund. Paul and his band joined Pete for a version of "The Kids Are Alright."

Simone, Nina   American singer known as the "High Priestess of Soul" who performed the song "Fast Food" for Pete Townshend's 1989 *Iron Man* project, which was based on the children's story by **Ted Hughes**. Townshend had been introduced to her music in the 1960s thanks to the impressive record collection of his friend **Tom Wright**. In the Who's early days, Roger Daltrey listed her as one of his favorite singers. Simone, who was born Eunice Waymon in 1933, attended New York's famed Julliard School of Music. She had a gold record with her 1959 version of the musical number "I Loves You Porgy." Subsequent singles made her quite popular in the UK during the '60s, and she ended that decade with a successful cover of the **Bee Gees** song "To Love Somebody." She then became known for confrontational protest songs. Nina Simone died on April 21, 2003, at the age of 70.

Sinclair, John *see* Hoffman, Abbie.

The Small Faces Mod group viewed by East Londoners in 1965 as the counterpart to the Who in West London and whose drummer, **Kenney Jones**, would take Keith Moon's place in the Who. Along with the Who, the Small Faces performed at what **Richard Barnes** called "the pop event of 1966," a concert that included many of the UK artists who ranked high in a *New Musical Express* poll from 1965. In January of 1968 the Small Faces played a disastrous tour of Australia with the Who, though only the latter was characterized as "unwashed, foul-smelling, booze-swilling no-hopers" by the New Zealand *Truth*. One of the other times the Who and the Small Faces crossed paths was a tour safely back in their homeland that also featured Joe Cocker and **Arthur Brown** at the end of 1968, shortly before the **Rolling Stones'** Rock And Roll Circus. Guitarist/vocalist Steve Marriott left the band by 1969 to form **Humble Pie** with **Peter Frampton**, and his former group became simply the Faces with the addition of **Rod Stewart** and eventual Rolling Stone Ron Wood.

The Faces had a hit with "Stay with Me" in 1971. In late 1973 Marriott took over **Steve Winwood**'s role of the father in the second performance of **Lou Reizner**'s production of *Tommy* for charity. That same year original Small Face **Ronnie Lane**, with whom Pete Townshend collaborated on **Meher Baba** projects and the *Rough Mix* album, left the Faces and did not join with Marriott, Jones, keyboardist Ian McLagan and some new members, including former **Thunderclap Newman** and Wings guitarist Jimmy McCulloch, when the Small Faces were revived briefly in 1977–78.

In 1990 Marriott died in a fire at the age of 43, and in 1997 Lane died of multiple sclerosis at the age of 51. Shortly thereafter *Mojo* magazine reported that an expanded version of the classic 1968 Small Faces album *Ogden's Nut Gone Flake* would serve as the soundtrack for an animated film. Kenney Jones said, "We need to re-write the story to make Happiness Stan bump into people and talk to them more, to make it more of a story. That means we needed another five songs at least, of which Pete Townshend is going to write a couple," presumably in place of Ronnie Lane. The project originated in part as a tribute to Lane and reunited Jones, Stewart, McLagan, and Wood for the new recordings and possibly some live appearances. In fact, the Faces were offered an appearance at the Prince's Trust charitable concert in June of 1996, but Stewart felt the band should decline due to a lack of practice. Roger Daltrey, John Entwistle, and Pete Townshend, temporarily eschewing the name "The Who," then agreed to appear and premiered their multimedia update of *Quadrophenia*.

Small, Henry   Canadian vocalist with the John Entwistle Band during its 1980s phase, when it also went by the name the Rock. Henry co-wrote most of the songs, primarily with guitarist Devin Powers, on the band's long-delayed album, which was released in 1996. Henry also spent some time in a long-lived Canadian band called Prism. Some of his work can be heard on that band's *From the Vaults* CD.

Smith, Curly   *see* Jo Jo Gunne.

Smith, "Legs" Larry   *see* The Bonzo Dog Doo-Dah Band.

Smith, Patti   Punkish rocker who led the Patti Smith Group in the last half of the 1970s and who recorded a foul-mouthed but snappy version of the Who's "My Generation" in Cleveland in early 1976. It surfaced as the B-side of her "Gloria" 45 and on a 1986 various artists compilation on the Arista label called *Rock at the Edge*. A version of "The Kids Are Alright" appears on a U.S. bootleg LP of hers.

Smith, Pete   Executive producer, along with Steve Vining and Alex Lawrie, of the 1998 London Philharmonic Orchestra album *Who's Serious*. In his liner notes Smith said that "Baba O'Riley" and Pete Townshend's *Quadrophenia* songs "possess a unique combination of musical sophistication and focused rock song format" and noted that "Townshend's songwriting has significantly incorporated classical music elements from a very early stage."

The Smithereens   New Jersey-based band that had some chart success in the late 1980s with songs like "Only a Memory" and "A Girl Like You" but it was clear that they had a soft spot for British Invasion songs from two decades earlier. Their six-song *Live* CD included a live version of the Who's 1970 single, "The Seeker," that was recorded in October of 1986 at a concert which aired on MTV. They've also been known to perform "Substitute" live. In November of 1987, drummer Dennis Diken wrote that "We've always dug the Who and were really heavily influenced by their music (especially the *Happy Jack*-era stuff for me personally). "The Seeker" was a lesser known track of theirs that we toyed around with in rehearsal and debuted at CBGB's in the spring of 1986. It'd become a big live favorite with our audiences... ." The Smithereens recorded a studio version of this song in the spring of 1987. It was released a year later on the flip side of their "Only a Memory" cassette single and turned up on their 1995 compilation CD, *Attack of the Smithereens*. The CD's liner notes state that the "slight ignorant lyric change" was courtesy of lead singer Pat DiNizio, who confused two verses at different points. Nevertheless, the entire band did a good job on the song.

The Smothers Brothers   American comedy duo comprised of real-life brothers, Tom and Dick Smothers. In the 1960s they hosted a variety show on American television and the Who appeared on it in September of 1967, just after they concluded their first American tour in support of **Herman's Hermits**. Half of this appearance was used in 1979 to provide the beginning for the Who movie *The Kids Are Alright*. The explosion at the end of "My Generation" caused **Bette Davis** to faint offstage into **Mickey Rooney**'s arms. In John G. Fuller's *Are the Kids All Right?* the creator of *The Kids Are Alright*, **Jeff Stein** said, "It proves that the Who were the greatest rock and roll band in the world." In 2000 this performance was ranked by the cable TV channel VH1 as the 10th greatest moment in rock 'n' roll history.

Snider, Todd   "Satiric troubadour" (that's what he was called by MCA Records, which is also the Who's label in America) whose 1994 single was entitled "My Generation (Part 2)," which does not resemble the original, either musically or lyrically. However, Todd did seem to be using his satiric skills to suggest that his generation needs to develop some admirable qualities, like Pete Townshend's.

Snow, Phoebe   Singer whose eponymous debut album in 1974 yielded the top five single "Poetry Man." During an internet interview, Phoebe said that Roger Daltrey was one of the performers with whom she'd like to record a duet someday. She had sung on a few of the songs (though not with Roger) during the 1995–6 *Wizard of Oz* concert for the Children's Defense Fund, at which Roger turned in a riveting performance as the Tin Man. This concert was released on compact disc and turns up on TV around the holidays. Phoebe and Roger also helped unveil the **British Rock Symphony** at a sold-out show in 1998.

Spalding, Phil   Bass player during the first half of 1994 "Daltrey Sings Townshend" concerts, after which John Entwistle would be introduced and take over. He also played bass on the London Philharmonic Orchestra's 1998 album *Who's Serious* and on the 1999 **British Rock Symphony** CD. From 1986 to 1996 he performed on albums for Ray Charles, **Elton John**, Matthew Sweet, Terence Trent D'Arby, GTR, and Michael Oldfield. He also performed on **Simon Townshend**'s 1999 CD, *Animal Soup*.

Spandau Ballet Successful 1980s group consisting of British schoolmates. "True," a single in 1983, was among their hits. By the close of the decade brothers Gary and Martin Kemp were turning their attention to acting and lead singer Tony Hadley pursued a solo career in the 1990s. In 1996 Hadley took part in a radio production of **Andrew Lloyd Webber** and **Tim Rice**'s musical *Jesus Christ Superstar* on BBC 2. The British heartthrob had the title role, Roger Daltrey was Judas, and comedian Julian Clary was King Herod.

Spear, Roger Ruskin *see* The Bonzo Dog Doo-Dah Band.

Spedding, Chris One of the most noteworthy session guitarists in rock, having worked with Jack Bruce, Lulu, Gilbert O'Sullivan, Dusty Springfield, **David Essex**, Donovan, **Roy Harper**, Brian Eno, and **Bryan Ferry**, among others. He was also a member of a band called the Sharks, whose third album, to be called *Music Breakout*, was produced by John Entwistle and **John Alcock** in 1974. According to the lengthy biography at chrisspedding.com, in September and October of that year the album was rejected by Island Records and other labels, and the Sharks soon broke up. "There were so many tensions that the only way we produced any music at all was with an incredible amount of hassle," Spedding recalled. "But that was probably the thing that was producing all the music." In 1976, Spedding compiled a list of his "guitar heroes" for *Melody Maker* magazine and called Pete Townshend and the **Rolling Stones**' Keith Richards the "two most famous and important rhythm guitarists in rock." Spedding was one of the musicians helping Roger Daltrey record a solo album in the early 1980s that was to be called *Pop Records*, but the results haven't been released as of this writing. Spedding played guitar on Roger Daltrey's 1984 solo LP, *Parting Should Be Painless*. Spedding also played guitar on projects for **Mike Batt** in 1984 and 1998 that each featured Roger Daltrey's vocals on one song.

Spike Nickname of Helen Wilkins, who was executive producer of Roger Daltrey's *Parting Should Be Painless* album and who compiled the *Scoop* and *Another Scoop* collections of Pete Townshend demos. In the late 1980s, Pete commissioned her to compile a boxed set from the body of Who archives and out-takes, but the project was shelved. Such a set would not appear until mid–1994 under the direction of **Chris Charlesworth**.

Spoon, Kief Name employed by Keith Moon when he drummed on John Lennon's *Sometime in New York City* album in 1972, two years after Lennon's **Beatles** broke up.

Springer, Jerry America's most infamous talk show host at the end of the millennium who also happened to be the mayor of Cincinnati until three days before 11 fans died at the Who concert in his city on December 3, 1979. In the midst of his family's flight from the Holocaust to New York City, Springer was born in London in 1944 barely a fortnight before Roger Daltrey. Springer earned a law degree at Northwestern University and in 1971 won a seat on the Cincinnati city council. In December of 1975, the Who and Wings performed concerts in Cincinnati and several months later an articulate young fan named Richard Klopp wrote a letter of complaint to various officials about fans being crushed due to the first come, first served "festival seating." As revealed in John G. Fuller's account of the subsequent tragedy, *Are the Kids All Right?*, Councilman Springer was the only person to acknowledge Klopp's prophetic letter. In fact, Springer is one of the officials thanked in Fuller's acknowledgments. On August 5, 1976, Springer said publicly that festival seating caused a "climate of disorder," but the coliseum's Brian Heekin said Springer was not qualified to comment on concerts. In 1977, Springer became one of the nation's youngest mayors at age 33 (though his successor would be even younger). However, his political career suffered some damage due to a prostitution scandal — the proof was in the form of his payment by personal check. J. Kenneth Blackwell was sworn in as the new mayor in late 1979, but in the first several days after the tragedy it was only Springer who said there should have been someone at the venue with the authority to order that doors be opened when it was obvious that disaster was looming.

The Squadronaires *see* Townshend, Cliff.

Squier, Billy Successful 1980s rock frontman from the Boston area whose band included **Alan St. Jon** and who sang and played guitar on "Rebel Without a Car" on the John Entwistle Band's *Van-Pires* soundtrack album.

Staehely, Al *see* Jo Jo Gunne.

Staehely, John *see* Jo Jo Gunne.

Stainton, Chris Frequent keyboard player for Joe Cocker starting in the 1960s and for **Eric Clapton** since 1980 who also has a number of other credits, including a batch with the Who. On the Who's double album *Quadrophenia* in 1973 Chris played keyboards on "The Dirty Jobs," "5.15" and "Drowned." Pete Townshend wanted Stainton to back the Who on the 1973 tour promoting the album, but Roger Daltrey didn't want anyone onstage with the Who. On the *Tommy* movie soundtrack in 1975 Stainton played organ on "1951/What About the Boy," "We're Not Gonna

Take It" and "Listening to You"/"See Me, Feel Me." In addition, he played piano on "There's a Doctor" and acoustic guitar with Alan Ross of **Ro Ro** on "Tommy Can You Hear Me?" In 1982 Stainton played on Pete Townshend's 1982 album *All the Best Cowboys Have Chinese Eyes* and two years later he backed **Simon Townshend** on his album *Sweet Sound*.

Stamp, Chris Manager of the Who with **Kit Lambert** from 1964 into the 1970s. Chris and **Terence Stamp** were the sons of an East End tugboat man. Chris and Kit met at Shepperton Studios as assistant movie directors. In 1963 they decided to tap into Britain's pop music craze and spent at least four months hunting for a relatively unknown group to showcase on camera. In July of 1964 Lambert and Stamp's old classmate **Mike Shaw** discovered the **High Numbers** at a gig. Around August 1 Stamp had the opportunity to see the band for himself, and within a month Lambert and Stamp had largely pushed publicist **Peter Meaden** and nominal manager Helmut Gorden out of the picture. **Richard Barnes** said that when the band needed an infusion of money, Stamp worked on the movie *The Heroes of Telemark*, which starred Kirk Douglas. Filming was in Norway, and once a week Stamp would wire most of his salary to Lambert. By November Lambert persuaded the High Numbers to revert to their previous name, the Who. When Lambert and Stamp created their New Action company, the only other people involved were Shaw and Kit's friend **Anya Butler**. Anya helped bring **Shel Talmy** in to produce records for the Who in 1965.

When the Who were considering what single to record in 1965 after "Anyway Anyhow Anywhere," Roger Daltrey reportedly resisted using "My Generation." In *Before I Get Old*, Stamp told Dave Marsh, "It really took a lot of persuading to get it going. It took me at least two months to persuade Roger and everybody that they should record it." According to *The Who Concert File*, it was Stamp's idea for Roger to stutter certain words while singing it. Chris spent much of 1966 making trips to New York fighting the lawsuit Talmy filed in March and thus was regularly trying to evade the opportunistic rock impresario Allan Klein, whom Talmy insisted be part of their settlement negotiations. Stamp also spent time trying to develop a rapport with Decca Records, the Who's stodgy American label. Stamp and Lambert also became the managers of the **Merseys**, who then released a version of the Pete Townshend composition "So Sad About Us" in July of 1966, before the Who released its own version.

By 1969 Lambert and Stamp had turned the day-to-day operations of the Who over to **John "Wiggy" Wolff**, and Wiggy and Townshend tried mightily but ultimately in vain to resist **Frank Barsalona**'s effort to recruit the Who for the now-legendary Woodstock festival. Due to growing animosity between Roger Daltrey on the one hand and Lambert and Stamp on the other, Daltrey anointed **Bill Curbishley** as his personal manager for his 1973 debut solo album, *Daltrey*. Roger then snapped when an investigation revealed just how much of the Who's money was unaccounted for and soon insisted that Lambert and Stamp turn over managing responsibilities of the Who to Curbishley.

Curbishley became the manager around the summer of 1974, and spent many months disentangling the Who contractually from New Action and Track Records. *Quadrophenia* was the last new Who album on which Lambert and Stamp were credited, as executive producers. However, in 1975 Stamp received credit as executive producer of the *Tommy* movie. In the spring of 1978 *Melody Maker* reported that Track had been liquidated (though it had essentially been dead for two years). According to Richard Barnes, around 1977 Townshend asked Stamp and Nik Cohn (the critic who'd inspired Pete to write "Pinball Wizard") to write a screenplay for a movie based on *Quadrophenia*. Stamp was ultimately credited as a story consultant. On the Who's 1987 U.S. album *Two's Missing* their version of **Bo Diddley**'s "I'm a Man" from 1965 was incorrectly attributed to Lambert and Stamp. Chris was thanked in the credits of Roger Daltrey's 1994 CD *A Celebration — The Music of Pete Townshend and the Who*. During the 1990s Daltrey kept trying to get a movie about Keith Moon off the ground, and at some point brought Stamp in as a partner. In June of 1995 Stamp wrote liner notes that were used when *A Quick One*, the Who's second album, was reissued on CD with bonus tracks.

Stamp, Terence Movie actor who is the brother of former Who co-manager **Chris Stamp**. Terence made his film debut in 1962 in Peter Ustinov's adaptation of Herman Melville's *Billy Budd* and earned an Oscar nomination. In 1965 Terence was to be flown first-class to the U.S. for a role in the movie *The Collector* but he exchanged his ticket for two coach seats so that Chris could visit the American offices of Decca Records for the first time. Terence also helped Chris and the Who economize by letting Chris stay in his suite.

During 1965 the Who released their records in the UK on the Brunswick label but on Decca in the U.S. The Who had heard that the Decca staff was quite conservative and out of touch, meaning that the Who's recording career could suffer in the U.S. as a result. The Who wanted Chris to assess the situation in person but couldn't afford to send him until Terence rode to the rescue. Chris confirmed their suspicions about Decca, but the trip was more fruitful for Terence, whose acting in the movie would earn him the Best Actor award at the Cannes Film Festival. In mid–1967 Stamp and actress Julie Christie were immortalized in the **Kinks** song "Waterloo Sunset" when Ray Davies sang, "Terry and Julie cross over the river, where they feel safe and sound."

In 1980 Terence played the villainous General Zod in *Superman II* (15 years before Roger Daltrey would menace the Man of Steel on the American TV series *Lois & Clark: the New Adventures of Superman*). In 1994 Stamp was acclaimed for his acting range in the cult movie *The Adventures of Priscilla, Queen of the Desert*. In 1999, he could be seen as Supreme Chancellor Valorum in *Star Wars: Episode I— The Phantom Menace* and in *The Limey*, which used the Who's 1970 single "The Seeker" on its soundtrack.

Stanley, Richard BBC science documentary director of the early 1970s who was one of many friends with whom Pete Townshend discussed the development of the rock opera *Tommy*. Stanley, who once lived in the same house as Pete and his wife, Karen, was one of several devotees of **Meher Baba** who typically attended the **Mike McInnerney** gatherings that Pete Townshend described in his 1999 liner notes for the *Avatar* boxed set. Stanley graduated with an advanced degree in filmmaking from London's Royal College of Art in 1968, the same year that he made a short film called *Lone Ranger*. According to John Atkins's *The Who on Record*, Townshend recorded four songs, mostly instrumentals, for the film's main theme (possibly titled "Spanish Foot"), title music, swimming pool sequence, and "Frankenstein sequence."

Lone Ranger earned Stanley a Golden Hugo from the Chicago Film Festival and the prize for best script at the Nyons Festival in France. According to Dave Marsh in *Before I Get Old*, the song "Something in the Air" was written for Stanley's use the year before it became a #1 hit for **Thunderclap Newman**. Stanley was part of an expedition into the heart of Brazil searching for a native tribe living a stone age lifestyle. In 1969 his film of this trek won a Golden Bear award for best documentary. He then joined the BBC science series *Horizon* and filmed more award-winning documentaries. He also crafted music promotion films in the early '70s for such performers as Santana, Yes and members of the **Beatles**. In 1970 Stanley was the cinematographer on the Isle of Wight movie, which was commercially released in 1995. In 1972 Stanley filmed a meeting of the Who at Roger Daltrey's home, and some of this black & white footage was used for the Who's 1979 movie *The Kids Are Alright*. Stanley moved to Finland in 1974 to work as a music producer and recorded with many top Finnish bands, but 10 years later he returned his focus to visual media. Townshend's friend Richard Stanley, who was born in Leicester, England in 1943, is not to be confused with the younger horror movie director and writer of the same name from South Africa.

Stanshall, Viv *see* The Bonzo Dog Doo-Dah Band.

Starkey, Zak Son of **Beatles** drummer Ringo Starr who is also a noted drummer in his own right. Zak was born on September 13, 1965, the oldest of Ringo's three children with Maureen Cox. Zak received his first full drum kit from Keith Moon, who was a close friend of Ringo's. Zak recalls that at big parties in the early 1970s only Keith would pay attention to any kids who were present. Tony Fletcher's definitive Moon biography *Dear Boy* provides several other insights into Zak's relationship with Keith. Zak wed Sarah Menikides in January of 1985. The birth of Zak's daughter Tatia rekindled his relationship with Ringo, which had deteriorated when Zak developed a drinking problem as a teen and after his parents divorced.

In the early 1980s Zak started working on a project that had been conceived in 1976 by Eddie Hardin, who had been **Steve Winwood**'s replacement in the **Spencer Davis** Group back in the 1960s. The goal was to turn Kenneth Graham's well known novel *Wind in the Willows* into a musical. This came to fruition in 1985 on an album by that name with help from many noted musicians including John Entwistle playing bass on "Piper at the Gates of Dawn." There was a live performance of the musical in Germany during 1991 (which wasn't released until 1998) but Entwistle didn't lend Eddie and Zak a hand that time. The same year that *Wind in the Willows* was first recorded Zak drummed on the title track of Roger Daltrey's 1985 solo album, *Under a Raging Moon*. He performed one of the song's drum solos in honor of Keith and teamed with **Mark Brzezicki** during the song's "outro." Soon thereafter Zak was the drummer on the John Entwistle Band's long-delayed album, *The Rock*, which was released in 1996 though recorded about a decade earlier. However, **Steve Luongo** stepped in to drum on the 1988 tour that followed the recording sessions.

In 1987 Zak drummed on an album for Michael D'Abo and then briefly joined the band Icicle Works but left before their next album was released. Zak joined his father for All Starr Band world tours in 1992 and '96. In 1994 Zak played drums behind Roger at "Daltrey Sings Townshend" concerts. That same year Zak's mother died due to leukemia. In 1996 and 1997 Zak drummed energetically and commendably for the Who on their "Quadrophenia" tours. A year later he drummed on the London Philharmonic Orchestra's 1998 album *Who's Serious*, which consisted of various Who songs played in a classical style. He also performed throughout the

1999 **British Rock Symphony** video headlined by Daltrey. In 2000 and 2002 he toured as part of the Who again.

Starr, Ringo *see* The Beatles.

Stars On Band of anonymous musicians who achieved surprising success by releasing albums consisting of multi-song medleys set to an unwavering rhythm of hands clapping. 1981 saw the release of *Stars on Long Play II*, which contained 21 seconds from the beginning of a bland version of "The Overture from Tommy" before morphing into disco whooping.

Stealers Wheel London pop group of the mid–1970s led by Gerry Rafferty and Joe Egan, whose song "You Put Something Better Inside of Me" was covered by Roger Daltrey as a non-album B-side in July of 1977. The song later turned up on Daltrey's *Best Bits* album and as a bonus track when his *Ride a Rock Horse* album was released on compact disc in the 1990s. It had been recorded by Ted Neeley of *Jesus Christ Superstar* fame back in 1973, the year that Stealers Wheel's self-titled debut album was released. That album produced the band's U.S. and UK Top 10 hit "Stuck in the Middle with You," which **Adam Faith** and Daltrey covered together in 1993.

The drummer on *Stealers Wheel* was Rod Coombes, who in 1972 drummed on John Entwistle's second solo album, *Whistle Rymes*, on the songs "Ten Little Friends" and "I Was Just Being Friendly." Coombes had been in **Ro Ro** and would later join the Strawbs. By the third Stealers Wheel album a couple years later Dave Wintour had become the band's bass player. He had played on Roger Daltrey's 1973 debut solo album *Daltrey* and on Daltrey's 1975 album *Ride a Rock Horse*. He also played bass on the *Tommy* movie soundtrack, on "Cousin Kevin." From 1973 to the early 1980s Wintour played bass on albums for Murray Head, **Rick Wakeman**, Adam Faith, **Leo Sayer**, **Steve Swindells**, Rick Springfield, Neil Sedaka, the Raspberries' Eric Carmen, Alexis Korner, and **Russ Ballard**, among others. He also played on the *Rocky Horror Picture Show* soundtrack. After Stealers Wheel split around 1975 Rafferty went on to hit it big solo with "Baker Street" in 1978 and recorded several more solo albums in the 1980s and 1990s. Egan maintained a low profile until the late 1990s, when he engineered several various artists compilations.

Steely Dan *see* Baxter, Jeff "Skunk."

Stein, Ben Renaissance man whose Comedy Central quiz show, *Win Ben Stein's Money*, has included some Who-related references. He has typically started episodes by uttering a quote in his trademark monotone, and once he slightly revised a well known Who lyric by saying, "Nobody knows what it's like to be the sad man, to be the bad man, behind blue eyes." On another occasion, after winning the show's concluding contest against the top-scoring contestant, he recited the closing line of the Who's "Won't Get Fooled Again." In other episodes, categories of questions have included "Townshend Acts not Involving Smashed Guitars" and "Thou Shalt Not Commit a Daltrey." (It should be noted that "Thou Shalt Not Commit a Daltrey" was the title of a *New Musical Express* article by Danny Kelly in that publication's March 2, 1991 issue.) Two dozen years before his quiz show's 1997 debut, Stein served as a speech writer and lawyer for U.S. President Richard Nixon and successor Gerald Ford. In addition to extensive writing for newspapers and magazines, he has written and published over a dozen books, half novels and half nonfiction. He is also a well known actor, and his role as a lifeless teacher in *Ferris Bueller's Day Off* was ranked among the 50 most famous scenes in American film.

Stein, Jeff The young Who fan commissioned to create the semibiographical movie *The Kids Are Alright*. The Who had played live only once in 1977, and Stein was disappointed in the lack of relatively current live footage available, so special concerts were arranged for him to film. Thus on May 25, 1978, Keith Moon performed live with the Who for the final time, and their second performance that day of "Won't Get Fooled Again" became the movie's closing number. Jeff's brother Kevin provided photos for the *30 Years of Maximum R&B* boxed set's booklet in 1994.

Stereophonics Alternative rock band from the UK that has had chart success since its 1997 debut, *Word Gets Around*, landed in the UK Top 10. In 2001 the CD entitled *Substitute: The Songs of the Who* included a version of "Who Are You" by Stereophonics with backing vocals from Noel Gallagher of **Oasis**. In addition, the final track of the CD features Kelly Jones of Stereophonics singing "Substitute" with the Who. The performance was from a November 27, 2000 concert to benefit the Teenage Cancer Trust.

Stewart, Dave *see* Eurythmics.

Stewart, Ian *see* The Rolling Stones.

Stewart, Rod Gravely-voiced British singer who had success with the **Jeff Beck** Group and the **Faces**, and as a solo artist ever since. According to **Richard Barnes**, when Stewart was a member of Long John Baldry's Hootchie Coochie Men in 1965, he was once wooing the same young woman as Keith Moon. As the story went, Stewart rode on a train with Keith Moon and the two struck up a conversation. It turned out they were both riding as far as Bournemouth with the intention of paying a visit to model Kim Kerrigan, who ultimately married Moon. However, according to Tony Fletcher's definitive Moon biography *Dear Boy*, the story isn't true, though Stewart did admit over 30 years later he did have a crush on Kim until he realized how much Keith cared for her. In 1969 and '70 **Lou Reizner** produced albums for Stewart, and when Reizner soon started developing his all-star orchestral production of *Tommy*, he reportedly wanted Stewart for the lead role though not surprisingly it went to Roger Daltrey. Stewart instead sang "Pinball Wizard" on Reizner's 1972 album. Stewart's version of "Pinball Wizard" also turned up on his first greatest hits LP. Stewart and Daltrey suggested that Reizner have his production performed live on stage. According to Barnes, Stewart tried to steal the show "but he failed miserably." When the movie version of *Tommy* was in development a couple of years later, the Who reportedly wanted Stewart for "Pinball Wizard" but **Elton John** talked him out of it.

Stigwood, Robert   Producer of some very well known movies in the 1970s who had been an early booking agent for the Who. In 1966 Stigwood's new Reaction label helped the Who immensely in its legal battle with **Shel Talmy** by being willing to release the Who's fourth single, "Substitute," on March 4, 1966. In *Before I Get Old* Dave Marsh noted that the Who's brief association with Reaction was crucial because established labels would probably shun any group facing litigation. The Who's other new recordings in 1966 were also on the Reaction label: the "I'm a Boy" and "Happy Jack" singles and the *Ready Steady Who* EP. The three Who 45s released in 1965 under Talmy were on the Brunswick label and Talmy continued to release Who 45s on Brunswick in 1966 until November when his dispute with the Who was settled. Stigwood's Reaction label also released early recordings by **Jimi Hendrix**, Cream, and Australia's **Bee Gees**. Stigwood, who was from Australia himself, managed the latter two acts as well. In 1967 Stigwood used **Frank Barsalona**'s negotiations with Murray the K over Mitch Ryder and the Who to get Cream on the Easter show as well. In the early 1970s Stigwood produced the movie version of *Jesus Christ Superstar*, and this gave him sufficient credibility to be named the producer of the *Tommy* movie in mid–1973. Stigwood's biggest movie successes, which also featured music prominently, came later in the 1970s as producer of the blockbusters *Saturday Night Fever* and *Grease*. After sequels to both movies proved to be duds in the early 1980s Stigwood maintained a low profile until producing the 1996 movie version of *Evita*.

Sting   *see*   The Police.

The Stone Canyon Band   *see*   Nelson, Rick.

Stone the Crows Early 1970s British soul band that included Les Harvey and Scottish singer Maggie Bell, who were introduced by Les's brother, Alex. Also in the band was Scotsman Jim Dewar, who later worked with **John Alcock** and John Entwistle. Bell portrayed Mrs. Walker in **Lou Reizner**'s all-star stage version of the Who's *Tommy* in 1972. Around this time she also sang on the Ellis album *Riding on the Crest of a Slump*, which Roger Daltrey produced. Former **Thunderclap Newman** guitarist Jimmy McCulloch helped the band finish its final album in 1972 after Les Harvey's fatal electrocution on stage at the age of 27. McCulloch, who would go on to play in Wings with ex–**Beatle** Paul McCartney as well as the reformed **Small Faces**, would also die at the age of 27 seven years later, due to a heart attack. Stone the Crows split up in June of 1973 and Bell had a solo career that netted two Top 40 singles in the UK by 1981. An early boost to her solo career was supporting the Who before 50,000 at their Charlton football stadium show in South London on May 18, 1974. Among her more recent credits is singing on the 1998 version of the Eddie Hardin/**Zak Starkey** *Wind in the Willows* album.

The Stones *see* The Rolling Stones.

The Stranglers One of the most durable and influential bands of the 1970s punk/new wave era though with much less media attention than many of their counterparts. At one point this band criticized the Who, and Pete Townshend countered with some very unkind comments in a *Melody Maker* interview late in the summer of 1977. However, the two sparring parties must have reconciled within two years because the Stranglers joined AC/DC and Nils Lofgren (who played with **Neil Young** in the early 1970s and joined Bruce Springsteen's band in 1984) as the supporting bands on the bill headlined by the Who on August 18, 1979 at Wembley Stadium. This concert was the Who's official London relaunch with new drummer **Kenney Jones** despite the fact that they had played at the Rainbow Theatre in North London on May 2nd of that year. 77,000 filled Wembley to its legal limit.

The Strawberry Alarm Clock A 1967 one-hit wonder from California that reached #1 with the song "Incense and Peppermints." A very rare album created for the Ford Motor Company consisted of five Who songs on one side and five by the Strawberry Alarm Clock on the flipside.

Streetwalkers Group formed by two of the founding members of **Family**, Roger Chapman and Charlie Whitney, shortly after that band broke up in 1973. Streetwalkers were among the groups on the bill that was headlined by the Who at three UK soccer stadiums on the 1976 "Who

Put the Boot In" mini-tour. It was at Charlton on this tour that the Who earned a longstanding entry in the *Guinness Book of World Records* for Loudest Pop Group. Bassist Phil Chen was one of Streetwalkers' earlier members. He played bass on the *Tommy* movie soundtrack, on "Amazing Journey," "Sensation," "Sally Simpson," "Go to the Mirror," and "Do You Think It's Alright?" A decade later Chen played on Pete Townshend's *White City* album. Over the years he also recorded with Donovan, **Jeff Beck**, and **Rod Stewart**. A later Streetwalkers member was future **Iron Maiden** drummer Nicko McBrain. By the end of 1977 the group had disbanded. Roger Chapman went on to work with **Geoff Whitehorn**.

Streiker, Lisa *see* Strike, Liza.

Streisand, Barbra Renowned American singer and actress who in 1985 made an MTV-style music video for her song "Emotion" featuring Roger Daltrey as her mate. In her biography *The Second Decade* she said that "Roger was really fun to work with. He brought a whole new dimension to the character of the husband. Although I felt bad for him; he kept wanting to make this into a feature." The video was released to movie theaters and accompanied screenings of Madonna's movie *Desperately Seeking Susan*.

Strike, Liza One of the singers for the *Tommy* movie. Around that time Pete Townshend promised her he would perform a rare solo concert for charity at the Roundhouse in April of 1974 but he thought the crowd would be very small. Pete was incredibly nervous that day, and **Richard Barnes** (who rendered her name as Lisa Streiker) theorized that this experience kept him from breaking away from the Who.

Strummer, Joe *see* The Clash.

Styx Chicago area pop/rock band that grew into one of the biggest musical acts from the second half of the 1970s into the early 1980s. Their many hit singles included "Lorelei," "Babe," "Lady," "Come Sail Away," "Fooling Yourself (The Angry Young Man)," "Blue Collar Man (Long Nights)" and "Too Much Time on My Hands." In 1984 Styx split up but they have reformed with differing lineups a few times since. In 1999 the **British Rock Symphony** CD included longtime Styx guitarist Tommy Shaw singing the Who's "See Me, Feel Me"/"Listening to You." Newer Styx member Glen Burtnik wrote songs for a kid-oriented project that Roger Daltrey was once pursuing.

Sutch, Lord *see* Little, Carlo.

Sweet 1970s pop/rock band from Britain with hits like "Little Willy,"

"Ballroom Blitz," "Fox on the Run" and "Love Is Like Oxygen" and which included a version of the Who's "My Generation" on the UK pressing of *Desolation Boulevard* though not on the American release. Band member Brian Connolly died of a heart attack in 1997 at the age of 52.

Swervedriver   Popular UK band of the 1990s that covered the Who's classic B-side "In the City" on the 1993 various artists tribute CD *Who Covers Who* and covered "Magic Bus" on one of their own releases. The former song also turned up on their "Last Train to Satansville" EP in 1993.

Swindells, Steve   Songwriter whose compositions have appeared on several of Roger Daltrey's albums. Swindells had played with the band Pilot and in the late 1970s was keyboard player in the Hawkwind spin-off the Hawklords. Shortly thereafter he provided the song "Bitter And Twisted" for the *McVicar* soundtrack. He also contributed "Martyrs And Madmen" and "Treachery" on Roger Daltrey's *Best Bits* album in 1982. When Roger sang the latter he said that foremost in his mind was the assassination of Egyptian leader **Anwar al-Sadat**, which was in the news at the time. Swindells's two *Best Bits* songs were finally released on CD in 1998 as bonus tracks on Daltrey's *One of the Boys* album. In 1984 Swindells wrote "Don't Wait on the Stairs" on Daltrey's solo LP *Parting Should Be Painless*. For over 20 years Swindells has recorded solo from time to time. He recently released a CD entitled *Y2K*.

The Swinging Blue Jeans   Group formed in Liverpool that had some success in 1963–64, starting with "Hippy Hippy Shake." They were sold to British youth as fashion leaders, and helped popularize leather jackets and of course blue jeans in certain circles. In 1964 they were one of the bands that opened for **Chuck Berry** at a concert that was the first large gathering of mods which Pete Townshend attended. The **Animals** met with approval from the mods because they were considered a "rhythm and blues group" but the sight of the rocker-like Swinging Blue Jeans getting booed off the stage and having objects hurled at them might have been an image in the back of Pete's mind when conceiving *Quadrophenia*. In fact, Chris May and Tim Phillips noted in their book *British Beat* that being booed off the stage happened to the Swinging Blue Jeans regularly on this tour. Something similar almost happened to the Who on July 5, 1969, when by coincidence they were sharing a bill with Chuck Berry at London's Royal Albert Hall. When the Who came on for the final set, trouble was caused by some rockers who had been hanging around after the **Rolling Stones** gave a free concert in the area that afternoon. The arrival of a flock of policemen kept history from repeating itself, or worse.

Szymczyk, Bill American record producer who had worked on several albums for the **Eagles** and who was brought in to handle the *Face Dances* album. The Who chose to work with someone new because the album would be their first with a new drummer, **Kenney Jones**, and their first for their new label, Warner Brothers. Though the Who wanted to record at Ramport Studios while Szymczyk chose Odyssey, the band did not lay all the blame on him for their dissatisfaction with the final product.

T. Rex *see* John's Children.

Take That *see* Barlow, Gary.

Talmy, Shel American producer who was working in Britain in late 1964 when he was recruited to produce the Who's first single. Talmy produced records for the **Kinks**, including their breakthrough hit "You Really Got Me." Thanks to **Anya Butler** and **Mike Shaw**, Talmy's wife heard Pete Townshend's demo of "I Can't Explain" and **Kit Lambert** then cut a deal with him that resulted in Talmy producing the version of the song that was released in January of 1965. He produced the Who's other two 1965 singles, "Anyway Anyhow Anywhere" and "My Generation," as well as their first album, *My Generation*. In the UK the B-side for "I Can't Explain" was Talmy's song "Bald Headed Woman," which the Kinks had recorded in October of 1964. According to John Atkins in *The Who in Print*, Talmy adapted it from an unspecified blues song. For "Anyway Anyhow Anywhere," Talmy told **Richard Barnes** that "nobody had ever done feedback before" but the Who's use of it on the 45 was intentional: "I set the mikes up the way I thought it would work and it worked perfectly the first time. I think the feedback was a few months ahead of its time, but it caught on eventually."

Despite the huge success of the next single, "My Generation," Lambert and Talmy grew increasingly intolerant of each other, which also affected Lambert's relationship with Talmy aide **Glyn Johns**; tensions between Lambert and Johns during the recording of *Who's Next* in 1971 could be traced back to Talmy's year with the Who. Because of the animosity between Lambert and Talmy and because the deal with Talmy greatly favored the producer, the Who's first single in 1966, "Substitute," was released on **Robert Stigwood**'s Reaction label. For the B-side the Who intentionally chose to rerecord "Circles," a song that had once been projected as their next A-side after "My Generation." They had recorded an earlier version with Talmy and even though the Who confused matters by pressing most of the B-side labels with the title "Instant Party," as expected it was Talmy who shouldered the burden of bringing the dispute to a head by suing the Who. The Who then shifted tactics and sought to disentangle "Substitute" from its legal dispute with Talmy by replacing the B-side "Circles"/"Instant Party" with a song Talmy couldn't lay claim to, the instrumental "Waltz for a Pig." Barnes said the title supposedly was an insult directed at Talmy. This instrumental was attributed to "The Who" or "The Who Orchestra" depending on the pressing but it was actually performed by the **Graham Bond** Organisation.

The Who continued to release new records on Reaction in 1966 and Talmy also released Who 45s on the Brunswick label; the master tapes of the 1965 recordings were finally accessed by the Who to release an expanded *My Generation* in 2002. Talmy was ultimately awarded 5 percent royalties on all Who records through their 1971 smash *Who's Next*. From 1966 to the present Talmy has helped a handful of different bands cover Who songs, including the **Rockin' Vicars** and the **Untamed**.

Taylor, Roger see Queen.

Telephone French punk/new wave group whose fifth and final album, 1984's *Un Autre Monde*, featured John Entwistle on French horn. **Glyn Johns** produced it.

Thomas, Mickey see Jefferson Airplane/Starship.

Thompson, Chris see Manfred Mann.

Thunderclap Newman Band that had its #1 single in 1969 produced by Pete Townshend. Thunderclap Newman consisted of postal clerk and musician Andy Newman, songwriter and drummer John "Speedy" Keene, and future Wings and **Small Faces** guitarist Jimmy McCulloch. Townshend had been friends with Newman and Keene for several years each. Newman was the person who got Pete interested in multi-tracking. The West London home of Keene's parents was where Pete wrote "So Sad About Us" in 1966. Keene was the author of the song "Armenia City in the Sky," which the Who performed on their 1967 album *The Who Sell Out*. In the late 1960s Keene was driving Pete to performances around the UK. In the liner notes for Pete's album *Scoop* he called Keene "a talented drummer [who] emerged as a great writer as soon as I opened my ears to him properly." According to Dave Marsh in *Before I Get Old*, Keene originally wrote "Something in the Air" during the previous year for a **Richard Stanley** film. It was subsequently used in the movies *The Magic Christian* and *The Strawberry Statement*. After "Something in the Air" hit it big the band released its only album, *Hollywood Dream*, which Townshend produced. As "**Bijou Drains**" he was the band's bass player. In a November

1970 issue of *Rolling Stone* Pete had to deny that he and Speedy Keene were the same person.

Over the next few years Townshend also served as executive producer of Andy Newman's *Rainbow* LP, and Keene released two solo albums. In addition to going on to record with the Small Faces and with ex–**Beatle** Paul McCartney in Wings, McCulloch also played with **Stone the Crows**. He also backed two other members of the Who on solo projects: He played guitar on John Entwistle's second LP, 1972's *Whistle Rymes*, on the songs "Apron Strings" and "I Feel Better," as well as on Roger Daltrey's third album, 1977's *One of the Boys*. McCulloch died in 1979 at the age of 27 due to a heart attack. On Pete Townshend's 1982 solo album *All the Best Cowboys Have Chinese Eyes* Andy Newman co-wrote the short song "Prelude," which Pete performed as an expanded instrumental on a 30-minute music video he produced. *Hollywood Dream* has been released on compact disc with bonus tracks.

Tipton, Glenn *see* Judas Priest.

Tommy and the Bijoux *see* Heron, Mike.

Tosh, Stuart Drummer for a few groups from 1974 to 1980 who also handled those duties on Roger Daltrey's third solo album, 1977's *One of the Boys*. He played on a few albums each for the band Pilot from 1974 to '76, for the **Alan Parsons** Project from 1975 to '79, and for 10cc from 1975 to 1980. During the 1990s he had a hand in several stage musicals, including 1995's *Only the Lonely: The Roy Orbison Story*.

Towns, Colin Keyboard player on more than a dozen albums by former Black Sabbath and Deep Purple vocalist Ian Gillan, starting around 1977. Towns wrote "How Does the Cold Wind Cry" on Roger Daltrey's 1984 solo album, *Parting Should Be Painless*. Towns released several of his own albums in the late 1990s.

Townsend, Godfrey The John Entwistle Band's guitar player and main vocalist. Godfrey also plays keyboard, and has over three decades of musical experience, including at least 25 years of performing, touring, and recording with such musicians as Mitch Ryder, Noel Redding of the **Jimi Hendrix** Experience, and Joey Molland of Badfinger. He has been living in New York City, and it was several spontaneous jams with John Entwistle there that led to his inclusion in the John Entwistle Band in 1995. One recent side project for Godfrey was playing guitar on Joe Lynn Turner's 1999 album *Under Cover, Vol. 2*. In 2001 Entwistle, Townsend, and **Steve Luongo** toured with **Todd Rundgren**, **Alan Parsons**, and Ann Wilson of **Heart** in the **Beatles** tribute billed as *A Walk Down Abbey Road*.

This was a fitting job for someone who fondly recalls spending a summer on Malta as a kid, playing Beatles songs on the piano with his uncle.

Townshend, Betty   Former singer who became Pete Townshend's mother. Betty Veronica Dennis sang with the popular dance band the Sidney Torch Orchestra before World War II. She was introduced to Cliff Townshend by Leslie Douglas, in whose band Betty and Cliff would perform during the War. In November of 1962 Betty arranged for the **Detours** to audition with Bob Druce, and their first documented gig for him was later that month. Around January of 1963 she sought Leslie's help in getting the Detours a few gigs at an American Servicemen's club, and succeeded. It was reported in 1998 that she had started to write her memoirs.

Townshend, Cliff   Professional clarinet and saxophone player who became Pete Townshend's father. Clifford Blandford Townshend recorded with several bands, such as Mark White's Jazz Club, but was known primarily for his long stint in the Squadronaires, which lasted into the 1960s. The back cover of Cliff's own four-track extended play record *The Singing Saxophone* provides biographical facts, though it misspells his surname as "Townsend." According to the record cover, Cliff Townshend was "a well-known figure playing clarinet at jam sessions and concerts before the war." Born in London in 1917 to show-business parents, he showed an early interest in music. He began playing guitar at 12 and at 14 switched to saxophone; the record claims "he used to sneak away from school to play in clubs." In 1935 he toured Scandinavia with a band led by drummer Joe Daniels; later, he played sax for several dance orchestras. In wartime Cliff Townshend served in the R.A.F. and was a "founder-member of the Dance Orchestra of the R.A.F.," a group that remained popular in Britain under the name Ronnie Aldrich and the Squadronaires.

In 1963 or '64 Cliff Townshend arranged with acquaintance Barry Gray for the **Detours** to have their first recording session (and their only one before becoming the Who). Many years later Cliff and Pete performed together, on BBC 1 in March of 1981. Cliff died in June of 1986. Pete dedicated his album *Another Scoop* to him: "A clarinet and saxophone player admired by his contemporaries, and loved by his family. 'I don't care what you call it, as long as it's real music, and as long as it swings'." According to Dave Marsh in his book *Before I Get Old*, Cliff tried unsuccessfully to assuage young Pete Townshend's insecurities about having a prominent nose by pointing to Squadronaires pianist Ronnie Aldrich, who had many successful solo albums. Pete recalled Cliff saying something like, "Look at Ronnie, look at Ronnie. He's the leader of a famous orchestra, he's got a beautiful wife, a beautiful house, a lovely car. What more can you want?

He makes music all his life, he's a respected man. What more can you want in life? He's got a big nose, Peter."

Townshend, Emma   Oldest of Pete Townshend's three children and a recording artist in her own right. Emma was born in 1969. Her father dedicated the song "Rough Boys" on his 1980 solo album *Empty Glass* to the **Sex Pistols** and to Emma and her sister Minta. Emma provided backing vocals on her dad's 1985 album *White City*. The short movie released in conjunction with that album included a bonus video of a Pete Townshend song called "Night School" and Emma provided backing vocals with her friend Justine Frischmann, later of the band Elastica. On February 9, 1986, **Chucho Merchan** organized a special concert in England to help victims of a volcano eruption in his homeland, and Pete was among the performers; Emma made her stage debut with him that night. A video of Pete's *White City* single "Face the Face" includes Emma singing a verse.

In a *San Francisco Chronicle* article on February 23, 1998, she pointed out that her youth was far less eventful than many would suppose. "I had this really ordinary suburban childhood. My dad would come back from being on the road, and he would make us sandwiches, take us to the science museum. People ask me, 'Did your dad have mad parties?' And I can't even think of one." She added that Roger Daltrey "has never been around to our house, as far as I can remember. And my mom would never have taken us anywhere (the late drummer) Keith Moon was." The occasion of this article was Emma's major label release, the album *Winterland*.

The March 1998 issue of the British magazine *Mojo* said that a "childhood steeped in music and the mechanics thereof (not only from Pete Townshend but also from maternal granddad **Edwin Astley** who composed countless early TV themes) has given her a control of form and melody" and that there was "intelligence everywhere." The review emphasized how different the album was from her father's style, which Emma herself explained in the *San Francisco Chronicle* article. "Guitar bands have always struck me as quite male," she said. "I listen to a lot of dance music, quite a lot of classical and jazz, old bluesmen playing the piano." Still, Emma didn't seem reluctant to talk about her high-profile relatives. "Of course it's an advantage," she said. "It's a huge marketing advantage." Unfortunately, Emma's label dropped her after one album. In 1999 Emma sang the theme song for the U.S. network television miniseries *The Magical Legend of the Leprechauns*, in which Roger Daltrey appeared. Her new song "Fly Away" was in a scene during the first episode, at the end of the second, and in promotional spots. At the beginning of 2000 she was among the vocalists on the acclaimed album *Pearl & Umbra* by Russell Mills & Undark.

Townshend, Paul   One of Pete Townshend's two brothers. A Who fan publication said he spent some time in Los Angeles in the early 1980s trying to get a record contract for a band of his, but didn't succeed. However, he is reportedly a very good guitarist. Paul has frequently helped his brother Simon (see entry below) on tour, beginning with Simon's American tour in the mid–1980s. In recent years he has also assisted Simon during recording sessions. In 1993 Paul helped with the staging of Pete's *Psychoderelict*. When the Simon Townshend Band toured the U.S. to promote its *Among Us* CD, the author had the privilege of having official permission to videotape the band's show at the Chicago House of Blues on November 14, 1997 thanks in part to the cooperation of Paul Townshend. In 2000 Paul received a telephone call from Roger Daltrey out of the blue, insisting that there was some sort of emergency that Paul needed to attend to. Paul was preparing for a children's birthday party and tried to resist Roger but ultimately couldn't. When he went to Shepherd's Bush to meet Roger he was greeted by a large recording crew plus a loud cheer from an elated crowd consisting of *The Simpsons*' production crew, plus Roger, John Entwistle, and actor Dan Castellaneta, the voice of TV's Homer Simpson. They were taping lines for an upcoming episode of *The Simpsons* and needed Paul to read Pete's lines when he failed to show. He was reportedly compensated handsomely for his time. The episode was the 250th of the series and kicked off its 12th season. In "A Tale of Two Springfields" it was up to the Who to stop a civil war of sorts. "Roger Daltrey showed up 20 minutes early (to record his dialogue) and I immediately lost respect for him as a rock star," joked executive producer Mike Scully in *TV Guide*.

Townshend, Pete   Guitarist and primary songwriter for the Who. Peter Dennis Blandford Townshend was born to Betty and Cliff Townshend (see entries above) on May 19, 1945, 10 days after Germany surrendered in World War II. His parents were performers who met through their work. In 1956 Pete saw the movie *Rock Around the Clock,* featuring Bill Haley and the Comets, and it swept away his basic notions of what music should and shouldn't be like. His grandmother bought him a primitive guitar and Pete began teaching himself how to play it. Townshend attended Acton County Grammar School with John Entwistle. They first played music together in a band called the **Confederates**. Both were later in the **Aristocrats** and the **Scorpions** before Entwistle was persuaded by Roger Daltrey in 1961 or '62 to join the **Detours**. Entwistle soon arranged for Townshend to be a member as well. Eventually the Detours settled on four members, with **Doug Sandom** on drums. In *Before I Get Old* Dave

Marsh said Sandom was a fine musician and quoted John Entwistle as saying he was "ten times better than we were."

At one important audition in Willesden, a promoter pointed to Townshend out in the hallway and said to Doug, Roger and John, "Get rid of him an I'll sign you" but Doug insisted, "Either you have us as we are, or you can get stuffed." In early 1964 the band learned that an act had appeared on TV calling itself the Detours, so a brainstorming session resulted in the new name the Who. Though it had been suggested by Pete's good friend **Richard Barnes**, Pete really wanted the new name to be the Hair or at least the Hair And the Who. Around late April of 1964 another big change was set in motion when a tirade by Pete pushed Doug out of the band. About 10 days later the band found a new drummer in the person of Keith Moon.

Townshend had written at least one song, called "It Was You," prior to Moon's arrival on the scene, and by the time new managers **Kit Lambert** and **Chris Stamp** brought producer **Shel Talmy** into the picture, Pete was ready to write hit singles. He had also borrowed some concepts about "auto destruction" that he picked up in art school and began smashing guitars to climax concerts. In 1966 Townshend began to experiment with longer compositions and concept albums with the title track of the Who's second album, *A Quick One*, and with aborted ideas like *Quads*, from which emerged the hit single "I'm a Boy." As he was developing *Tommy* Pete became a follower of **Meher Baba**, whom Pete would periodically make the focus of songs and side projects. Most notably, he and other Baba disciples released three tribute albums from 1970 to 1976; Pete's album *Who Came First* was a spin-off.

Pete and the former Karen Astley were married on May 20, 1968. They have two daughters, Emma (see entry above) and Minta, and a young son named Joseph. *Tommy* obviously expanded the boundaries of rock and pop in 1969 but Townshend aimed even higher with *Lifehouse*. Unfortunately, a variety of factors such as finances, confusing concepts and personality clashes kept the project from being completed. Still, the remainder formed one potent album: *Who's Next*. Pete's next project did get completed, and in 1973 the Who released the double album *Quadrophenia*. It was made into a well-regarded movie in 1979, four years after *Tommy* made its splash on film. *Tommy* earned Townshend an Academy Award nomination for Best Adapted Score.

The Who had two more albums of newly recorded material in the 1970s, *The Who by Numbers* in 1975 and *Who Are You* in 1978. In between Townshend and **Ronnie Lane** released the critically acclaimed *Rough Mix*. The death of Who drummer Keith Moon in September of 1978 worsened

Townshend's dependencies on drugs and alcohol. After 11 fans were killed at a Who concert in Cincinnati 15 months later, Townshend was in the worst condition of his life. Pete released a very successful solo album in 1980, *Empty Glass*, from which the single "Let My Love Open the Door" climbed as high as the Who's best performer, "I Can See for Miles" back in 1967. Both reached the Top 10. *All the Best Cowboys Have Chinese Eyes* followed in 1982. The Who released albums with new drummer **Kenney Jones**, *Face Dances* in 1981 and *It's Hard* in 1982, but within a year Townshend dissolved the band. In 1983 he took an editorial position at Faber & Faber. They published his 1985 collection of short musings called *Horse's Neck*. That same year Pete released the album *White City — A Novel*, which was also made into a short film. Toward the end of 1985 and into early 1986 Pete played live with a band he called **Deep End**. In 1989 the Who reunited for a tour. That same year Pete released *The Iron Man*, based on the story by **Ted Hughes**.

About a decade later Pete was executive producer when this tale was adapted as the animated feature *The Iron Giant*. In 1991 Pete received the Living Legend Award during the third annual International Rock Awards ceremony in London. In 1993 Pete released his concept album *Psychoderelict*, and *The Who's Tommy* was a hit on Broadway, winning five Tony Awards. In 1999 BMI bestowed a two million performance award on Townshend for "Pinball Wizard." Beginning in 1999 Pete's Eel Pie label became very active, most notably by releasing the six-disc *Lifehouse Chronicles*. In 2001 Pete received the Ivor Novello lifetime achievement award for songwriting. Townshend's life has been the focus of three books: *Townshend: A Career Biography* by **Chris Charlesworth** in 1984; *Behind Blue Eyes: A Life of Pete Townshend* by Geoffrey Giuliano in 1996; and *Pete Townshend: The Minstrel's Dilemma* by Larry David Smith in 1999. On January 13, 2003, Pete was briefly arrested for having visited child porn websites but the Internet Watch Foundation later confirmed that he had alerted them several times of sites he had discovered. Many peers, such as Roger Daltry, **Elton John**, **David Bowie** and **Bob Geldoff**, defended Pete, and on May 7, he was cleared by London's Metropolitan Police.

Townshend, Simon   Singer, guitarist, songwriter, and youngest brother of Pete Townshend. Simon was born in 1960. Though not credited as a vocalist on the Who's smash 1969 album *Tommy*, Simon helped sing the ascending "rise, rise, rise," line in the song "Smash the Mirror." From 1974 to 1976 Simon released his first three 45s. His second A-side was entitled "Janie," which is the name of his wife. Both took part in the photo shoots for the booklet that accompanied the Who's *Quadrophenia* album in 1973. In 1975 he sang "Extra, Extra, Extra" and "Miracle Cure" on the *Tommy* movie soundtrack. **Tony Butler** was among the musicians who backed Simon during a concert in 1977. Shortly thereafter he, Simon, and **Mark Brzezicki** formed On the Air and released a couple of records before Tony and Mark joined **Big Country** in 1982. In 1983 Pete produced Simon's first album, *Sweet Sound*. The single "I'm the Answer" received some airplay, and Simon toured the U.S. The album *Simon Townshend's Moving Target* was released in 1985. A protracted contractual dispute was partly to blame for the 10-year void between *Moving Target* and Simon's 1996 album *Among Us*. During that span Simon would only release a pair of 45s in 1988 with a new On the Air lineup. He then sang "Man Machines" on Pete's *Iron Man* album, his 1989 musical adaptation of the **Ted Hughes** tale. On Pete's *Psychoderelict* album in 1993 Simon co-wrote the song "Flame" with Brzezicki and others. Simon's demo was a bonus track on one of Pete's "English Boy" CDs in Europe. Roger Daltrey recruited Simon to tour with him in 1994 and Simon debuted his song "The Way It Is" for audiences during at least one of those shows. Simon played guitar and was part of the chorus on the London Philharmonic Orchestra's 1998 album *Who's Serious*. On the **British Rock Symphony** CD in 1999 he backed several well known vocalists including Daltrey, Paul Rodgers of **Bad Company** fame and **Animals** frontman Eric Burdon. Simon also appeared in the 1999 British Rock Symphony video headlined by Daltrey. He was actually on camera more than Roger was, in part because he played guitar throughout. Simon also sang lead on two **Beatles** songs, "Blackbird" and "Norwegian Wood." On the latter he was backed on vocals by Alvin Fields. Singers whom Simon backed on the video included Gary Brooker of Procol Harum fame and Paul Young.

Simon started to make up for lost time by following up 1996's *Among Us* with *Animal Soup* in 1999 and *Bare Bodies Bare Assets* in 2000. Simon's son Ben, who has drummed with his father since 1996, joined Simon on the Ultimate Rock Symphony tour of Australia with headliners such as Jack Bruce and Billy Thorpe. Simon's website, simontownshend.com, included this tongue-in-cheek complaint about the Australian tour: "Roger Daltrey smashed my beautiful Maton acoustic on stage in Australia for absolutely no reason whatsoever. To make matters worse the company director who was at the time considering my sponsorship sat in the front row and witnessed the whole ugly event. Of course, I didn't get the deal, he had changed his mind and to top the lot the press the next day had twisted the story and announced that Roger had smashed **Peter Frampton**'s guitar…. Of all the nerve!"

In March and April of 2000 Simon had a prominent role in another

British Rock Symphony tour. Headliners included **Billy Preston**, **Darlene Love**, and Nikki Lamborn. One of Simon's most recent releases was an EP on compact disc entitled *Ages*. In February of 2001, about 45 seconds of Simon's song "Save Me from Me" was used in an episode of NBC's series *Providence*. On March 21 Simon and Ben performed live with Roger Daltrey in Vail, Colorado, to benefit the U.S. Disabled Ski Team. Simon's new recording project in 2002 was *.bom* which reunited him with **Mark Brzezicki**. For the Who's 2002 tour Simon was part of the band, a few years after singing lead on "The Dirty Jobs" on the *Quadrophenia* tours.

Townson, Chris   Drummer for **John's Children** who filled in for Keith Moon on Aug 18, 1966 and again on June 4 and 5, 1967. The first time Moon was ill but the second time he missed some concerts due to a self-inflicted injury. Moon had strained his stomach muscles while goofing around during the Who's previous performance on May 27 and/or during a recording session on May 28. **Julian Covey** of Machine filled in on May 29 and June 3. John's Children was one of the bands signed to the Who's Track Records label, which debuted in 1967. *The Who Concert File* notes that from May 21 through 27, 1966, "an unknown deputy drummer filled in" for Keith because he was recovering from being accidentally hit in the face with Pete Townshend's guitar on May 20. After John's Children broke up in 1968 Townson drummed in the London club band Sparks and Jook until it split up in 1975. He then formed the band Jet with two other former members of John's Children. John's Children reunited in the 1990s.

Towser *see* Jason.

The Tubes   Critically acclaimed rock band of the late 1970s and early '80s known for their visually stimulating concerts. On September 9, 1978, the day after Keith Moon's death, in tribute the Tubes closed their Knebworth Festival concert with a Who medley consisting of "Baba O'Riley" and "The Kids Are Alright." They were joined onstage by **Todd Rundgren**, who soon produced one of their albums. Rundgren joined the Tubes for the same songs at the end of a concert in New York City on July 18, 1979. The Tubes also performed those two songs in their video *Live at the Greek*. The Tubes had a Top 10 hit single with "She's a Beauty" in 1983, disbanded a few years later, and reunited in 1993.

Turner, Tina   One of rock and pop's leading ladies. In St. Louis, Annie Mae Bullock had sung with Ike Turner's band for a couple of years, married him in 1958, and was known as "Tina" by 1960 when they landed the Top 40 hit "A Fool in Love." More hits followed in 1961 and 1962 but their most memorable song of the '60s was probably "River Deep, Mountain High" in 1966. It ended up being Phil Spector's last "Wall of Sound" single; its lack of chart success in the U.S. kept him from producing another record for three years. It was a big hit in the UK, however, and Ike and Tina saw success in the U.S. return with several hits in the early 1970s, including the top five cover "Proud Mary." In 1975 she made a memorable appearance as the Acid Queen in *Tommy* and named her debut solo album that year *Acid Queen*. In addition to the song "Acid Queen" it also included her cover of the Who's "I Can See for Miles." She and Ike divorced around that time but Tina maintained a low profile for the rest of the 1970s.

She made a comeback with a top 40 cover of Al Green's "Let's Stay Together" in 1984 but she did even better with her next single, the #1 smash "What's Love Got to Do with It." She soon had two more Top 10 hits with "Private Dancer" and "Better Be Good to Me." In 1985 another movie role, in *Mad Max: Beyond Thunderdome*, led to the #2 hit theme song "We Don't Need Another Hero." After 1986 she had less commercial success but her albums still sold respectably. In 1991 Ike and Tina Turner were inducted into the Rock and Roll Hall of Fame. Two years later Tina's life story was told in the movie *What's Love Got to Do with It* and the soundtrack yielded another new hit, "I Don't Wanna Fight." In 2000, at the age of 60 and with a new album, she embarked on what was reportedly a farewell tour.

The Turtles *see* Flo and Eddie.

Twiggy Well known model-turned-actress who defined fashion in the UK during the 1960s while still in her teens. In his Keith Moon biography *Dear Boy* Tony Fletcher noted that Keith met her around 1960 while working as a delivery boy for butchers. Keith used to claim that she failed to hide the crush she had on him, but Fletcher suspects it was the other way around. Twiggy, whose real name was Lesley Hornby, found much less success as a recording artist in the 1960s so she turned more toward acting by the 1970s. In the July 10, 1976 issue of *Melody Maker* Twiggy appeared with Roger Daltrey in a photo when he was honored by a disabled children's charity. About 10 years later she and Daltrey starred in a filmed musical production of **Hans Christian Andersen**'s *The Little Matchgirl*. Around that time she had received a Tony nomination for her work in the musical *My One and Only* with Tommy Tune. In her autobiography she made mention of Roger while complaining how difficult it is to get a hit single in England: "The problem with England is the Radio One playlist. If you can't get on it, it's almost impossible to get a hit record. I remember when I was doing 'Matchgirl' with Roger Daltrey him bemoaning the same which amazed me. You can hardly get more famous in the rock world than Roger Daltrey of the Who and even he couldn't make the playlist with the single he'd just put out. There are hundreds of records that never get heard. A rather sad, limiting state of affairs, down to the vagaries of the producer's decision, I suppose." In mid–1999 she appeared in the off–Broadway musical *If Love Were All*.

Tyrannosaurus Rex *see* John's Children.

The Ultimate Rock Symphony *see* The British Rock Symphony.

The Untamed Little-known British band that covered the Who's "It's Not True" with help from **Shel Talmy**. This was one of several times when Talmy produced a cover of a Who song for some other band. Around 1993 the song appeared on a compilation CD entitled *English Freak Beat Volume 5*. The liner notes for this album state: "Why, one might ask, would anyone try to challenge the Who with such a close copy of their own version (lacking only such trivial elements as Pete's windmill guitar and Keith's smashing drums…like nobody would notice?). Well, in this case it wasn't the band but the producer, one Shel Talmy, whose recent handling of the Who had resulted in a 'tribute' B-side (on their rare Atco 45) called 'Waltz for a Pig.' Seems Shel wanted to prove he could do it without them… well, nice try. The Untamed were actually quite a good band; all five of their singles are worth finding."

Utopia *see* Rundgren, Todd.

Vallance, Jim Songwriter who teamed with **Bryan Adams** to write two songs, "Rebel" and "Let Me Down Easy," on Roger Daltrey's 1985 album *Under a Raging Moon*. "Let Me Down Easy" was released as a single and reached #86 in the American charts. Vallance gained experience as a songwriter (under the pen name Rodney Higgs) as the original drummer in the Canadian band Prism, to which **Henry Small** belonged for awhile. Vallance disliked touring and quit after the band's 1975 debut album. Three years later he met Adams in a music store and the two formed a very successful partnership for the next 11 years. He has co-written several songs each, including a few hits, for Aerosmith, Glass Tiger, **Joan Jett**, the **Scorpions** and 38 Special. Vallance also hit it big as primary writer of "What About Love" for **Heart**.

Van Halen American hard rock band that quickly established itself with its self-titled debut album in 1978 and remained popular into the new century. With **Sammy Hagar** as their second lead vocalist they issued a live cover of the Who's "Won't Get Fooled Again" as a CD single in 1993. Long before they had a record deal, the band reportedly played songs from the Who's *Live at Leeds* on stage and attempted to play them note for note. According to Geoffrey Giuliano in his Pete Townshend biography *Behind Blue Eyes,* guitar virtuoso Eddie Van Halen phoned Pete at some unspecified time to say, "Pete, I've just been listening to Live at Leeds. Christ, man, that's one great album. You play some fantastic mistakes!"

Van Zandt, "Little Steven"   Guitarist for Bruce Springsteen's E Street Band who organized a variety of performers as "Artists United Against Apartheid" to protest the racial separation policy in South Africa. The result was the 1985 *Sun City* album on which Pete Townshend played some guitar. At the turn of the century Van Zandt was appearing in the acclaimed series *The Sopranos* on cable TV's HBO.

Vedder, Eddie   *see*   Pearl Jam.

The Velvet Underground   *see*   Reed, Lou.

Vitale, Joe   Drummer who has recorded frequently with **Joe Walsh** since 1972 and with Crosby, Stills, and Nash since 1977, sometimes including **Neil Young**. Vitale played drums, flutes and keyboards on John Entwistle's fifth solo album, 1981's *Too Late the Hero*. Walsh and Vitale appeared on the album's back cover.

Volman, Mark   *see*   Flo and Eddie.

Voormann, Klaus   *see*   Paddy, Klaus and Gibson.

Wakeling, Dave   *see*   The English Beat.

Wakeman, Rick   Noted progressive rock keyboard player who was the arranger, principal musician, and one of the costars of Roger Daltrey's second movie, 1975's *Lisztomania*. In the late 1960s Wakeman was a session musician, most notably for **David Bowie**, before joining the progressive rock band the Strawbs for two albums in the early 1970s. He then jumped to Yes in time for their fourth album, *Fragile*, which yielded the hit song "Roundabout" in 1972. That year he also played on another Yes album and released his first solo LP, *The Six Wives of Henry VIII*. Wakeman soon left Yes but would periodically rejoin over the years while continuing to release solo albums. His second solo effort, *Journey to the Center of the Earth*, was very successful commercially. The next year he teamed with Ken Russell on *Lisztomania*. Wakeman wrote the track "Hibernation" and he worked with Russell to add lyrics to **Franz Liszt**'s "Excelsior

Song." Wakeman has continued to do respectably on a variety of fronts, such as movies and television.

Walsh, Joe   Rock guitarist who has had success since 1969 as a member of the **James Gang** and the **Eagles** and as a solo artist. The James Gang was his first band, but he was only a member for two years. He released the first of many solo albums in 1972 and his second the next year went gold thanks to the Top 40 hit "Rocky Mountain Way." **Joe Vitale** has often been Walsh's drummer. On Keith Moon's only solo album, 1975's *Two Sides of the Moon*, Walsh played guitar and arp synthesizer on "Solid Gold" and "The Kids Are Alright," and guitar on "One Night Stand," "Back Door Sally," and "Move Over Ms. L," including the solo on the latter. Walsh joined the Eagles in 1976 but continued to release solo albums. On his 1978 album *But Seriously Folks…* he thanked John Entwistle for unspecified help. That album yielded the Top 20 hit "Life's Been Good." Walsh played guitar, percussion and keyboards on Entwistle's 1981 album *Too Late the Hero*, which also prominently featured Vitale. When Walsh found out that Pete Townshend wanted someone else to take on most of the electric guitar playing during the Who's 1989 reunion tour, Walsh offered to do so. The job had gone to **Steve Bolton**. In 1990 Walsh and Entwistle were in the short-lived supergroup **the Best**. In the song "Fairbanks Alaska" on Walsh's 1992 album *Songs for a Dying Planet* one verse mentions The Who. In 1994 Walsh reunited with the Eagles for a very popular tour. When the Eagles were inducted into the Rock and Roll Hall of Fame at the ceremony in January of 1998, Walsh thanked the other two James Gang members for being terrible singers and thus forcing him to learn how to sing, and he thanked Pete Townshend for taking him under his wing.

Warnes, Jennifer   Very successful American singer both on her own and in duets. She has received three Oscars for "Best Song" and two Grammy Awards. Her number one singles include "Up Where We Belong," with Joe Cocker, "(I've Had) The Time of My Life," with Righteous Brother Bill Medley, and her solo song "Right Time of the Night." Warnes was an original cast member of the **Smothers Brothers** *Comedy Hour* in the late 1960s. In 1969 she covered the Who's "See Me, Feel Me" on her album *See Me, Feel Me, Touch Me, Heal Me*.

Waters, Muddy   Legendary Chicago blues guitarist whose music Pete Townshend was exposed to by the impressive record collection of his friend **Tom Wright**. Around 1964 the Who would sometimes cover one of Waters's 1954 hits, "I Just Want to Make Love to You," which was written by Willie Dixon. Dixon also wrote hits for **Howlin' Wolf**, including at least one covered by the Who live. Muddy Waters was born McKinley Morganfield in Mississippi on April 4, 1915. In 1941 folklorist Alan Lomax, who was collecting songs for the Library of Congress, recorded Waters with portable recording equipment. In 1943 Waters decided to pursue a musical career in Chicago. Waters appeared frequently on the national R&B charts from 1948 to 1958, with multiple hits in 1951, 1954, and 1956. During that span Dixon played an increasingly important role as Waters's songwriter. Waters recorded regularly until his death on April 30, 1983 in Westmont, Illinois. He was inducted into the Rock and Roll Hall of Fame in 1987 (and Willie Dixon followed in 1994). In October of 1989, Pete Townshend and **Eric Clapton** appeared together on the British TV talk show *Saturday Matters* and performed an acoustic version of Waters's song "Standin' Around Cryin'."

Watson, Bruce *see* Big Country.

Watt-Roy, Norman   Played bass on Roger Daltrey's *Parting Should Be Painless* album in 1984. He has also recorded with the **Clash** and Frankie Goes to Hollywood. In the late 1970s he was in Ian Dury and the Blockheads, as was **Mickey Gallagher**, who also played on that Daltrey album. Since backing Daltrey he has been a member of fellow Blockhead Wilko Johnson's band.

Watts, Charlie *see* The Rolling Stones.

Webber, Andrew Lloyd *see* Lloyd Webber, Andrew.

Weider, Johnny   Guitar, bass, and violin player in the New **Animals**, **Family** and **Ro Ro**. Weider played violin on the song "Nightmare (Please Wake Me Up)" on John Entwistle's second solo album, 1972's *Whistle Rymes*. In 1975 he played bass on the **John Alcock**/John Entwistle *Flash Fearless* album.

Weill, Kurt   German-born composer of the first half of the 20th century. He wrote the music for **Bertolt Brecht**'s *The Threepenny Opera*. Weill's wife Lotte Lenya, an Austrian actress, appeared in it; her name turned up in Bobby Darin's huge hit "Mack the Knife" in 1959. *The Threepenny Opera*, which debuted in 1928, was based on **John Gay**'s *The Beggar's Opera* from two hundred years earlier. Roger Daltrey played the street singer in the 1989 movie *Mack the Knife*, which was an adaptation of the *Threepenny Opera*. Roger launched into the title song just before the appearance of stars **Raul Julia** and **Richard Harris**. *Rolling Stone* reviewer Peter Travis liked Daltrey's rendition of the song but thought his character was overused to take advantage of Daltrey's celebrity. In 1983 Roger had played Macheath in a BBC production of the *Beggar's Opera*.

West, Leslie   Guitarist who was a co-founder of the hard rock band Mountain in 1969. West had been in a locally popular Long Island band called the Vagrants, which actually released a version of "Respect" shortly before that became a huge hit for Aretha Franklin in 1967. By 1969 West recorded a solo album entitled *Leslie West — Mountain* and the trio Mountain grew out of those recording sessions. They netted gold records each of the next two years but after 1971 West used the name Mountain sporadically for bands he led. In 1971 West and **Al Kooper** recorded several songs with the Who, including a version of the **Holland/Dozier/Holland** composition "Baby Don't You Do It." This didn't surface until bonus tracks were added to the *Who's Next* album 1995. West also played on a different version of "Love Ain't for Keeping," which surfaced as an *Odds and Sods* bonus track in 1998. During those sessions West also played with the Who on a different version of "Won't Get Fooled Again" than the one put on *Who's Next*, but that version was not officially released until 2003, when that album was expanded as a two-CD set. On September 17, 1997, Leslie joined John Entwistle and drummer **Steve Luongo** onstage to play the **Kinks**' "You Really Got Me" during a John Entwistle Band gig at London's Shepherds Bush Empire. West also joined that band at a June 1998 concert in New York to play "Summertime Blues." Around this time West played guitar and sang on "Don't Be a Sucker" for the John Entwistle Band's *Van-Pires* soundtrack album.

West, Mae   American actress whose suggestive screen presence made her quite popular, particularly during the 1930s. By late 1976 she was in her eighties but made one last movie, called *Sextette*. Keith Moon appeared in one scene with West and her movie husband, Timothy Dalton. **Alice Cooper**, who was one of several other celebrities who also had a role in the movie, was quoted in Tony Fletcher's Moon biography *Dear Boy* as saying *Sextette* was "one of those movies that should never have been made."

White, Jay   *see*   Nelson, Rick.

Whitehorn, Geoff   Guitarist who backed Roger Daltrey and the Who in the 1990s. In 1975 Whitehorn toured and recorded with ex–**Stone the Crows** singer Maggie Bell, who opened for **Bad Company** on a U.S. tour. Whitehorn joined **John "Rabbit" Bundrick** and others in Crawler in 1976 and stayed with them until they folded in 1979. That year he joined Roger Chapman, previously of **Family** and **Streetwalkers**, in a band called the Shortlist, which over the next decade toured Europe extensively and recorded 10 albums, three of which Whitehorn co-produced with Chapman. Whitehorn joined Bad Company in mid–1990 for a U.S. tour and stayed until the return of Mick Ralphs in April 1991. By December he had joined the reformed Procol Harum and worked with them throughout the 1990s. Since 1993 he has also worked extensively with Bad Company frontman Paul Rodgers. In 1994 he toured behind Roger Daltrey and in mid–1996 he performed with the Who at the Hyde Park *Quadrophenia* concert and for six nights at Madison Square Garden. Whitehorn played guitar on the London Philharmonic Orchestra's 1998 album *Who's Serious*, which consisted of various Who songs played in a classical style. He also played guitar on the 1999 **British Rock Symphony** video headlined by Roger Daltrey and on the British Rock Symphony CD the same year.

The Who   Band that has been widely hailed as the world's greatest live rock act, if not the greatest rock band, period. In the early 1960s Roger Daltrey of the **Detours** coaxed John Entwistle into his band and Entwistle soon enlisted his friend Pete Townshend, with whom he had played in bands called the **Confederates**, the **Aristocrats**, and the **Scorpions**. The Detours eventually settled in as a quartet with drummer **Doug Sandom.** However, on January 30, 1964, a band called Johnny Devlin & the Detours appeared on the TV show *Thank Your Lucky Stars* and Daltrey's Detours knew they had to change their name quickly. The subsequent brainstorming session reached its peak when **Richard Barnes** suggested "The Who." Pete Townshend wasn't immediately sold, but Roger Daltrey was. In February they started using their new name between two of their weekly appearances at West London's Oldfield Hotel.

Another big change came in April when Doug Sandom left the band. About 10 days later Keith Moon made his memorable debut, also at the Oldfield. By July the band's relatively new manager, Helmut Gorden, had yielded much of his authority to publicist **Peter Meaden**, who persuaded the band to embrace the mod movement and change its name to the **High Numbers**, a name based on mod slang with positive connotations. They also released a 45. However, **Kit Lambert** and **Chris Stamp** appeared on the scene and quickly supplanted Gorden and Meaden. In November the band's name reverted to the Who to stay. In early 1965 they began recording with producer **Shel Talmy** and their first two 45s as the Who, "I Can't Explain" and "Anyway Anyhow Anywhere," were both quite successful. However, shortly after the Who released its third single, the mythic "My Generation," Daltrey was kicked out of the band temporarily. Rumor had it that Boz Burrell, then in the band Boz's People and later a member of

Bad Company, would be Roger's replacement. Pete Townshend and Kit Lambert also considered merging the three remaining members of the Who with **Paddy, Klaus and Gibson**.

The huge success of "My Generation" provided the impetus to readmit Roger. Roger talked about this period in an interview with Gary Herman for his biography *The Who*: "We did nearly split up at the time of My Generation, it was a big thing, arguments between me and Moon, and I was gonna leave the group and form one with Pete." Richard Barnes said that "John and Keith weren't too sure about working with Pete and wanted to form a group of their own without either Pete *or* Roger." At the end of 1965 the Who released their first album, *My Generation,* but in March of 1966 were in the thick of a legal battle with Talmy. Their second album, *A Quick One*, was released at the end of 1966. In the meantime, the Who had enough success with singles to draw attention from television shows in many countries. For example, the Who appeared on TV in France on October 27, in Denmark on October 28, in West Germany on November 1, and in the Netherlands and Sweden as well. All three U.S. television networks also showed interest in the Who around this time, yet it would be several months before the band touched down on American soil. The Who were on NBC's *Today Show* on November 12, on ABC's *Where the Action Is* on November 22, and on *CBS Reports* around Dec 1.

The Who released the clever album *The Who Sell Out* in November of 1967 from which its best-selling single emerged, the Top 10 hit "I Can See for Miles." The Who then needed 18 months to produce the groundbreaking *Tommy*. This double album "rock opera" obviously expanded the boundaries of rock and pop in 1969 but Townshend aimed even higher with his next project, *Lifehouse*. Unfortunately, a variety of factors such as finances, confusing concepts, and personality clashes kept the project from being completed. Still, the remainder formed one potent album in 1971: *Who's Next*. Pete's next project did get completed, and in 1973 the Who released the double album *Quadrophenia*. It was made into a well-regarded movie in 1979, four years after *Tommy* made its splash on film.

Due to growing animosity between Roger Daltrey on the one hand and Lambert and Stamp on the other, Daltrey anointed **Bill Curbishley** as his personal manager for his 1973 debut solo album, *Daltrey*. Roger then became enraged when an investigation revealed just how much of the Who's money was unaccounted for and soon insisted that Lambert and Stamp turn over managing responsibilities of the Who to Curbishley. Curbishley became the manager around the summer of 1974, and then many months were spent disentangling the Who contractually from New Action and Track Records.

The Who had two more albums of newly recorded material in the 1970s, *The Who by Numbers* in 1975 and *Who Are You* in 1978. Keith Moon died mere weeks after *Who Are You* was released providing some comfort for the mourners was the fact that a special performance had recently been arranged for use in the 1979 semi-documentary *The Kids Are Alright*. By the end of 1978 the Who had decided to persevere with a new drummer, **Kenney Jones**, and the band began touring with new vigor in 1979. The issue of *Time* dated December 1 featured the Who on the cover, but this uplifting recognition was soon forgotten when 11 fans were crushed to death at a Who concert in Cincinnati.

A different sort of tragedy was the focus on December 28 when the Who took part in the Concerts for the People of Kampuchea. Highlights were included in a UK television broadcast in January of 1981 and the Who earned one side of the double album that followed in March. The Who were still impressive enough in 1979 with Kenney on drums to be named the year's best band by *Rolling Stone* readers. The Who released two albums with Kenney, *Face Dances* in 1981 and the underrated *It's Hard* in 1982, but within a year Townshend announced that he was dissolving the band. The band reformed for the enormous Live Aid benefit in mid–1985 but largely avoided each other until embarking on a reunion tour in 1989 (without Kenney). They were inducted into the Rock and Roll Hall of Fame in 1990.

Starting in 1994 with a boxed set called *30 Years of Maximum R&B*, the entire catalog of Who recordings were overhauled. In 1996 and 1997 the Who regrouped again to tour with a semi-staged, semi-filmed production of *Quadrophenia*. Who songs suddenly started turning up quite often on the soundtracks of major motion pictures such as *Apollo 13*, *Jerry Maguire*, *Rushmore*, *Summer of Sam*, *Austin Powers 2*, *American Pie*, and *Almost Famous*, plus as theme songs for CBS's two popular *CSI* series. The Who performed some shows in 1999 consisting of the three founding members plus **Zak Starkey** and **John "Rabbit" Bundrick**, and toured with this lineup in 2000. Their concert in New York for the Robin Hood Foundation raised a startling $10 million. "I think it's going into the *Guinness Book of Records* as the highest amount of money raised in one night for one foundation by one band," Roger Daltrey told the *Boston Globe* in June of 2000. At the New York concert for victims of the September 11, 2001, tragedy, the Who's set was the biggest hit among the various performances. Shortly after John Entwistle's death in 2002, Pete, Roger, Zak and Rabbitt were joined by **Simon Townshend** and **Pino Palladino** on tour.

The Who Orchestra *see* Bond, Graham.

Wholey, Dennis American public television talk show host and best-selling author who interviewed various alcoholics, including some celebrities, for a 1984 book, *The Courage to Change: Hope and Help for Alcoholics and Their Families*. For about a dozen pages early in the book Pete Townshend related his pertinent experiences. Graham Chapman of **Monty Python's Flying Circus** was also quoted briefly about Keith Moon further into the book. Pete was quoted again in two later chapters. Wholey, who was born in 1937, was a member of the Hardly-Worthit comedy troupe in the 1960s. They performed during Murray the K's Easter Show in 1967, which also featured the Who making its first big splash in the U.S.

Wickham, Vicki *see* LaBelle, Patti.

Wiggy *see* Wolff, John "Wiggy."

Wilkins, Helen *see* Spike.

Williams, Bryan Trombone player on John Entwistle's second solo album, 1972's *Whistle Rymes*, on the songs "I Wonder" and "Who Cares?" He also played organ on "Nightmare (Please Wake Me Up)." According to Randy Poe's liner notes for the U.S. CD released in 1997, Williams' primary job was as a carpenter and he ended up on the album because he had been paneling John's dining room at the time. Williams also played trombone on John's next album, *Rigor Mortis Sets In*, on the songs "My Wife" and "Peg Leg Peggy."

Williams, John Australian-born classical guitarist who performed a duet on June 30, 1979 with Pete Townshend on "Won't Get Fooled Again" at the Secret Policeman's Ball for Amnesty International. In addition to appearing on a twelve-inch record with two songs Townshend performed solo that night, this version of "Won't Get Fooled Again" was issued as a seven-inch record by the Island label (with the B-side blank). Williams was initially taught music by his father and studied guitar in Europe. By the early '60s he had performed in three European capitals as well as the USSR, Japan, and the U.S. He has released a number of acclaimed albums. Some of Williams's noteworthy collaborators besides Townshend include Itzhak Perlman, André Previn, and Cleo Laine. He is not the same John Williams who is known for scoring movies such as the *Star Wars* and *Indiana Jones* series. To help distinguish this, johnwilliamsguitar.com is his official website.

Williamson, Sonny Boy Wrote the song "Eyesight to the Blind," which was used on the Who's *Tommy* album, sometimes under an alternative title, "The Hawker," and with a vocal track that was changed for some reason around 1973. A version also turned up on Pete Townshend's 1986 ***Deep End*** *Live!* album. Williamson released the song in early 1951 but the Who were first exposed to the 1959 version by **Mose Allison.** Williamson, whose real name was Aleck "Rice" Miller, was born in Mississippi in 1899, moved to Chicago in 1937, and died in Arkansas in 1965. He toured Britain and appeared on the television show *Ready Steady Go* a couple of years before his death. He is considered the second performer to use the name "Sonny Boy Williamson" even though he was 15 years older than the "first," John Lee Williamson, who was born in Tennessee and died in Chicago in 1948.

Wilson, Ann *see* Heart.

Wilson, Brian *see* The Beach Boys.

Winger *see* Beach, Reb.

Wings *see* The Beatles.

Wintour, Dave *see* Stealers Wheel.

Winwood, Steve Singer and keyboard player who has experienced success in groups and as a solo performer. He got his start in the 1960s as a member of the **Spencer Davis** Group from 1963 to '67, a span that included the hit single "Gimme Some Lovin'." From 1967 through 1974 he was a member of the intermittent band Traffic. That span also included working with **Eric Clapton** in the short-lived band Blind Faith in 1969 and appearing in **Lou Reizner**'s all-star stage version of the Who's *Tommy* in 1972 as Tommy's father. In early 1973 Winwood and three other members of Traffic were among the musicians who joined Townshend to support Clapton at his comeback concert. Winwood's solo success began with his 1980 album *Arc of a Diver*. In 1984 Roger Daltrey covered "Gimme Some Lovin'," which Winwood wrote with his brother Muff and Davis, as a B-side for the twelve-inch single of "Walking in My Sleep." In 1989 Winwood joined the Who onstage to sing "Eyesight to the Blind" for a charitable performance of Tommy that was released on video. Winwood received special thanks on the John Entwistle Band's 1999 CD *Left for Live*.

Wolff, John "Wiggy" Longtime employee of the Who. In the spring of 1966 he was hired to be a driver for the Who, one of several replacements for **Richard Cole**. Wiggy was responsible for the hiring of **Bob Pridden** later that year. Wiggy had the honor of accompanying the Who on their first trip to America in March of 1967; **Chris Stamp** was the only other person to join them. By 1969 Stamp and **Kit Lambert** had turned the day-to-day operations of the Who over to Wiggy, and he and

Pete Townshend tried mightily to resist **Frank Barsalona**'s effort to recruit the Who for the now-legendary Woodstock festival. Luckily for fans of the Who, Barsalona prevailed. Wiggy was one of several of the Who's associates to be immortalized in John Entwistle's solo composition, "Cell Number Seven," on his 1975 *Mad Dog* album. The song was about the Who and a number of associates being jailed briefly for some post-concert hotel destruction in Montreal on December 2, 1973. Almost two years later Wiggy and Entwistle were arrested at a post-concert party in Houston. According to *The Who Concert File*, when the Who made its official London relaunch with **Kenney Jones** on drums before 77,000 fans on August 18, 1979, Wiggy's ambitious plan for a "breath-taking pyramid of laser light" was scuttled when safety inspectors ordered him to pull the plug.

Wood, Ron   UK guitarist who has spent most of his career in groups—the Creation, the **Jeff Beck** Group, the Faces, and the **Rolling Stones**—but who has found time to make a few solo albums that served as assemblages of his friends. In the early 1960s Wood attended Ealing Art School at the same time as Pete Townshend. In early 1973 he was among the musicians who joined Townshend to support **Eric Clapton** at his comeback concert. On 1975's *Tommy* movie soundtrack Wood played guitar on "Acid Queen" and "There's a Doctor." In September of that year he also played on three Keith Moon solo songs that were produced and directed by **Steve Cropper** for a second Moon album. The songs, "Naked Man," "Do Me Good," and "Real Emotion," were released over 22 years later as bonus tracks on the *Two Sides of the Moon* CD. Also guesting on these tracks was **David Bowie**. In 1976, around the time that Wood jumped from the Faces to the Stones, he and **Ronnie Lane** released the *Mahoney's Last Stand* album, which **Glyn Johns** produced. Guests included **Kenney Jones**, who'd been in the Faces as well as the **Small Faces** with Lane, and Pete Townshend. Kenney and Pete played on "Tonight's Number" and Pete supplied percussion on "Car Radio." On whodirect.com, the Who's official online "store," one could purchase a litho of Ron's painting of Pete Townshend and Keith Moon for $825.

Wray, Link   Influential American rock guitar pioneer who introduced a distorted "fuzz-tone" sound in the 1950s on his million-selling instrumental "Rumble." Though he was unable to replicate this success after the '50s, Pete Townshend is just one of several guitarists who has sung Wray's praises, most notably in March of 1974 when Pete wrote comments for the back cover of the album *The Link Wray Rumble*. In *Before I Get Old* Dave Marsh mentioned that Wray visited the Who in March of

1971 while the band was recording *Who's Next* and he was greeted with a hug from a nude Keith Moon, whom he'd never met.

Wright, Tom   American photographer who introduced Pete Townshend to blues, R&B, jazz, and marijuana. Wright studied photography at Ealing Art School, which Townshend also attended. After the two became friends, Wright was deported for being caught with marijuana. The two were reunited when Wright became a roadie for the Who's first tour of the U.S., in 1967. Wright and **Bob Pridden** were the two mainstays of the Who's road crew in 1968. By May of 1969 Wright was managing Detroit's Grande Ballroom, and the Who started that year's U.S. tour there. When the second convention of Who fans was held in London in 1998, an exhibit of Wright's Who photos was scheduled nearby. In *The Who: Maximum R&B* **Richard Barnes** said that Wright's massive record collection first exposed Townshend to "Jimmy Reed, **Chuck Berry, James Brown, Bo Diddley, John Lee Hooker**, Snooks Eaglin, **Mose Allison**, Jimmy Smith, **Muddy Waters**, Lightin' Hopkins, **Howlin' Wolf, Slim Harpo**, Buddy Guy, Big Bill Broonzy, Sonny Terry & Brownie McGhee, Joe Turner, **Nina Simone**, Booker T., Little Richard, Jerry Lee Lewis, Carl Perkins, the Isley Brothers, Fats Domino, the Coasters, Ray Charles, Jimmy McGriff, Brother Jack McDuff, John Patton, Bobby Bland, the Drifters, [**Smokey Robinson** and] the Miracles, the Shirelles, [and] the Impressions." Barnes also listed jazz artists including Charlie Parker, Charles Mingus, John Coltrane, **Miles Davis**, Milt Jackson, Wes Montgomery, Jimmy Guiffre, and Dave Brubeck.

Wyckham, Vicki   *see*   LaBelle, Patti.

Wyman, Bill   *see*   The Rolling Stones.

Xtreems   An obscure garage band from Saint Louis, Missouri that recorded a 45 on the Star Trek label featuring a cover of the Who's "Substitute." As noted in the Borderline/Delerium Records online "Fuzz, Acid & Flowers" archive, based on the Vernon Joynson book of the same name, this 1967 single was their only release. Nevertheless, "Substitute" and/or the flip side, "Facts of Life," has appeared on at least five different compilation albums. Both can be found on *A Journey to Tyme, Vol. 2* and "Substitute" appears on *The Garage Zone, Vol. 2* on the Moxie label. The former album was remastered and reissued in 1998 in the UK on the Phantom label.

Yankovic, Weird Al   By far the most successful American purveyor of parodies of popular songs. His 1980 song "Another One Rides the Bus," which is about a bus ride with far too many passengers, contains the line:

"The window doesn't open and the fan is broke and my face is turnin' blue, I haven't been in a crowd like this since I went to see the Who." On his 1984 album *In 3-D*, his medley of rock songs set to polka music ends with the Who's "My Generation." Al claims to be unrelated to polka king and fellow accordionist Frankie Yankovic.

The Yardbirds *see* Led Zeppelin.

Young, Neil Member of the popular group Crosby, Stills, Nash and Young but also quite successful on his own. When John Entwistle's first solo album, 1971's *Smash Your Head Against the Wall*, was finally released on CD in Europe more than 20 years later, John's version of Young's "Cinnamon Girl" was a bonus track. The song was intended for the original album but Entwistle decided not to use anyone else's songs and quickly wrote "My Size," a line from which supplied the album's name. When Neil gave a speech inducting Paul McCartney into the Rock & Roll Hall of Fame, he reminisced about being a young musician in the 1960s who was blown away by what the **Beatles**, the **Rolling Stones**, and the Who were doing. In 1996 Pete Townshend was among the performers at Young's annual benefit for the Bridge School, a Northern California facility for disabled children that opened in 1987. The Who and **Pearl Jam** were among the acts that played at the 13th annual benefit in 1999.

Young, Roy Influential British pianist who switched to horn for Roger Daltrey's self-titled debut solo album in 1973. In the early 1960s Young was under contract to perform at the Star-Club in Hamburg, Germany, and felt obligated to decline an offer from **Beatles** manager Brian Epstein to return to England to procure a record contract. Young played keyboards and sang with Cliff Bennett and the Rebel Rousers on their 1966 album *Driving You Wild*, but his most notable work came in the 1970s. The Roy Young Band released albums in 1971 and 1972, and he recorded with **David Bowie** and Long John Baldry by the end of that decade. In 1995 he recorded an album with two early associates of the Beatles, **Howie Casey** and Tony Sheridan.

Zappa, Frank Notorious leader of the Mothers of Invention, a Los Angeles band formed in 1965. Despite being an accomplished musician and composer, he is probably best known for writing vulgar lyrics and articulately defending his peers during U.S. Senate hearings on popular music. The Mothers of Invention were one of the few American groups at Woodstock that impressed Roger Daltrey. Keith Moon worked with Zappa shortly thereafter when he portrayed a nun in Zappa's movie *200 Motels*, which was released in the U.S. in late 1971. Among the stars of the movie were Theodore Bikel, ex–**Beatle** Ringo Starr, and the future **Pamela Des Barres**, then known as Pamela Miller. Moon also employed Zappa's frequent backing vocalists, **Flo and Eddie**, on his only solo album. Zappa died of cancer in 1993 at the age of 52.

Zelda *see* Astley, Zelda.

The Zombies   British Invasion quintet which included **Rod Argent** and which managed to have more success in America than in their native UK, beginning with the 1964 #2 hit "She's Not There," sung by **Colin Blunstone**. The Zombies gave up two weeks after recording the number one hit "Time of the Season," and it fell to Columbia Records staff producer **Al Kooper** to fight to have the record released. Argent and Blunstone would later contribute to Roger Daltrey's 1977 solo album, *One of the Boys*.

Zummo, Vinnie   Frequent guitarist for successful 1980s performer Joe Jackson who provided the flamenco solo on "Perfect World" on Roger Daltrey's 1992 solo album, *Rocks in the Head*. Around the same time he also recorded with Shawn Colvin and Art Garfunkel. In 1998 he and his wife Janice, a singer, released an album of jazz versions of familiar children's songs, *So to Bed … So to Rise: Jazz Wake-Ups and Lullabies*.

Bibliography

Books

Atkins, John. *The Who on Record: A Critical History, 1963–1998*. Jefferson, North Carolina: McFarland & Company, Inc., 2000.
Barnes, Richard. *The Who: Maximum R&B*. New York: St. Martin's Press, 1982.
Fletcher, Tony. *Dear Boy: The Life of Keith Moon*. London: Omnibus Press, 1998. (Published in the United States by Harper Collins under the title *Moon: The Life and Death of a Rock Legend*.)
Hanel, Ed. *The Who: The Illustrated Discography*. London: Omnibus Press, 1982.
Joynson, Vernon. *Tapestry of Delights: A Comprehensive Guide to British Music of the Beat, R&B, Psychedelic and Progressive Eras, 1963–1976*. Glasgow: Borderline Books, 1998.
Marsh, Dave. *Before I Get Old: The Story of the Who*. New York: St. Martin's Press, 1983.
May, Chris, and Tim Phillips. *British Beat*. London: Socion Books, 1974.
McMichael, Joe, and "Irish" Jack Lyons. *The Who Concert File*. London: Omnibus Press, 1997.
Neill, Andy, and Matt Kent. *Anyway Anyhow Anywhere: The Complete Chronicle of the Who 1958–1978*. New York: Friedman/Fairfax, 2002.
Wolter, Stephen, and Karen Kimber. *The Who in Print: An Annotated Bibliography, 1965 through 1990*. Jefferson, North Carolina: McFarland & Company, Inc., 1992.

Internet

The All Music Guide (AMG), www.allmusic.com
The Musicians' Olympus, maintained by Miguel Terol, http://www.geocities.com/SunsetStrip/Palladium/9932/index.htm
www.thewho.net

INDEX

*A number in **boldface** refers to the main entry. When (two) appears after a number, the reader should check two different entries on that page. For reasons of space, index listings for the Who, Roger Daltrey, John Entwistle, Keith Moon and Pete Townshend have been omitted (though each has a full biographical entry in this book).*

Aaronson, Blair **1**
About Face 41, 107, 141
AC/DC **1**, 176
"Acid Queen" 37, 49, 51, 95, 104, 110, 145, 146, 152, 189, 200
Acock, Bimbo **2**
Acoustic Alchemy 73
Adam and the Ants **2**
Adams, Bryan **2**, 115, 125, 190
Adamson, Stuart 32
Aerosmith 190
"After the Fire" 32, 45, 49, 163
Agent 31
The Alarm 160
Alcock, John **2**, 47, 48, 53, 62 *(two)*, 67, 70, 101, 104, 130, 145, 167, 176, 193
Aldrich, Ronnie 111, 182
"All Lovers Are Deranged" 142
"All Shall Be Well" 11, 49, 53
All the Best Cowboys Have Chinese Eyes 11, 24, 37, 41, 45, 74, 94, 118, 139, 141, 143, 169, 181, 186

All This and World War II 28, 147
Allison, John **3**
Allison, Mose **3**, 199, 201
Altham, Keith **4**
The Altones **4**, 25
"Amazing Journey" 47, 95, 133, 149, 177
The Amboy Dukes 136–137
Amen Corner 73
Amnesty International 130, 198
Amos, Tori 10
Amy, Curtis 51
"And I Moved" 7, 45, 129
"And Then It's Alright" 150
Andersen, Hans Christian **4**, 189
Andes, Mark 101
Andwella's Dream 21
Angie **5**, 7
The Animals **5**, 20, 31, 88, 93, 112, 178, 187, 193
Ann-Margret **5**
Another Scoop 11, 13, 18, 40, 128, 142, 149, 167, 182
"Another Tricky Day" 42

Antonioni, Michelangelo 84
Anya *see* Butler, Anya
"Anytime You Want Me" 94, 99
"Anyway Anyhow Anywhere" 37, 41, 59, 94, 98, 108, 110, 152, 169, 179, 195
Appice, Carmen **3**
"Apron Strings" 181
Arbus, Dave **6**
Arc 30, 78
Argent **6** *(two)*, 16
Argent, Rod **6** *(two)*, 34, 203
The Aristocrats **7**, 53, 69, 158, 184, 195
Armatrading, Joan **7**, 9, 104 *(two)*, 123
"Armenia City in the Sky" 180
ARMS 105, 114
Arrival 109
Artists for Research into Multiple Sclerosis (ARMS) 105, 114
Artists United Against Apartheid 191
"Ascension Two" 43, 105

Index

Asher, James 5, 7
Ashford & Simpson 32
Ashton, Tony **8**, 74
Asia 69
Asner, Ed **8**
Aspery, Ron **8**
The Assembled Multitude **8**
Astley, Edwin *see* Astley, Ted
Astley, Hazel 11
Astley, Jon 7, **9**, 11 *(two)*, 12, 94, 104, 115, 117, 134–136
Astley, Layla 9, 12
Astley, Ted 9, **10**, 11, 12, 13, 121, 159, 183
Astley, Virginia 9, **11** *(two)*, 12
Astley, Zelda 9, **12**
Atfield, Donald 49
Atlas, Charles **12**
Atomic Rooster 35, 39
Auger, Brian 55
Avatar **13**, 171
"Avenging Annie" 60
Avory, Mick 6, 108
Axton, Hoyt 23

Baah, Rebop Kwaku 42
Baba, Meher **12**, 94, 114, 117, 125, 134–135, 142, 146, 148, 153–154, 164, 171, 185
"Baba O'Riley" 6, **13**, 31, 49, 83 *(two)*, 117, 136, 140, 148, 152, 154, 165, 188
Babe Ruth 160
Baby Buddha **13**
"Baby Don't You Do It" 79, 92, 110, 194
The Babys 45
Back Door **8**
"Back Door Sally" 1, 76, 101, 192
Back Street Crawler 42
Backtrack 7 102
Bacon, Francis 33
Bacon, Kevin 14
"Bad Attitude" 128, 160
Bad Company **14**, 42, 59, 115, 152, 187, 194–195, 196
Badfinger 72, 136, 181
Bailey, Richard 15
Baird, Roy **15**, 57, 126
Baker, Ginger **15**, 35–36

Baker, Ray Robert **16**, 146
"Bald Headed Woman" 115, 179
Baldry, Long John 8, 101, 149, 174, 202
Baldwin, Billy 75
Balin, Marty 100
Ball, Kenny **16**, 32, 53
Ballard, Russ 6, **16**, 68, 97, 126, 160, 173
The Band 87
The Banger Sisters 125
Bangladesh 28
The Bangles 92
Banks, Tony 80
Bannen, Ian 31
"Barbara Ann" 24
Barcelona, Frank *see* Barsalona, Frank
Barclay, John **17**, 26
Barclay, Nickey 74–75
The Bards **17**
"Barefootin'" 139
"Bargain" 13
Barham, John 17
Barker, Clive 33
Barker, Robert *see* Parker, Robert
Barlow, Gary 17
Barnacle, Gary **18**
Barnacle, Steve **18**
Barnes, Richard 2, 4, 6, 15, **18**, 23, 25, 26, 35, 37, 39, 53, 61, 64, 75, 90, 91, 103, 104, 107, 108, 111, 115, 124, 126, 127, 145, 146, 147, 150, 151, 156, 161, 164, 169–170, 174–175, 177, 179–180, 185, 195–196, 201, 205
Barnett, Andy **19**, 125
Barney *see* Barnes, Richard
Baron, Steve **19**
The Barron Knights **20**
Barry, Dave **20**
Barsalona, Frank **20**, 90, 113, 169, 175, 200
Barton, Gordon **21**
Batt, Mike **21**, 34, 47, 67, 119, 148, 167
Baum, L. Frank **22**
Baverstock, Jack **22**, 90, 127, 129
Baxter, Jeff "Skunk" **23**, 31, 47, 100, 138
Bayless, Lily **23**, 113

Beach, Reb 24
The Beach Boys 1, 24, 27, 49, 58
The Beachcombers 4, 25, 71, 131, 156
Beachill, Peter 17, **26**
Beard, Tony **26**
The Beat 69
The Beatles 8, 17 *(two)*, 20 *(two)*, 24, **26**, 33–34, 36, 39, 47, 49, 55, 64, 71, 72, 77, 80, 82, 86, 87, 91 *(two)*, 95 *(two)*, 103, 108, 115, 118, 121, 124, 125, 127, 132 *(two)*, 134, 136, 138, 139, 142, 143, 144, 146–147, 147, 150–151, 154, 158, 162, 167, 171, 172, 176, 181, 181–182, 187, 202 *(two)*, 203
Beck, Jeff 15, **29**, 56, 96, 102, 105, 114, 115, 133, 141, 174, 177, 200
Beckett, Peter **29**
The Bee Gees **30**, 77, 134 *(two)*, 164, 175
The Beggar's Opera 38, 79, 95, 193–194
Begin, Menachem 154
"Begin the Beguine" 142
"Behind Blue Eyes" 56, 143, 174
The Bel-Airs 64
Bell, Graham **30**, 78, 146
Bell, Maggie 146, **176**, 194
Bell and Arc 30, 78
Belly 38
Bender, Ariel 150
Bennett, Cliff 202
Benson, A.C. 67–68
Benson, George 38
Benson, Jonathan **30**, 118
Berlin 34
Berry, Chuck 5, **31**, 53, 65, 101, 161, 178, 201
Berry, Dave 124
The Best 23, **31**, 69, 192
Best, George **31**, 121, 123
Best Bits 9, 96, 155, 173, 178
Bethnal **31**
Big Country **32**, 41, 44–45, 51, 73, 141, 187
Bikel, Theodore 203
Bilk, Acker 16, **32**, 53
Biondolillo, Jimmy **32**
Birch, Dyan 109

Bird, Ronnie 32
The Birdman 33
Birkett, David 33
Bishop, Elvin 100
"Bitter and Twisted" 178
Björk 17, 18, 26, 33
Black, Gene 34
The Black Crowes 57, 116
Black Oak Arkansas 3
Black Sabbath 71, 181
Blackwell, J. Kenneth 168
Blades, Jack 33, 77, 137
Blake, Peter 33, 138
Bland, Bobby 201
Blind Faith 16, 49, 199
Bloch, Gene 34
Blondie 32, 34
Blood, Sweat & Tears 109
The Blossoms 120
The Blue Beats 132
The Blue Belles 110
The Blues Brothers 56, 93
Blues Incorporated 15
The Blues Magoos 90
The Blues Project 109
Blunstone, Colin 34, 203
Blur 60, 107
Boddicker, Michael 34
The BoDeans 44
"Body Language" 41
"Bogey Man" 71
Bolan, Marc 102–103, 111
Boland, Neil 34, 36, 44
Bolin, Tommy 100
Bolton, Steve "Boltz" 35, 39, 192
Bond, Graham 15–16, 35, 180
Bonham, John 77, 116, 136
The Bonzo Dog Doo-Dah Band 34, 36, 133, 158, 160
Booker T. and the MGs 47, 56, 201
The Boomtown Rats 80
"Boris the Spider" 29, 70, 100, 151
"Born on the Bayou" 55
Boruff, David 37
Bowie, David 37, 56, 75, 78, 133, 152, 186, 191, 200, 202
Bown, Alan 37, 150
"The Boys of Summer" 22, 67
Boz's People 14, 59, 195
Bradbury, Ray 38

Branigan, Laura 26, 34, 38
"Breaking Down Paradise" 16
Brecht, Bertolt 38, 79, 106, 193
Brecker, Michael 38
The Breeders 38
The British Rock Symphony 5, 11, 15, 29, 33, 37, 38, 43, 54, 77, 81, 87, 95, 116, 120, 143, 152, 161, 166 (two), 173, 177, 187–188, 195
Britton, Terry 78
Bronco 150
Brooker, Gary 187
"Brooklyn Kids" 11
Broonzy, Big Bill 201
Broudie, Ian 117
Brown, Arthur 35, 39, 69, 86, 113, 164
Brown, Charles 40, 93
Brown, Georgia 6
Brown, James 40, 201
Brown, Peter 2
Brown, Vicki 41, 133
Browne, Jackson 22, 41, 163
Browne, John 41
Brubeck, Dave 201
Bruce, Jack 15–16, 35, 97, 167, 187
Bruford, Bill 3
Brzezicki, Mark 9, 32, 41, 45, 141, 172, 187–188
"Bucket T" 49
Buckler, Rick 32
Buddy's Song 15, 22, 57, 60, 160
Buffett, Jimmy 115
Bundrick, John "Rabbit" 7, 39, 42, 45, 63, 81, 94, 104, 194, 197
Burchill, Julie 43
Burdon, Eric 5, 187
Burke, Clem 34
Burnett, Chester *see* Howlin' Wolf
Burnett, T-bone 43
Burr, Clive 98
Burrell, Boz 14–15, 59, 152, 195
Burridge, Emily 44
Burrows, Tony 99
Burtnik, Glen 177
Buscemi, Steve 44
Bush, Kate 68

Butcher, Harry 15, 35
Butler, Anya 44, 112, 162, 169, 179
Butler, Jean 48
Butler, Joe 45
Butler, Peter "Dougal" 44, 131
Butler, Tony 9, 32, 41, 42, 44, 81, 94, 104, 163, 187
Butler, Yancy 45
The Butts Band 150
Byrd, Bobby 40
Byrd, Charlie 45, 106
Byrd, Ricky 45, 101, 125
The Byrds 41

C Average 140
"Cache, Cache" 160
Cale, John 48, 90
"Call Me Lightning" 18, 76, 101
Canned Heat 93
"Can't Explain" *see* "I Can't Explain"
Can't Wait to See the Movie 2, 16, 18, 26, 29, 34, 37, 60, 77, 82, 84, 96, 97, 160, 163
Capaldi, Jim 42
Capehart, Jerry 51
Carey, Drew 121
Carin, Jon 46, 142
Carlsen, Dave 46, 62
Carmen, Eric 173
Caron, Leslie 15
Carroll, Dina 49
Carroll, Lewis 22, 47, 119, 148
Carter, John 99
The Carter-Lewis Duo 99
Casey, Howie 47, 202
Cash, Pat 19, 98, 124
Cassidy, David 47
Cassidy, Shaun 47, 154
Castellaneta, Dan 184
"Cat Snatch" 128
Cavaleri, Nathan 47
A Celebration: The Music of Pete Townshend and the Who 43, 46, 49, 118, 135, 141, 155, 170
"Cell Number Seven" 8, 33, 44, 96, 200
Cerveris, Michael 47
Cetera, Peter 84
Chambers, Martin 72, 143

Index

Chambers, Paddy **138**
"Champagne" 6, 147
Chandler, Chas 5, 88, 112
The Chanter Sisters 3, **48**, 77–78
Chaos & Co. 132
Chapman, Graham 130, 198
Chapman, Phil 9
Chapman, Roger 74, 176–177, 194–195
charitable performances 14, 28, 33, 42, 45, 46, 49, 50, 56, 62, 80, 81, 86, 94, 98 *(two)*, 102, 104, 105, 110, 114, 124–125, 128–129, 130, 140, 142, 158, 163, 164, 166, 174, 177, 183, 188, 189, 191, 197, 198, 199, 202
Charles, Ray 166, 201
Charles, Ronnie 146–147
Charlesworth, Chris 25, **48**, 146, 167, 186
Cheap Trick 1
Cheech and Chong 160
Chen, Phil 177
Cher 34, 84, 117
Chicago **48**, 77, 125
The Chieftains **48**
Children's Defense Fund 166
Children's Health Fund 163
Chong, Tommy 160
The Chosen Few 30, 78
Christian, Roger 24, **49**
Christie, Julie 171
"Christmas" 95
Churchill, Chick 3
Chyna **49**, 63
Cincinnati 19, 104, 168, 186, 197
"Cinnamon Girl" 202
"Circles" 35, 73, 99, 179–180
Circus 109
Clapton, Eric 10, 15–16, 29, 35, 36, **49** *(two)*, 68, 77, 97, 103, 105, 107, 108, 114, 123, 138, 139, 168, 193, 199, 200
Clark, Dave 17, 46
Clark, Kenneth 10
Clarke, Dave 46
Clarke, Simon 106–107
Clary, Julian 167

The Clash 18, **51**, 78, 104, 193
Claypool, Les 14
Clayton, Merry **51**, 120, 146
Cleese, John 130
Clempson, Dave "Clem" 17, 97
Clooney, Rosemary 76
"C'mon Everybody" 51–52
The Coasters 201
Cochise 78
Cochran, Eddie **51**
Cochran, Karl 71
Cockburn, Bruce 44
Cockney Rebel 68, 139
Cocker, Joe 21, 50, 51, 56, 75, 143, 147, 164, 168, 192
Cohen, Allen 13
Cohn, Nik 170
Cold Justice 60
Cole, B.J. **52**, 73
Cole, Gary **52**
Cole, Richard **52**, 116, 199
Collins, Albert 47
Collins, Frank 109
Collins, Judy 26, 90
Collins, Mel 109
Collins, Phil 18, 29, 80–81, 153
Colosseum 97
Coltrane, John 201
Colvin, Shawn 203
Colyer, Ken 66
"(Come and) Get Your Love" 16
The Comedy of Errors 161
The Commodores 30
The Confederates 7, 16, 32, **52**, 69, 147, 158, 161, 184, 195
Connollly, Brian 178
"Content" 121
Conway, Deborah 53
Cooder, Ry 43
Cook, Norman 75
Cook, Paul 159
Coombes, Rod 148–149, 173
Cooper, Alice 3, 39, **53**, 152, 194
Copeland, Stewart 142
Corabi, John 71
Cosby, Bill 84
Costello, Elvis 8, 18, 43
Cotten, Gordon 155

Cotton, Mike 111
The Count Five **54**
Counting Crows 44
"Country Fool" 90, 127
Courtney, David **54**, 74, 126, 156–157, 161
"Cousin Kevin" 14, 133, 146, 173
Covey, Julian **55**, 74, 188
Covington, Joey 100
The Coward Brothers 43
Crane, Vincent 39
Crawler 42, 194
"Crazy Like a Fox" 101
The Crazy World of Arthur Brown 35, **39**, 68, 86, 113
Cream 16, 35, 49, 51, 96, 175
The Creation 200
Creedence Clearwater Revival 55, 86
Cregan, Jim **55**, 74
Crenshaw, Marshall 44
The Crickets 50
Cropper, Steve 28, **55**, **56**, 138, 200
Crosby, Stills and Nash 191, 202
Cross, Christopher 138
Crow, Sheryl **56**
The Crowd **56**
Crowded House 53
The Crystals 120
Culture Club 77
Curbishley, Bill 15, **57**, 81, 105, 113, 116, 126, 127, 162, 170, 196
Curbishley, Jackie **57**
The Cure 17
Curved Air 148
Cusack, John 105, 141

D'Abo, Michael 172
Dale, Dick **58**
Dalton, Timothy 194
Daltrey 6 *(two)*, 16, 52, 54, 57, 60, 74, 96, 113, 157, 170, 173, 196, 202
Daltrey, Carol 58
Daltrey, Gillian 58
Daltrey, Harry 58
Daltrey, Irene 58
Daltrey, Jackie 60
Daltrey, Jamie 60
Daltrey, Rosie 60
Daltrey, Simon 60
Daltrey, Willow 60

Index

Damn Yankees 33, 137
"Dancing in the Street" 79, 123
Dandy, Jim 3
D'Angelo, Beverly 92
Daniels, Joe 182
Daniels, Phil **60**
D'Arby, Terence Trent 166
Darin, Bobby 193
Davies, Cyril 94, 118
Davies, Dave 29, 108
Davies, Marion 111
Davies, Ray 108, 171
Davis, Bette **60**, 153, 166
Davis, Cam 74
Davis, George **61**
Davis, Jesse Ed 75
Davis, Miles **61**, 84, 89, 201
Davis, Spencer 9, 32, 46, **61**, 93, 172, 199
Davison, Brian "Blinky" 30
Day, Morris 84
"Day of Silence" 13
Deacon, Mike 3, **62**
The Dead *see* the Grateful Dead
Dead Sea Fruit **62**
Deakin, Graham 3, **62**, 130
Deal, Kelley 38
Deal, Kim 38
Dean, Elton 101
"Dear John" 55
de Balzac, Honore 124
De Burgh, Chris 26
Decan, Mike *see* Deacon, Mike
Dee, Kiki 23, 62, 84, 134
Deep End 43, 49, 57, 61, **62**, 69, 77, 86, 94, 107, 118, 128, 135, 139, 141, 142, 186, 199
Deep Purple 8, 32, 100, 116, 181
Def Leppard 98
Delaney and Bonnie 50
The Del-Phis 123
DeNiro, Robert 44
Denny, Sandy 42, **63**, 111, 146
Densmore, John 150
Des Barres, Michael 63
Des Barres, Pamela **63**, 203
Desperately Seeking Susan 177

The Detours 3, 18, 26, 58, 63, 65, 66, 69, 75, 85, 103, 104, 107, 132, 147, 150, 155–156, 159, 161, 182 *(two)*, 184–185, 195
Device 34
Devlin, Johnny 64, 195
Dewar, Jim 3, 176
DeYoung, Dennis 160
Diamond, Neil 34, 37
Di'Anno, Paul 98
Dickinson, Peter **65**
Diddley, Bo 19, 31, **65**, 114, 170, 201
"Dig" 17, 26
Diken, Dennis 165
DiNizio, Pat 166
Dion, Celine 37, 77, 125
Dire Straits 47, 109
"The Dirty Jobs" 168, 188
"Dirty Water" 105
"Disguises" 99
Dives, Angela 63, **65**
Dixon, Willie 96, 193
"Do Me Good" 56, 200
Do Re Mi 53
"Do the Dangle" 47, 111
"Do You Think It's Alright?" 62, 95, 149, 177
"Doctor, Doctor" 98
"Dogs Part Two" 100
"Doing It All Again" 55
Dokken 24
Domino, Fats 86, 139, 201
Donegan, Lonnie 58, **66**
Donelly, Tanya 38
Donovan 42, 167, 177
"Don't Know Myself" 77
"Don't Let Go the Coat" 13
"Don't Let the Sun Go Down on Me" 24, 102
"Don't Wait on the Stairs" 178
"Don't Worry Baby" 1, 24, 49, 76 *(two)*, 159
The Doobie Brothers 23
The Doors 51, **66**, 96, 150
Dorsey, Tommy 147
Douglas, Kirk 169
Douglas, Leslie 182
Downes, Julia 139
Doyle, Jerry 23
Dozier, Lamont *see* Holland/Dozier/Holland
Drains, Bijou **66**, 90, 180
Drake, Pete 20

The Dream Academy 11, 26
The Drifters 201
"Driftin' Blues" 40, 93
"Drowned" 168
Druce, Bob 64, 182
Dulfer, Candy 12, 72
Dunbar, Aynsley 55
Duncan, Kirk 3, 130
Duncan, Lesley 3, **67**
Dury, Ian 78, 193
Dylan, Bob 43, 87, 109, 122, 133

The Eagles 22, 41, **67**, 103, 179, 192
Eaglin, Snooks 201
"Early Morning Cold Taxi" 59
"Early Morning Dreams" 118, 135
Earth, Wind & Fire 118
East of Eden 6
The Easybeats 143
Echo and the Bunnymen 117
Eddy, Duane 53, 82
Edison Lighthouse 99
Edmunds, Dave 52
Egan, Joe 173
Eilbacher, Lisa 52
Elastica 183
Elgar, Edward **67**
Elliman, Yvonne **68**, 75
Elliott, Stuart 17, **68**, 139
Ellis 176
Ellis, Herb 45, 106
Ellis, Ian 63
Eltworth, John **68**
Emerson, Lake and Palmer 8, 31, 35, 39, **68**, 98
"Emotion" 177
Empty Glass 7, 13, 41, 42, 45, 94, 105, 129, 141, 153, 160, 182, 185
The English Beat **69**
"English Boy" 118, 128, 135, 187
Eno, Brian 167
Entwistle, Alison 71
Entwistle, Christopher 71
Entwistle, Herbert 69
Entwistle, Queenie Maud 69
Epstein, Brian 202
Erasure 18
Errington-Townsend, John 62

Index

The Escorts 4, 25, 71, 118, 131, 138
ESP 71
Essex, David 15, 71, 74, 78, 83, 146, 167
Estefan, Gloria 81
Eurythmics 11, 72, 108, 128
Evans, Mal 72
The Everly Brothers 21, 73
Every Mother's Son 132
"Evolution" 114
"Extra, Extra, Extra" 149, 187
"Eyesight to the Blind" 3, 40, 50, 86, 104, 147, 198, 199

The Fabulous Poodles 73
Face Dances 2, 33, 42, 67, 105, 114, 179, 186, 197
"Face the Face" 183
The Faces 19, 104, 114, 164, 174, 200
Fairport Convention 63
Fairweather-Low, Andy 42, 73, 105, 115
Faith, Adam 15, 54, 60, 72, 74, 76, 97, 126, 156–157, 173
Faithfull, Marianne 105, 120
"Fake It" 9, 117, 135
The Fall 117
"Fallen Angel" 84
Family 8, 55, 74, 176, 193, 194
The Famous Flames 40
Fanny 74
"Fantasia Upon One Note" 144
Farr, Gary 68
Fassert, Charles 24
"Fast Food" 163
Fatboy Slim 68, 75
"Feeling" 97
Feliciano, José 56
Felix 142
Fender, Freddy 75
Fenn, Sherilyn 75
Fenton, Shane 75
Ferguson, Jay 101
Ferrer, José 76
Ferrer, Miguel 76
Ferry, Bryan 41, 46, 76, 101, 109, 167
"The Ferryman" 11, 13

"Fiddle About" 36
Fieger, Doug 23
Fields, Alvin 39, 187
Fine Young Cannibals 69
"Fire" 39–40, 113
Firehouse 137
The Firm 115
Fishof, David 39
"5.15" 39, 54, 107, 141, 155, 168
"Flame" 41, 187
The Flamin' Groovies 76
Flash Fearless Versus the Zorg Women Parts 5 & 6 2, 47, 48, 53–54, 62 (two), 67, 70, 101, 104, 130, 145, 193
Flatley, Michael 48
Fletcher, Tony 4, 25 (two), 35, 46, 52, 71, 75, 90, 110, 118, 131, 137, 156, 172, 175, 189, 194, 205
Flo and Eddie 76, 203
The Flowerpot Men 99
Fontaine, Dick 76
Fontana, Wayne 22
"Football Fugue" 10
Foran, Barry 64
Forbert, Steve 155
Ford, Gerald 174
Ford, Perry 99
Foreigner 26, 33
"Forever's No Time at All" 134–135
Foster, David 33, 37, 77, 139
Foster, Gina 63, 77
4" Be 2" 160
The Four Tops 137
The Fourmost 64, 132
Fox, Michael J. 34, 37, 77
Framed 111
Frampton, Peter 39, 77, 78, 97, 134, 136, 164, 187
Frankie Goes to Hollywood 193
Franklin, Aretha 115, 194
Franklin, Juanita "Honey" 48, 77
Free 15, 42, 115
"Free Me" 16, 60, 126
Freed, Alan 86
Freedman, Dick 20
Frehley, Ace 71, 115
Frey, Glenn 67
"A Friend Is a Friend" 43

Frischmann, Justine 183
The Fruit-Eating Bears 129
The Full Metal Rackets 19, 98, 125
Fury, Billy 72, **78**

Gabriel, Peter 17, 26, 49, 80
Gallagher, Mickey 30, **78**, 193
Gallagher, Noel 137, 174
Gallagher and Lyle **78**, 103
Garcia, Jerry 83
Gardner, Simon 107
Garfunkel, Art 22, 163, 203
Garland, Judy 124
Garrett, Leif **79**
Garvey, Nick 131–132
Gay, John 38, **79**, 95, 193
Gaye, Marvin **79**, 92, 123
Geldof, Bob 28, **80**, 105, 186
General Public 69
Generation X 97
Genesis 18, 29, **80**, 98, 153
George, Gloria 111
Gerry and the Pacemakers 56, 142
Gers, Janick 98
Gerson, Gregg **81**
"Get Your Love" 16
"Getting in Tune" 94, 110
Getz, Stan 45
Ghent, Valerie 32
Gibb, Barry **30**, 134
Gibbons, Steve 1, 57, **81**, 127
Gibson, Mel 120
"Giddy" 28
Gilbert, Tony 10
Gillan, Ian 32, 181
Gilliam, Terry 130
Gilmour, David 7, 41, 55, 63, 77, 107, 115, 128, 141–142
"Gimme Some Lovin'" 9, 61, 199
"Gimme That Rock 'n' Roll" 47
"Give Blood" 7
"Giving It All Away" 54, 60, 157
Glass, Philip 148
Glass Tiger 190

Index

Glennie-Smith, Nick **82**
Glitter, Gary **82**, 144
Glover, Danny 120
"Go to the Mirror" 15, 95, 136, 177
Gogmagog 71, 98
"Goin' Fishin'" 24
"Going Out of My Head" 68, 75
"Going Strong" 76
Goldberg, Whoopi **82**
Goodhand-Tait, Philip 109
Gooding, Cuba, Jr. 92
Goodman, Benny 121
Goodman, John 43
Goodman, Steve 23
Goose Creek Symphony 33
Gorden, Helmut 91, 112, 126–127, 155, 169, 195
Gordon, Coral **49**, 63
Gordy, Berry 92–93
Gorky Park 158
Gorman, John 158
Gorman, Tim **82**
"Got Love If You Want It" **85**, 90, 127
Government Mule 141
Grabham, Mick 3
Graham, Bill 84, 132
Graham, Kenneth 172
The Grateful Dead **83**, 96, 141
Gray, Barry 64, 155, 182
Great Guitars 45, 106
Grech, Rick 16
Griffith, Nanci 48
Grimes, Carol 30
Grimms 158
Groening, Matt **83**
Grosvenor, Luther 150
GTR 166
Guiffre, Jimmy 201
"Guitar and Pen" 9
Gunne, Jo Jo *see* Jo Jo Gunne
Guy, Buddy 201

Hackett, Steve 2, 80
"Had Enough" 7, 10
Hadley, Tony 119, 147, 167
Hagar, Sammy 56, **83**, 191
Hagman, Larry 15, 72, **83**
Hain, Kit **84**
Haley, Bill 184

Halford, Rob 106
Hall & Oates 8, 163
Halpin, Scott **84**, 96
Hancock, Herbie 61, **84**, 129
Handel, George Frideric 85
Handy, W.C. 143
Happy Birthday 13, 114, 142
"Happy Jack" 92, 123, 162, 165, 175
Hardin, Eddie 2, 8, 21, 62, 172, 175
Hardin, Tim 149
Harper, Roy **85**, 167
Harpo, Slim **85**, 90, 127, 201
Harrington, David 148
Harris, Emmylou 52
Harris, Jet 161
Harris, Richard 38, 79, 86, 106, 146, 159, 193
Harris, Steve 98, 125
Harrison, George 8, 17, 26–28, 108
Harry, Deborah 32, 34
Hart, Corey 10, 19
Harvey, Alex 176
Harvey, Les 176
Havens, Richie **86**, 146
"The Hawker" 198
Hawkes, Chesney 15, 22, 57, 160
Hawkins, Ronnie 87
Hawkins, Screamin' Jay **86**
Hawkwind 150, 178
Hayward, Justin 3, 22, 48, 62, 130, 134
Head, Murray 41, 173
Headstone 35
Hearing Education and Awareness for Rockers (H.E.A.R.) 14
Heart 30, 34, 39, 71, 84, 87, 116, 121, 139, 154, 181, 190
"The Heart Has Its Reasons" 2
"Heart to Hang Onto" 14, 42, 140
"Hearts of Fire" 16
"Heat Wave" 92–93, 94, 123
Heath, Frederick 107
"Heaven and Hell" 97
Heavy Jelly 30

Heckstall-Smith, Dick 16
Heekin, Brian 168
Helm, Levon 87
Hendrix, Jimi 5, 23, 46, 61, 85, **88**, 108, 111, 112–113, 116, 131, 156, 175, 181
Henley, Don 22, 67
Henrit, Bob 6
Henson, Jim **89**
Herd 77
"Here for More" 59
"Here 'Tis" 19, 65
Herman, Woody 45
Herman's Hermits 20–21, 89, 142, 166
The Heroes of Telemark 169
Heron, Mike 67, **90**
Hester, Paul 53
Higgs, Rodney 190
The High Numbers 3, 18, 22, 26, 59, 65, 79, 85, 90, 92, 95, 105, 108, 111–112, 124, 126, 144, 161, 169, 195
Highlander 60
Hilfiger, Tommy **91**
Hill, Benny 111
Hinkle, Bob 76
Hoffman, Abbie **91**
Hoffs, Susanna 92
Hogan, Paul 92
Holland, Jools 128
Holland, Nicky 11
Holland/Dozier/Holland 79, **92**, 110, 123, 194
The Hollies 8, 22, 71
Hollywood Dream 180–181
Honey Cone 93
Honeychild 32
Hooker, John Lee 40, **93**, 201
Hope-Evans, Peter 42, 45, 63, 81, **94**, 104
Hopkins, Lightnin' 201
Hopkins, Nicky 3, 29, **94**, 115
Horse's Neck 186
Hoskins, Bob 79, **95**
Hot Tuna 100
"Hound Dog" 47
The House That Track Built 102
The Housemartins 75
Houston, Cissy 115
Houston, Thelma 29, 39, **95**

Houston, Whitney 77, 115
"How Does the Cold Wind Cry" 181
"How Many Friends" 94
Howlin' Wolf 84, **95**, 103, 193, 201
Hue & Cry 32
Hugg, Mike 122
Hughes, Graham 57, **96**, 162
Hughes, Ted 11, 17, 26, 43, 49, 53, 77, 93, **97**, 104, 124, 128, 135, 141, 163, 186, 187
Hull, Alan 30
Humble Pie 17, 77, **97**, 164
Hunt, Marsha 102
Hunter, Ian 45, 152
"The Hunting of the Snark" 22, 47, 119, 148
Hynde, Chrissie 51, 128, 143

I Am 13, 135
"I Can See for Miles" 14, 27, 136, 139, 186, 189, 196
"I Can't Explain" 37, 59, 68, 75, 76, 79, 98, 108, 115, 152, 158, 160, 162, 179, 195
"I Don't Even Know Myself" 77
"I Don't Mind" 40, 94
"I Eat Heavy Metal" 93
"I Feel Better" 181
"I Gotta Dance to Keep from Crying" 149
"I Just Want to Make Love to You" 96, 192
"I Need You" 27
"I Put a Spell on You" 86, 129
"I Saw Her Standing There" 28
"I Want It All" 145
"I Wonder" 198
"I Won't Run Anymore" 53
Icicle Works 172
Idle, Eric 36
Idol, Billy **97**
Iglesias, Julio 34, 82
"I'll Be Your Baby Tonight" 74
"I'm a Boy" 54, 175, 185

"I'm a Man" 65, 94, 114, 170
"I'm Free" 60, 95, 104, 146
"I'm the Face" 22, 85, 90, 127
"Imagine a Man" 94
The Impressions 201
"In My Life" 28
"In the City" 178
The Incredible String Band 90
Indigo Girls 22
Innes, Neil 36, 158
"Instant Party" 35, 73, 179–180
An Irish Evening 48
The Iron Giant **97**, 124, 186
Iron Maiden 19, 70–71, **98**, 125, 177
The Iron Man 3, 11, 17, 26, 40, 43, 49, 53, 77, 93, 97, 104, 124, 128, 135, 141, 163, 186, 187
The Islands 125
The Isle of Wight Festival 36, 69, 89, 96, 171
The Isley Brothers 201
"It Don't Satisfy Me" 160
"It Was You" 64, 90, 127, 132, 155–156, 185
"It's a Boy" 41, 133
"It's Alright" 150
It's Hard 73, 82, 103, 105, 125, 186, 197
"It's Not True" 21, 94, 137, 190
"It's Your Turn" 73
"I've Had Enough" 153
The Ivy League **98**

Jackson, Janet 30
Jackson, Joe 203
Jackson, Michael 34
Jackson, Milt 201
Jagger, Mick 126, 141, 142, 151–152
The Jam 32, **99**
The James Gang **99**, 192
Jan and Dean 49
Jason **100**
Jay and the Americans 20
Jefferson Airplane/Starship 23, 83, **100**
Jesus Christ Superstar 68, 119, 134, 147, 167, 173, 175

Jethro Tull 101
Jett, Joan 45, **100**, 190
Jewel 22, **101**
Jo Jo Gunne **101**
Jobson, Eddie 3, **101**
John, Elton 24, 52, 67, **101**, 108, 118, 132, 133, 135, 138, 147, 166, 175, 186
"Johnny B. Goode" 31
Johns, Glyn 7, 9, 50, 51, 67, 78, 82, 96, **103**, 112–113, 114, 151, 179, 180, 200
Johns, John 104
John's Children 55, **102**, 111, 113, 188
Johnson, Lonnie 66
Johnson, Wilko 193
Johnston, Bruce 24, 27
"Join My Gang" 134
"Join Together" 79, 92, 107
Join Together 135
Jones, Brian 151
Jones, Davy 37
Jones, Grace 26, 150
Jones, John Paul 29, 115–116
Jones, Kelly 174
Jones, Kenney 1, 3, 7, 9, 15, 28, 33, 42, 45, 80, 81, 94, **104**, 114 *(two)*, 115, 141, 152, 160, 164, 176, 179, 186, 197, 200 *(two)*
Jones, Mick 33
Jones, Quincy 34
Jones, Rickie Lee 34
Jones, Steve 159–160
Jones, Tom 17, 26, **105**, 108
"Jools and Jim" 7, 43
Judas Priest 57, 98, **105**, 141
Julia, Raul 38, 79, **106**, 193
"Jungle Bunny" 62
"Just You and Me, Darling" 40

Kampuchea 28, 104, 197
Kane, Eden 111
Kantner, Paul 83
Karstein, Jim 50
"Kashmir" 39, 87, 116
Katrina & the Waves 82
Katz, David 125

Kaufman, Murray *see* Murray the K
Kaylan, Howard 76
The KBC Band 82
Keene, Speedy 66, 180
"Keep Me Turning" 42
"Keep on Working" 7, 45
Kelly, Mike 106
Keltner, Jim 28, 136
Kemp, Gary 167
Kemp, Gibson 138
Kemp, Martin 167
Kennedy, Terry 99
"Kensington High Street" 62
Kessel, Barney 45, 106
Khan, Chaka 84, 85
Kick Horns 63, 106
Kidd, Johnny 55, 64, 96, 107
"The Kids Are Alright" 76, 101, 150, 154, 163, 165, 188, 192
The Kids Are Alright 24, 28, 31, 61, 120, 140, 143, 152, 153, 166, 171, 197
Kilminster, Ian 150
King, B.B. 47, 51
King, Carole 51
King, Jonathan 98
King, Stephen 120
King Crimson 3, 14, 68, 109
Kingdom Come 40
Kings Road 107
Kingsley, Ben 15
The Kinks 6, 29, 91, 94, 108, 127, 171, 179, 194
Kiss 71, 115, 125
Kisselbach, Don 76
Kissoon, Katie 108
Kissoon, Mac 108
Klein, Allan 20, 169
The Knack 23
Knight, Gladys 85
Knopfler, David 73
Knopfler, Mark 47
Kokomo 108, 118
Kooper, Al 79, 92, 109, 194, 203
Korner, Alexis 15, 35, 66, 173
Kossoff, Paul 42
Krieger, Robbie 150
Kronos Quartet 148
Kwaku Baah, Rebop 42

"La-La-La Lies" 94

LaBelle, Patti 110, 115
The Ladybirds 111
Laine, Cleo 6, 123, 198
Lake, Greg 68
Lambert, Constant 111–112, 144
Lambert, Dave 111
Lambert, Kate 50
Lambert, Kit 5, 23, 26, 39, 44, 57, 59, 65, 70, 88, 91, 102, 103, 111, 127, 129, 132, 138, 144, 162, 169–170, 179, 185, 195–196, 199
Lamborn, Nikki 15, 143, 188
Lamm, Robert 48, 125
Lane, Brian 57
Lane, Nathan 22, 114
Lane, Ronnie 9, 10, 13, 14, 42, 50, 67, 78, 90, 94, 103, 104–105, 109, 114, 123, 135, 152, 164, 185, 200
lang, k.d. 52
Langston, Cy 59, 68, 97
Larden, Dennis 132
Lasley, David 115
"The Last Time" 151
The Law 9, 15, 105, 115
Lawrie, Alex 165
"Lazy Fat People" 20
Lazy Racer 82
"Leaving Here" 92
Led Zeppelin 10, 29, 39, 52, 57, 63, 77, 85, 87, 96, 98 *(two)*, 105, 115 *(three)*, 124, 136
Lee, Arthur 120
Lee, Spike 117
Left for Live 143, 199
"A Legal Matter" 33, 94
Leisure Process 18
Lemmy 150
Lennon, John 17, 20, 24, 26–28, 49, 91, 132, 136, 138, 167
Lennox, Annie 72, 108, 128
Leno, Jay 76
Lenya, Lotte 193
"Leon" 109, 161
"Let It Be" 28–29, 39, 80, 95, 120
"Let Me Down Easy" 2, 125, 190
"Let My Love Open the Door" 13, 105, 128, 141, 185

"(Let's Go) to the Chop" 3
"Let's See Action" 13, 94
Letterman, David 161
Level 42 18
Levenson, Keith 39
Lewis, Gary 109
Lewis, Gavin 42
Lewis, Jerry Lee 43, 52, 106, 201
Lewis, Ken 99
Liberace 117
"Life to Life" 122
Lifehouse 4, 38, 49, 103, 113, 144, 158, 185, 196
Lifehouse Chronicles 10, 13, 46, 94, 128, 136, 144, 186
Lightnin' Slim 85
Lightning Jack 92
The Lightning Seeds 117
Lily *see* Bayless, Lily
The Lincoln Trust 49
Lind, Jon 9, 117, 135, 153
Lindisfarne 30
Linscott, Jody 63, 115, 118
"Listening to You" 39, 95, 147, 150, 163, 169, 177
Liszt, Franz 28, 30, 118, 191
Lisztomania 15, 28, 30, 57, 60, 118, 134, 191
Little, Carlo 118, 131
"A Little Is Enough" 41
"The Little Match Girl" 5, 60, 189–190
Little Mothers 78
Little Richard 143, 201
The Little River Band 30
Little Steven *see* Van Zandt, "Little Steven"
Live Aid 28, 33, 46, 80, 105, 197
Live at Leeds 9, 10, 52, 89, 191
Livingstone, Rick 31
Lloyd Webber, Andrew 68, 119, 147, 167
Lochrie, Jaz 42
Lodge, John 62, 130
Lofgren, Nils 1, 176
Loggins and Messina 137
The London Philharmonic Orchestra 10, 11, 22, 43, 118, 119, 135–136, 165, 166, 172, 187, 195

Index

The London Symphony Orchestra 9, 11, 12, 86, **119**, 146–147, 153
Lone Ranger 171
"Long Live Rock" 2, 3, 72, 78
Longhair, Professor 139
Loog Oldham, Andrew 126, 151
"Looking for You" 84
Lord Sutch 29, 71, 94, 118–119
Lorimer, Roddy 107
Los Lobos 44
The Lost Boys 24, 102
Love **120**
Love, Darlene 15, 29, 39, **120**, 143, 188
Love, Mike 1
"Love Ain't for Keeping" 194
"Love Hurts" 73
"Love Is" 45
"Love Is Coming Down" 10
"Love on the Air" 142
"Love, Reign O'er Me" 147, 153
The Lovin' Spoonful 45, 159
Lowe, Jez 30
"Lubie Come Back Home" 94
Ludwinski, Chris 160
Lulu 124, 167
Luongo, Steve 71, 87, 108, **120**, 139, 143, 154, 172, 181, 194
Lydon, Jimmy 160
Lydon, John 159–160
Lyle, Graham **78**
Lynch, David 75
Lynch, John 31, **121**
Lynch, Kelly 75
Lynn, Vera 10, **121**
Lynyrd Skynyrd 51, 110
Lyte, MC 23

MacArthur, Neil 34
MacColl, Kristy 73
The Machine 55, 74, 188
Mack the Knife 38, 60, 79, 86, 106, 193
"Mad Dog" 48, 78
Mad Dog 2, 8, 44, 47, 48, 62, 70, 78, 96, 101, 200
Madonna 118, 177
"Magic Bus" 65, 85, 128, 129, 140, 150, 178

Magness, Ron **142**
Malkovich, John 75
"Man Machines" 187
"Man with Money" 21, 73
Manchester, Melissa 115
Mancini, Henry 121
Manhattan Transfer 34
Mann, Manfred 48, 109, **122**, 125, 138, 142
Manzanera, Phil 128, 141, 142
Margereson, Dave 46
Marin, Cheech 160
Markee, Dave **122**
The MarKeys 56
Marley, Bob 42
Marriott, Steve 45, 77, 97, 146, 164
Marsden, Gerry 56
Marsh, Dave 4, 6, 7, 9, 29, 83, 88, 103, 109, 116, 117, 126, 155, 169, 171, 175, 180, 182, 184–185, 200, 205
Marsh, Rodney 31, **123**
Martha and the Vandellas 79, 92–93, **123**
Martin, George 103
Martin, Marilyn 134
"Martyrs and Madmen" 9, 178
Marvin, Hank 31, 53, 161
"Mary Anne with the Shaky Hands" 109
Maryville Academy 129
Mason, Dave 55
Matlock, Glen 160
McAnuff, Des **124**
McArdle, Andrea **124**
McBrain, Nicko 98, 125, 177
McCallum, Val **124**
McCartney, Paul 17, 24, 26–29, 47, 55, 80, 82, 118, 125, 132 (two), 139, 142, 158, 176, 181, 202
McConnell, Page 141
McCulloch, Jack 35
McCulloch, Jimmy 35, 164, 176, 180–181
McDaniel, Ellas 65
McDonald, Michael 23, 110
McDuff, Brother Jack 201
McEnroe, John 19, 98, **124**
McGear, Mike 158

McGhee, Brownie 201
McGoohan, Patrick 10
McGough, Roger 158
McGriff, Jimmy 201
McGuinness, Paul 21
McGuinness Flint 78
McHugh, Paddy 109
McInnerney, Katie 125, 134
McInnerney, Mike 13, **125**, 134, 171
McIntosh, Robbie 2, 122, **125**
McLagan, Ian 131, 164
McLaughlin, Mary 35
McMahon, Gerard 81, **125**
McMaster, Andy 131–132
McVicar 8, 15, 16, 42, 57, 60, 68, 74, 104, 117, 123, 126, 135, 178
McVicar, John 55, 57, **126**
Meaden, Peter 22, 57, 81, 85, 90, 111–112, **126**, 151, 169, 195
Meaney, Colm **127**
Meat Loaf **127**, 139, 160
Meaty, Beaty, Big and Bouncy 57, 96, 162
Medicine Head 94
Medley, Bill 192
Meehan, Tony 55, 161
Meg *see* Patterson, Meg
"Meher Baba M4 (Signal Box)" 117
Melville, Herman 170
Menken, Alan 147
Mercer, Johnny 122
Merchan, Chucho 63, 72, 94, **128**, 142, 183
Mercury, Freddie 122, 144, 155
The Merseys 23, 112, **129**, 169
Messiah 85
Metallica 14
Metheny, Pat 86, **129**
Michael, George 44, 108
Michaels, Roy 142
Middleton, Ross 18
Midler, Bette 26, 115, **129**
Midnight Oil 104
Midnight Postcards 74
Miller, Frankie 3
Miller, Glenn 121
Miller, Pamela **63**, 203
Miller, Steve 20, 83, 103

Index

Millington, Jean 74–75
Millington, June 75
Mills, Russell 183
Mingus, Charles 201
"Miracle Cure" 147, 149, 187
The Miracles 149, 201
"Mirror, Mirror" 125
Mirror Stars 73
Mitchell, Mitch 88, 131, 156
mods 5, 19, 31, 44, 73, 90, 99, 102, 126–127, 178
Molland, Joey 181
The Monkees 37, 136
Mono Pacific 44
The Monterey Pop Festival 5, 27, 83, 88, 149, 163
Montgomery, Wes 201
Monty Python's Flying Circus 30, 36, 107, **130**, 198
The Moody Blues 3, 22, 26, 48, 62, **130**, 134
Moon, Alfred 25, 131
Moon, Kim 34, 131, 175
Moon, Kitty 131
Moon, Leslie 131
Moon, Linda 131
Moon, Mandy 131
Moore, Johnny 40
Moore, Mary Tyler 8
Moore, Roger 10
Moreshead, John 55
Moroder, Giorgio 14
Morrison, Jim 66
Morrison, Van 108
Most, Mickie 89
The Mothers of Invention 202
Mötley Crüe 71
Motorhead 150
"Motoring" 92–93, 94, 123
The Motors **131**, 133
Mott the Hoople 14, 45, 150, 152
Mountain 20, 194
"Move Better in the Night" 122, 125
"Move Over Ms. L" 28, 72, 77, 192
Moyet, Alison 109, 117
"Much Too Much" 94
Mulhearn, Daniel 113, **132**
The Muppets **89**

Murphy, Eddie 110
Murray the K 21, 109, 149, 175, 198
Music & Rhythm 43, 105
"My Baby Gives It Away" 152
"My Generation" 10, 14, 17, 20, 40, 54 *(two)*, 59, 61, 67, 98, 105, 122, 136, 137, 138, 141, 151, 153, 158, 165, 166 *(two)*, 169, 178, 179, 195–196, 202
My Generation 40, 65, 70, 94, 98, 103, 179–180, 196
"My Size" 202
"My Way" 52
"My Wife" 68, 198

"Naked Eye" 84
"Naked Man" 56, 200
Napier-Bell, Simon 102
Nash, Johnny 42
The Naturals 64, **132**
The Nazz 154
"Near to Surrender" 16
Neeley, Ted 173
Neil, Fred 136
Nelson, Rick **132**
Neville, Aaron 118
"New Life" 49
"New Song" 9
Newhart, Bob 121
Newman, Andy 180–181
Newman, Margo 41, **133**
Newman, Randy 34
Newman, Tony **133**
Newton, Juice 37
Newton-John, Olivia 30 *(two)*, 41, 132, **133** *(two)*, 148–149, 157
The Nice 30, 68
Nicholas, Paul **134**
Nicholls, Billy 9, 13, 63, 65, 107, 117–118, 126, 128, **134**
Nicholls, Morgan 136
Nicholson, Jack **136**
Night 125
Night, Holly 34
Night Ranger 33, 137
"Night School" 183
"Nightmare (Please Wake Me Up)" 193, 198
Nilsson, Harry 77, **136**
"1951/What About the Boy" 14, 95, 106, 168
Nirvana **136**

Nixon, Richard 174
"No More Mr. Nice Guy" 54
Noone, Peter **89**, 142
"Nothing Is Everything" 13
"Now and Then" 146
Nugent, Ted 33, 127–128, **136**, 155

Oakes, Bill 68
Oasis 17, **137**, 174
O'Brien, Conan 14
Ocean, Billy 15, 77
"Oceans Away" 109
O'Connor, Sinead 49
O'Day, Alan 138
Odds & Sods 10, 52, 92, 194
Oldfield, Mike 2, 73, 141, 166
Oldham, Andrew Loog 126, 151
Omartian, Michael 137
"One Night Stand" 33, 76, 101, 132, 192
"One of the Boys" 81
One of the Boys 6, 28, 34, 50, 55, 60, 73, 81, 126, 152, 155, 161, 178, 181 *(two)*, 203
Ono, Yoko 106
O'Parvardigar 13
Orbison, Roy 181
Orbital 10
Oscar 134
O'Sullivan, Gilbert 167
"Out in the Street" 54, 99
The Outlaws 134
"Over the Top" 93
"Overture from Tommy" 8, 117, 121, 173
"The Ox" 70, 94

Paddy, Klaus and Gibson 59, 71, 112, **138**, 196
Page, Jimmy 29, 52, 57, 98, 105, 115 *(three)*
Pale Horse 46, 62
Palin, Michael 130
Palladino, Pino 115, **138**, 197
Palmer, Carl 8, 35, 39, 68–69
Palmer, John "Poli" 8, 74
Palmer, Robert 37, 44, 118, 150
"Parade" 109, 161

Index

Parker, Charlie 61, 89, 147, 201
Parker, Robert **139**
Parmeinter, Chris 22, 156
Parr, John **139**
Parsons, Alan 67, 68, 71, 87, 121, 122, **139**, 154, 181 *(two)*
Parsons, John 73
Parsons, Tony 43
Parting Should Be Painless 32, 38, 60, 72, 76, 78, 84, 96, 135, 167 *(two)*, 178, 181, 193
"Parting Would Be Painless" 84
Parton, Dolly 23
Patches 157
Patterson, Meg 50, **139**
Patton, John 201
Paul, Adrian **140**
Paxton, Tom 90
Pearl Jam 128, **140**, 202
Peck, Kathy 14
Peel, John 94
"Peg Leg Peggy" 198
"Peppermint Lump" 5, 7
"Perfect World" 125, 203
Perkins, Carl 201
Perlman, Itzhak 198
The Pet Shop Boys 17, 108
Petty, Tom 73
Phillips, Sam 44
Phillips, Simon 31, 32, 41, 62, 105 *(two)*, 115, **141**
Phillips-Gorse, Josh 42
Phish **141**
"Pictures of Lily" 23, 37, 113, 119
"The Pig Must Die" 22, 47, 119, 147
Pigott, Steve 115
"Pile Driver" 77
Pilot 139, 178, 181
"Pinball Wizard" 11, 36, 37, 80, 100, 102, 105, 119, 124, 137, 146, 161, 170, 175, 186
Pink Floyd 7, 41, 46, 55, 63, 80, 82, 85, 95, 107, 108, 115, 128, 139, **141**
The Pioneers **142**
"Piper at the Gates of Dawn" 172
Pitchford, Dean 14
Pitney, Gene 111
The Pixies 38

Pizzaman 75
Plant, Robert 116
The Plastic Ono Band 138
Plath, Sylvia 97
Player 29–30
Playing for Keeps 122
"Please Don't Touch" 107
"Please Please Please" 40, 94
Plews, Dave 107
Poco 8, 56
The Pointer Sisters 34
The Police 17, **142**
Pop, Iggy 127
Pop Records 167
Popcorn Blizzard 127
Pope, Alexander 79
Porter, Angela 5
Porter, Cole **142**, 146
Powell, Cozy 97, 98, 106
Powell, Robert 15
Powers, Devin 34, 165
"Praying the Game" 10
"Prelude" 181
The Presidents 103, 151
Presley, Elvis 58, 144
Preston, Billy 15, **143**, 188
The Pretenders 21, 44, 45, 51, 72, 125, 128, **143**
The Pretty Things 22
Previn, André 198
Price, Alan 5, 123
"The Price of Love" 33, 34, 37, 77
Pridden, Bob 137, **143**, 199, 201
Priest, Maxi 18, 77
Primus 14
The Prince's Trust 164–165
Prine, John 56
Prior, Maddy 3
Prism 165, 190
"The Prisoner" 55, 126
Proby, P.J. 82, **144**
The Proclaimers 73
Procol Harum 3, 41, 187, 195
Professor Longhair 139
"Proud" 16
Pryor, Richard 86
The Psychedelic Furs 44, 46
"Psycho Montage" 118, 135
Psychoderelict 9, 13, 42, 43 *(two)*, 91, 94, 107, 108, 117, 117–118, 118, 135, 146, 184, 186, 187

Public Image Ltd 159
Purcell, Henry **144**, 158
"Pure and Easy" 143–144
Puttnam, David 15

Quadrophenia (album) 57, 70, 82, 84, 97–98, 103, 113, 127, 140, 141, 142, 144 *(two)*, 165 *(two)*, 170, 172, 178, 185, 186–187, 188, 195, 196–197
Quadrophenia (movie) 15, 40, 56, 60, 70, 79, 119, 122, 129, 153–154, 163, 170, 185, 196
Quads 185
Quatro, Patti 74
Quatro, Suzi 62, 74
Queen 122, **144**, 155
A Quick One 27, 59, 67, 73, 92, 123, 170, 196
"A Quick One While He's Away" 27, 151
Quicksilver 14
"Quicksilver Lightning" 14
Quiet Riot 137

Rabbit *see* Bundrick, John "Rabbit"
Rabin, Buzz 20
Radio Stars 103
"Rael" 39
Rafferty, Gerry 52, 173
The Raiders 17
Raitt, Bonnie 40, 41, 115
Ralphs, Mick 14–15, 195
The Ramones **145**
The Raspberries 173
Rat Race Choir 120
Raven, Paul 82
The Ravishing Beauties 11
Rea, Chris 115
"Ready for Love" 84
Ready Steady Who 24, 49, 175
"Real Emotion" 56, 200
"Rebel" 2, 190
"Rebel Without a Car" 168
Rebop 42
Redding, Noel 46, 181
Reed, Jimmy 201
Reed, Lou 3, **145**
Reeves, Jim 16, **146**
Reeves, Martha **123**

The Regents 24
Reizner, Lou 28, 30, 51, 60, 63, 72, 86 *(two)*, 119, **146**, 159, 164, 175, 176, 199
Renaissance 153
Revere, Paul 17
Reynolds, Art 95
Rhythm Heritage 138
Rice, Tim 68, 119, 147, 167
Rich, Buddy 147
Richard, Cliff 133, **147**, 157, 161
Richards, Keith 64, 126, 150–151, 167
Richardson, Warren S. 33
Richie, Lionel 34
Ride a Rock Horse 16, 17, 37, 55, 60, 96, 97, 109, 161, 173
Riding on the Crest of a Slump 176
The Righteous Brothers 8, 192
Rigor Mortis Sets In 2, 8, 47, 62, 70, 111, 148, 198
Riley, Terry 13, **148**
Riverdance 48
Ro Ro **148**, 169, 173, 193
"Road Runner" 31, 65
Robertson, Robbie 87
The Robin Hood Foundation 197
Robinson, Guy 107
Robinson, Smokey **149**, 201
Robinson, Tom 2
The Rock 34, 70, 83, 165, 172
"Rock and Roll" 98, 124
The Rock and Roll Hall of Fame 31, 40, 41, 51, 52, 56 *(two)*, 65, 67, 73, 80, 93 *(two)*, 96, 100, 108, 123, 131, 133, 149, 152, 159, 161, 163, 189, 192, 193, 197, 202
The Rockin' Vicars **149**, 180
Rocks in the Head 44, 45, 48, 60, 81, 96, 118, 125, 135, 203
Roden, Jess 37, **150**
Rodgers, Paul 15, 115, 187, 195
Rodgers and Hammerstein 56, 110, 124

Rogers, Kenny 30
Rogers, Simon 117
The Rolling Stones 9, 11, 12, 27, 31, 39, 48, 51, 54, 64, 85, 95, 96, 103, 105, 107, 109, 114–115, 119, 126, 141, 142, 143, 149, 150, 164, 167, 178, 200, 202
Ronson, Mick **152**
Ronstadt, Linda 41, 115
Rooney, Mickey 61, **153**, 166
Ross, Alan 148–149, 169
Rota, Nino 122
Roth, David Lee 26, 83
Rotten, Johnny 159–160
"Rough Boys" 105, 141, 153, 183
Rough Mix 9, 10, 14, 42, 50, 67, 78, 90, 94, 103, 109, 114, 123, 135, 152, 164, 185
Roxy Music 3, 76, 101, 141, 142
The Royal Philharmonic Orchestra 22, 67, 153
Rudd, Raphael 119, **153**
Rudd, Virginia 153
Rude Awakening 60, 75
"Run Run Run" 101
The Runaways 3, 100
Rundgren, Todd 47, 71, 75, 87, 121, 139, **154**, 181, 188
Ruskin Spear, Roger 36, 111, 133
Russell, Ken 15, 30, 72, 118, 134, 191
Rutherford, Mike 80–81
The Rutles 36
Ryder, Mitch 20–21, 175, 181

Sadat, Anwar al- **154**, 178
Sade 26
St. John, Kate 11
St. Jon, Alan **155**, 168
"Sally Simpson" 50, 62, 66, 95, 177
Samuels, Fuzzy **155**
Sanborn, David 38, 118, **155**
Sanders, Dave 107
Sanders, Tim 106–107
Sandom, Doug 26, 59, 64, 69, 88, 126, 131, **155**, 184–185, 15

Santana, Carlos 50, 171
"Satin and Lace" 55
"Satisfaction" 151
Satriani, Joe 141
"Saturday Night's Alright (for Fighting)" 102, 135
The Savages 118–119
"Save It for Later" 69
Sayer, Leo 34, 52, 54–55, 60, 74, 82, 123, 133, 134, 147, **156**, 173
The Scaffold **158**
Scarlatti, Alessandro 144, **158**
Scoop 12, 25, 41, 105, 106, 129, 160, 167, 180
Scorpions 1, **158**, 190
The Scorpions 7, 53, 63, 69, **158**, 184, 195
Scorsese, Martin 88
Scott, Sandy *see* Halpin, Scott
Screaming Lord Sutch and the Savages 29, 71, 94, 118–119
Scully, Mike 184
"Sea and Sand" 153
Seal 49
Sean, Sherman *see* Merchan, Chucho
The Searchers 142
Sebastian, John 45, 117, **159**
Sedaka, Neil 173
"See Me, Feel Me" 39, 45, 86, 95, 147, 161, 163, 169, 177, 192
"See My Way" 59
"The Seeker" 28, 59, 165, 171
Segovia, Andrés 45
Selena 84
Sellers, Peter 10, 86, 146, **159**
"Sensation" 95, 133, 149, 177
Senseless Things 136
The Sex Pistols **159**, 183
Sextette 54, 131, 194
Sha Na Na 36, **160**
Shacklock, Alan 17, 68, 97, **160**
The Shadows 31, 53, 55, 147, **161**
Shaffer, Paul 39, **161**
Shakespeare, William 120, **161**

Index

"Shakin' All Over" 23, 96, 107
Shankar, Ravi 17
Shannon, Del 20, 133
The Sharks 167
Shatlock, Alan *see* Shacklock, Alan
Shaw, Artie 106, 147
Shaw, Mike 26, 44, 57, 111–112, **162**, 169, 179
Shaw, Tommy 33, 39, 137, 177
Shelton, Anne 10
Shepard, Vonda **163**
Sheppard, Neil 148–149
"Sheraton Gibson" 99–100
Sheridan, Tony 47, 202
Sherman, Brad 23
The Shirelles 201
Shirley, Jerry 97
The Shortlist 195
"Shot of Rhythm & Blues" 107
"Shout and Shimmy" 40
The Showmen 90, 127
Sidwell, Neil 107
Siegler, John 17, **163**
"Signal 30" 151
Silk Tones 49
Silver, Long John 3, 54
Simon, Carly 41, 125
Simon, Paul 38, **163**
Simone, Nina **163**, 201
Simpson, Ray 32
Simpson, Valerie 32
Sinclair, John 91–92
Singer, Eric 71
The Singing Saxophone 182
"Single Man's Dilemma" 34
Sinise, Gary 75
"Sister Disco" 9
Skip Bifferty 30, 78
Slade 23
Slammin' Babes 75
Slaughter 137
Slaughter, Ricky 131
Slick, Grace 100
"Slip Kid" 94
Small, Henry **165**, 190
The Small Faces 41, 45, 77, 97, 104, 114, 131, 146, **164**, 176, 180–181, 200
"Smash the Mirror" 104, 149, 186
Smash Your Head Against

the Wall 36, 70, 96, 97, 202
Smith, Adrian 19
Smith, Curly 101
Smith, Jimmy 201
Smith, "Legs" Larry 34, 36
Smith, Patti **165**
Smith, Pete **165**
The Smithereens **165**
"Smokestack Lightning" 84, 95–96
The Smothers Brothers 61, 153, **166**, 192
The Snakes 131
Snider, Todd **166**
Snipes, Wesley 45
Snow, Phoebe 39, **166**
"So Sad About Us" 38, 47, 99, 112, 129, 154, 169, 180
"Sodding About" 151
Soft Machine 148
"Solid Gold" 74, 192
"Somebody Told Me" 72
"Something in the Air" 147, 171, 180
Son of Dracula 77, 131, 136
"The Song Is Over" 94
Spalding, Phil **166**
Spandau Ballet 119, 147, 167
Spear, Roger Ruskin 36, 111, 133
Spear of Destiny 18
Spector, Phil 103, 120, 189
Spector, Ronnie 81
Spedding, Chris 22, **167**
The Spice Girls 95, 107
Spike **167**
Spinetti, Henry 22
Spirit 101
Spiritual Cowboys 72
Spooky Tooth 106, 150
Spoon, Kief 28, **167**
Spooner, Bill "Sputnik" 33
"Spoonful" 84, 95–96
Springer, Jerry **168**
Springfield, Dusty 72, 108, 124, 167
Springfield, Rick 173
Springsteen, Bruce 21, 122, 176, 191
The Squadronaires 10, 182

"Squeeze Box" 38, 56, 74, 75
Squier, Billy 155, **168**
Staehely, Al 101
Staehely, John 101
Staines, Chris 63
Stainton, Chris 105, 115, **168**
Stamp, Chris 5, 20, 23, 44, 57, 65, 70, 88, 91, 111–114, 127, 129, 161, **169**, 170, 185, 195–196, 199
Stamp, Terence 169, **170**
"Standin' Around Cryin'" 50, 193
Stanley, Richard **171**, 180
Stanshall, Viv 36
Stardust 15, 71, 74, 83, 131
Starkey, Zak 2, 8, 19, 29, 39, 43, 44, 62, 118, **172**, 176, 197
Starr, Charlie 143
Starr, Ringo 26, 28–29, 77, 115, 136, 147, 172, 203
Stars On 173
The Stars Organization for Spastics (SOS) 146
"Start Me Up" 39, 54, 152
Stealers Wheel 52, 74, 149, **173**
Steeleye Span 3, 22
Steely Dan 23, 137
Stein, Ben **173**
Stein, Jeff 143, 166, **174**
Stein, Kevin 174
Stereophonics 137, **174**
Stevens, Don 13
Stewart, Al 139
Stewart, Dave 11, 72, 128
Stewart, Ian 152
Stewart, Rod 29, 34, 56, 77, 138, 147, 164, **174**, 177
Stigwood, Robert 16, 30, 35, 112–113, 134, **175**, 179
Stills, Stephen 155, 191
Sting 17, 142
The Stone Canyon Band 132–133
Stone the Crows 3, 146, **176**, 181, 194
The Stones *see* the Rolling Stones
The Stormsville Shakers 109

Index

"The Story So Far" 16
Strange Frequency 60
The Stranglers **176**
Strauss, Richard 118
The Strawberry Alarm Clock **176**
The Strawbs 2, 111, 149, 173, 191
Stredder, Maggie 111
"Street Fighting Man" 152
"Street in the City" 10
Streetwalkers 74, 98, **176**, 194
Streiker, Lisa *see* Strike, Liza
Streisand, Barbra 34, 37, 51, 74–75, **177**
Strike, Liza **177**
Strummer, Joe 51, 60
"Stuck in the Middle" 55, 74, 97, 173
The Style Council 73
Styx 33, 39, 137, 160, **177**
"Substitute" 15–16, 35, 105, 145, 149, 150, 160, 165, 174, 175, 179–180, 201
Substitute: The Songs of the Who 37, 56, 99, 137, 140, 141, 174
The Sugarcubes 33
Summers, Andy 142
"Summertime Blues" 23, 51, 101, 152, 194
Sun City 191
Supertramp 20
Sutch, Lord 29, 71, 94, 118–119
The Swanees 40
Sweet **177**
Sweet, Matthew 26, 35, 166
Swervedriver **178**
Swift, Jonathan 79
Swindells, Steve 9, 173, **178**
The Swinging Blue Jeans 5, 31, 71, **178**
Sylvester, Terry 71
Szymczyk, Bill 67, **179**

T Rex 102, 111
Take That 17
Tales from the Crypt 44
Talmy, Shel 21, 35, 44, 94, 103, 108, 112, 149–150, 162, 169, 175, **179**, 185, 190, 195–196

Tangerine Dream 148
Tarantino, Quentin 44
"Tattoo" 140
Tauber, Richard 10
Taupin, Bernie 24, 101–102, 135
Taylor, James 38, 115
Taylor, Mick 15
Taylor, Roger 145
Tchaikovsky, Bram 131–132
Tears for Fears 11, 94
The Teenage Cancer Trust 137, 174
"Teenage Idol" 58, 132
Telephone **180**
The Temptations 56
10cc 181
Ten Years After 3, 21
Terry, Sonny 201
Tex, Joe 139
That'll Be the Day 71, 74, 78, 131
The The 26
"There Is Love" 54, 157
"There's a Doctor" 149, 169, 200
"There's a Heartache Following Me" 16, 146
"They Are All in Love" 94
Thin Lizzy 3
"Thinking" 52
30 Years of Maximum R&B 65, 174, 197
.38 Special 190
Thomas, Mickey 23, 100
Thompson, Chris 122, 125
Thompson, Richard 43
Thoms, Peter 107
Thorne, Mike 32
Thorpe, Billy 187
The Three Blazers 40
Three Dog Night 16
The Threepenny Opera 38, 79, 106, 193
Throwing Muses 38
Thunderclap Newman 35, 66, 147, 164, 171, 176, **180**
Thunderthighs 3, 145
"Till the Rivers All Run Dry" 14, 50, 135
Tipton, Glenn 98, 106
"To Barney Kessell" 106
"To the Chop" 3
"Together" 72, 136, 138

Tommy (album) 3, 8–9, 13, 19, 28, 30, 47, 51, 60, 63, 66, 72, 80, 86 *(two)*, 97–98, 102, 107, 110, 113, 117, 119 *(two)*, 121, 124, 125, 129, 133, 146, 147, 148, 157, 159, 164, 171, 175, 176, 185–186, 186, 196, 198, 199
Tommy (movie) 5, 14, 15, 30, 36, 37, 40, 41, 50–51, 60, 62, 72, 85, 94–95, 96, 101–102, 104, 106, 113, 118, 131, 133 *(two)*, 134, 135, 136, 145, 149, 150, 152, 155, 168, 170, 173, 175 *(two)*, 177, *(two)*, 185, 187, 189, 196, 200
Tommy and the Bijoux 67, 90
"Tommy Can You Hear Me?" 95, 149, 169
Too Late the Hero 70, 105, 135, 149, 191, 192
"Too Much of Anything" 94
Torch, Sidney 182
Torme, Bernie 32
Torrence, Dean 49
Tosh, Stuart 139, **181**
Toto 55, 141
The Tourists 72
Towns, Colin 17, 26, **181**
Townsend, Godfrey 71, 87, 121, 139, 154, **181**
Townshend, Ben 60, 187–188
Townshend, Betty **182**, 184
Townshend, Cliff 10, 64, 111, **182** *(two)*, 184
Townshend, Emma 128, 160, **183**, 185
Townshend, Joseph 185
Townshend, Karen 10, 130, 142, 171, 185
Townshend, Minta 160, 183, 185
Townshend, Paul 83, **184**
Townshend, Simon 8, 9–10, 11, 15, 18, 32, 39, 41, 45, 60, 143, 152, 166, 169, 184, **186**, 197
Townson, Chris 55, 102, **188**
Towser 100
Traffic 42, 50, 55, 61, 199

Train 54
Travolta, John 133
"Treachery" 9, 155, 178
Trower, Robin 3
The Tubes 33, 110, 154, **188**
Tune, Tommy 189
Turner, Ike 188–189
Turner, Joe 201
Turner, Joe Lynn 181
Turner, Tina 18, 34, 78, 82, 108, 109, 145, **188**
The Turtles 17, 76
Twiggy 5, **189**
200 Motels 28, 63, 131, 202–203
Two Rooms 102, 135
Two Sides of the Moon 1, 19, 28, 33, 37, 44, 56, 58, 62, 72, 74, 76 *(two)*, 77, 101, 131, 132, 136, 138, 159, 192, 200
Two's Missing 65, 93, 114, 123, 170
Tyler, Bonnie 108
Tyler Moore, Mary 8
Tyrannosaurus Rex 102, 111
Tyson, Cicely 61

U2 21
U.K. 101
Ulrich, Lars 14
The Ultimate Rock Symphony 39, 187
Under a Raging Moon 2, 16, 32, 41, 45, 60, 69, 82, 84, 96, 122, 125, 139, 142, 143, 144, 160, 163, 172, 190
"Under My Thumb" 151
"Underture" 86
"Unforgettable Opera" 44, 48
The Untamed 21, 180, **190**
Urchin 19
Ustinov, Peter 170
Utopia 47, 154

Valentino, Bobby 73
Vallance, Jim 2, **190**
Van Damme, Jean-Claude 45
Vandross, Luther 115
Van Halen 26, 83, **190**
Vanilla Fudge 3
Van-Pires 71, 155, 168, **194**

Van Zandt, "Little Steven" **191**
Vedder, Eddie 129, **140**
Vee, Bobby 157
The Velvet Underground 48, 90, 145
The Vernon Girls 111
Vicious, Sid 160
Vining, Steve 165
Vitale, Joe 70, **191**, 192
Volman, Mark 76
Voormann, Klaus **138**

Wadleigh, Michael 91
Wagner, Richard 118
Waite, John 45
"Waiting for a Friend" 135
Wakeling, Dave 69
Wakeman, Rick 2, 8, 18, 57, 111, 118, 173, **191**
"Walking" 61
"Walking in My Sleep" 9, 61, 199
The Wallflowers 44
Walsh, Joe 31, 35, 67, 70, 100, 191, **192**
Walton, Mercy Dee 3
"Waltz for a Pig" 15–16, 35, 180, 190
Warnes, Jennifer **192**
Was (Not Was) 26
Waters, Muddy 50, 96, **192**, 201
Waters, Roger 82, 108
Watson, Bruce 32
Watt-Roy, Norman 78, **193**
Watts, Charlie 14, 105, 115, 152
"The Way of the World" 6, 74, 157
Wayne, Jeff 71
Wayne, Pat 25
Webber, Andrew Lloyd 68, **119**, 147, 167
Weider, Johnny 3, 5, 74, 148, **193**
Weill, Kurt **193**
Weinberg, Max 14
Weller, Paul 99
The Wellingtons 120
"We're Not Gonna Take It" 95, 106, 149, 155, 168–169
West, Leslie 20, 39, 79, 92, 108, 109, 120–121, **194**

West, Mae 54, **194**
Westbrook, Darren 143
Wetton, John 37
Wheeler, Kenny 17, 26
"When I Was a Boy" 94
"When I'm Sixty-Four" 28, 147
"Whiskey Man" 70
Whistle Rymes 2, 21, 70, 77, 148, 173, 181, 193, 198
White, Jay 132
White, Mark 182
White, Peter "Chalky" 44
White City 18, 34, 41, 43, 45, 94, 107, 128, 138, 141, 142, 177, 183, 186
"White City Fighting" 142
"White City Lights" 117, 135
Whitehorn, Geoff 15, 42, 177, **194**
Whitesnake 48, 98
Whitney, Charlie 74, 176
"Who Are You" 46, 94, 105, 128, 136, 137, 159, 174
Who Are You 7 *(two)*, 9, 10, 42, 73, 99, 103–104, 156, 185, 197
The Who by Numbers 94, 103, 114, 185, 197
Who Came First 13, 16, 96, 100, 114, 121, 125, 134–135, 146, 185
"Who Cares?" 198
Who Covers Who 178
The Who Orchestra 15, 35
The Who Sell Out 12, 59, 180, 196
Wholey, Dennis 130, **198**
Who's Better Who's Best 19
"Who's Gonna Walk on Water" 45, 125
Who's Missing 92
Who's Next 4, 6, 13, 83, 103–104, 110, 113, 179–180, 185, 196, 201
Who's Serious 10, 11, 43, 118, 119, 135–136, 165, 166, 172, 187, 195
The Who's Tommy 47, 124, 186
Wickham, Vicki 110
Wiggy *see* Wolff, John "Wiggy"

Wild Uncertainty 21
Wilkins, Helen **167**
Williams, Bryan **198**
Williams, Deniece 23
Williams, Everton 32
Williams, John **198**
Williams, Vanessa 117
Williamson, Mark 17
Williamson, Sonny Boy 3, **198**
Willis, Pete 98
Wilson, Ann 39, 71, **87**, 116, 121, 139, 154, 181
Wilson, Brian 24, 49
Wilson, Dennis 25
Wilson, Nancy 87
Winger 24
Winger, Kip 24
Wings 28, 47, 164, 168, 176, 180–181
Winter, Edgar 127
Winter, Johnny 127
Winterland 183
Wintour, Dave 173
Winwood, Steve 16, 50, 61, 105, 114, 146, 164, 171, **199**
Witchblade 45
With Love 13, 94, 135
"Without Your Love" 60, 126, 135
The Wizard of Oz 22, 41, 101, 114, 155, 166
Wolff, John "Wiggy" 21, 113, 143, 169, **199**

The Wombles 22
Wonder, Stevie 77, 108
"Won't Get Fooled Again" 46, 71, 79, 83, 84, 94, 110, 117, 123, 128, 174 *(two)*, 191, 194, 198
Wood, Ron 29, 50, 56, 103, 104, 114, 164, **200**
Wood, Roy 146
Wooden Ships 83
Woodstock 21, 55, 86, 88, 91–92, 113, 159, 160, 170, 200, 202
Woolfson, Eric 139
The Worried Men 74
Wray, Link **200**
Wright, Gary 17
Wright, Richard 35
Wright, Syreeta 143
Wright, Tom 40, 61, 65, 85, 93, 95, 149, 163, 192, **201**
"Written on the Wind" 60
Wyckham, Vicki 110
Wyman, Bill 105, 115, 151–152
Wynette, Tammy 52

The Xtreems **201**

Yamashita, Tatsuro 32
Yankovic, Frankie 202
Yankovic, Weird Al 145, **201**

The Yardbirds 29, 49, 51, 52, 102, 115–116
Yes 3, 34, 171, 191
"You and Me" 74, 157
"You Better You Bet" 2
"You Don't Have to Jerk" 18
"You Put Something Better Inside of Me" 173
"You Really Got Me" 108, 179, 194
"You'll Never Walk Alone" 56, 110
Young, Angus 2
Young, Neil 1, 51, 176, 191, **202**
Young, Paul 35, 187
Young, Roy 47, **202**
Young, Tim 10
"Young Man Blues" 3
"You're So Clever" 129

Zappa, Frank 28, 63, 76, **202**
"Zelda" 12
The Zombies 6, 34, 109, **203**
"Zoot Suit" 22, 90–91, 127
Zummo, Vinnie **203**

www.ingramcontent.com/pod-product-compliance
Ingram Content Group UK Ltd.
Pitfield, Milton Keynes, MK11 3LW, UK
UKHW041952140426
5217IPUK00015B/761